"This is a timely book that brings back the commonsense, in addition to the applied forensics, approach to due diligence. In light of recent dramatic due diligence failures, deal participants need to make sure they fully understand the company that is undergoing a corporate transaction. **Due diligence issues are often exacerbated in cross-border deals, making this book's global focus very relevant.**"

JAMES H. ZUKIN
Senior Managing Director
Houlihan Lokey Howard & Zukin Capital

"It's hard to find a book more timely than *Due Diligence for Global Deal Making*. The rapid growth of global markets in the last decade of the twentieth century increased the risk of fraud and problems in understanding legal and financial documents and assessing operations. Arthur Rosenbloom, a top authority on due diligence, has correctly diagnosed the situation and edited a useful and strategically important book. **Many of the recent financial scandals to which we are witness might have been avoided had the lessons appearing in this work been heeded.**"

VLADIMIR KVINT, PH.D.
Professor of Management Systems and International Business
Fordham University
Author, *The Global Emerging Market in Transition*
Contributing Editor, *Forbes Global* magazine

"The fact of globalization makes reading *Due Diligence for Global Deal Making* **a must for those contemplating cross-border transactions.** The work offers a much needed discussion of the strategic planning, human relations, and critical operational components of the due diligence process."

MARK LOWENTHAL
Former President
Revlon Europe and the Middle East

Due Diligence
FOR Global
Deal Making

A complete list of our titles is available at
www.bloomberg.com/books

BLOOMBERG PROFESSIONAL LIBRARY

Due Diligence FOR Global Deal Making

THE DEFINITIVE GUIDE TO
Cross-Border Mergers and Acquisitions, Joint Ventures, Financings, AND Strategic Alliances

EDITED BY

ARTHUR H. ROSENBLOOM

BLOOMBERG PRESS
Princeton

First edition published 2002
1 3 5 7 9 10 8 6 4 2

Library of Congress Cataloging-in-Publication Data

Due diligence for global deal making : the definitive guide to cross-border mergers and acquisitions, joint ventures, financings, and strategic alliances / edited by Arthur H. Rosenbloom.
        p. cm.
    Includes bibliographical references and index.
    ISBN 1-57660-092-0
        1. Consolidation and merger of corporations--Handbooks, manuals, etc.
2. International business enterprises. 3. Joint ventures. 4. Strategic alliances (Business)
I. Rosenbloom, Arthur H.

HD2746.5 .D84 2002
658.1'6--dc21   2002008649

Acquired and edited by Kathleen A. Peterson

Preface

EFFECTIVE DUE DILIGENCE in *all* transactions—but especially those involving parties across national borders—is a critical component of the deal process. This is an absolute if parties are to be spared the enormous loss of time, money, and reputation (not to mention personal anguish) of deals that fail to meet expectations. Cross-border due diligence encompasses all of the elements found in purely domestic transactions, overlain with an extra level of complexity due to its international character. (Thus, a double-barreled benefit for readers of this book!)

Paradoxically, the transactions in which strategic, operational, financial, tax, legal and people/organizational due diligence is practiced effectively often don't make the headlines but are observable only dimly in the accreted earnings of the acquirer. However with failed or aborted transactions, the story is otherwise. Daimler-Chrysler's shrunken market capitalization evidences a corporate marriage flawed in many cultural, financial, and operational ways. Better due diligence might have made a difference.

Could better legal due diligence have more effectively anticipated the European Union's anti-monopoly response, now on appeal, in General Electric-Honeywell? Perhaps. Had Enron, Global Crossing, Sunbeam, Adelphia, or WorldCom been the subject of cross-border deal offers, would the many issues surrounding these companies that later surfaced have been unearthed by means of effective due diligence? Unprovable, of course, but reasonably likely, we assert.

In many respects, twenty-first century cross-border due diligence resembles the classic due diligence of prior periods, but in two distinct ways it does not. One is the specter of international terrorism, whose implications for cross-border due diligence are the subject of the Appendix to this book. A second is the proliferation of intellectual property-driven transactions in fields like biotech, software, and communications. These sorts of deals require new levels of due diligence resourcefulness, and we have more than a little guidance for you in this regard in the pages that follow.

To the corporate executives, attorneys, accountants, consultants, and the graduate students and others who aspire to become skilled in any of these areas, and to those who teach these aspirants, we hope and believe that you'll find in this volume a wealth of practical advice on how to become more effective professionals in cross-border due diligence. Good luck and good deals to you all.

Acknowledgments

P UTTING TOGETHER a book like this is a work of the heart as well as the mind. All of the contributors to this volume either advise clients in cross-border deals, have been corporate executives engaged in the process of doing deals, or teach graduate students in this field. (Some of us do more than one of these.) From professional experience, we know how integral a role effective due diligence plays in the cross-border transactional process. As practitioners, we're pleased to share our insights with you because we believe that better due diligence means making better deals that result in greater increase in shareholder wealth. Such due diligence also may result in deals that, for good reason, should be aborted—an outcome that also serves shareholder interests.

Thanks are due to many staff persons at each of our places of work through whose efforts our chapters have emerged. Special thanks are due to Orietta Ramirez of CFC Capital LLC, who coordinated the general production of the manuscript, and Kathleen Peterson, Senior Acquisitions Editor at Bloomberg Press, for her valuable advice at every step of the way from conceptualization to manuscript production.

Contents

5 Legal Due Diligence

About the Contributors

Linda D. Arrington has spent nine years in banking at Chase Securities (and its predecessor institutions). Her investment banking experience has covered corporate finance activities in the retail industry group, media and telecommunications group, mergers and acquisitions group, private equity group, debt capital markets, and cross-border M&A analysis while covering clients in Johannesburg, South Africa. Ms. Arrington holds an M.B.A. from Columbia Business School and a B.S. degree from William Smith College. **(Chapter 3)**

Robert T. Bossart is of counsel in the New York office of Greenberg Traurig, LLP and chair of the firm's corporate international tax group. Formerly an international tax partner with the New York office of a Big Five CPA firm, he specializes in corporate and international tax matters. Mr. Bossart's client responsibilities include U.S. multinationals as well as non-U.S. multinationals investing in the United States. With more than twenty-five years of experience advising multinational manufacturing and service corporations, Mr. Bossart has frequently been involved in helping companies develop global tax strategies, including funding and movement of intellectual property, cross-border structuring and financing, mergers and acquisitions, transfer pricing issues, manufacturing/ distribution/Internet reengineering, revenue agent examinations, and strategic repatriation planning. In addition to an LL.M. in taxation from New York University's Graduate School of Law, Mr. Bossart holds a B.S. from the Wharton School of the University of Pennsylvania, an M.B.A. from Cornell University's Johnson Graduate School of Management; and a J.D. from Fordham Law School. **(Chapter 6)**

Geoff Cullinan is a director in Bain & Company's London office, where he leads the European private equity practice and the London M&A practice. Mr. Cullinan has more than twenty-five years of general management, strategy consulting, and investor experience in a wide range of industries, including consumer products, retail, automotive, chemicals, engineering, and financial services. Prior to joining Bain, Mr. Cullinan was chief executive officer of Hamleys Plc, a retail business in the toys and games industry. Previous to this, Mr. Cullinan was the founder and managing director of OC&C Strategy Consultants and the head of the European consumer goods practice for Booz Allen & Hamilton Inc. He has a B.A. degree from the University of Essex and earned an M.B.A. with highest distinction from IMEDE, Lausanne.   *(Chapter 2)*

Jorge M. Diaz is a partner at Ernest & Young LLP with more than twenty-eight years of experience working with organizations in various industries including telecommunications, international banking, domestic banking, investment funds, fresh produce, professional sports, real estate, airlines, manufacturing, and distribution. He has provided audit and business advisory services to many international public and privately held companies, and has expertise in initial and secondary public offerings, capital formation, and mergers and acquisitions. Mr. Diaz is actively involved in the international business community and has assisted numerous clients in accomplishing financial and operational objectives, including privatizations. He is a member of the Florida Institute of Certified Public Accountants, the California Society of Certified Public Accountants, the Florida International Bankers Association, the Florida International University Council of 100, and the Greater Miami Chamber of Commerce. Mr. Diaz has a Bachelor of Accounting degree from the University of Southern California.

(Chapter 4)

Nelson M. Fraiman is codirector of the W. Edwards Deming Center for Quality, Productivity and Competitiveness and professor in the Division of Decision, Risk and Operations at Columbia Business School. Professor Fraiman joined the business school faculty after a seventeen-year career at International Paper Company, where he was chief technology officer for eight manufacturing divisions. He specializes in the retailing, consulting, and process industries and studies general areas of operations management and technology. Professor Fraiman holds B.S., M.S., M.B.A., and Ph.D. degrees, all from Columbia University.

(Chapter 3)

Tom Holland is a director in Bain & Company's San Francisco office, where he heads the global business consulting firm's worldwide private equity practice. For nearly twenty years, Mr. Holland has worked with companies in a variety of industries, including technology, telecommunications, transportation, consumer goods, and manufacturing. He has advised clients on growth strategies, cost and asset restructuring, reengineering, and mergers and acquisitions. He has also helped clients facing major turnarounds or repositionings in turbulent industries, such as telecommunications, transportation, and aerospace. Prior to joining Bain, Mr. Holland held positions with Clorox and Bain Capital. He earned his M.B.A. with distinction from Stanford University and holds a B.S. degree in engineering from the University of California at Berkeley. *(Chapter 2)*

James B. Mintz, president of James Mintz Group, Inc., has spent the past twenty-five years conducting investigations worldwide, primarily for law firms and general counsel. Mr. Mintz helped pioneer the use of sophisticated resources by law firms in the late 1970s, as an in-house investigator at the Washington, D.C., law firm of Wald, Harkarader & Ross. He cofounded Investigative Group, Inc. in 1984, serving as its president for a decade, and founded the James Mintz Group in 1994. Mr. Mintz has participated in seminars on corporate investigations, including the Practicing Law Institute's "Conducting Complex Fact Investigations—Techniques and Issues for Lawyers." His articles have appeared in the *Wall Street Journal,* the Conference Board's *Across the Board* magazine, *Directors & Boards,* and *Corporate Legal Times.* Mr. Mintz can be reached at jmintz@mintzgroup.com. *(Chapter 8)*

Carolyn E.C. Paris is a fellow at the W. Edwards Deming Center for Quality, Productivity and Competitiveness at Columbia Business School. She was previously a partner at the law firm of Davis Polk & Wardwell in New York City, specializing in corporate finance, including domestic and international acquisition finance, structured finance, and bankruptcy/

workouts. Ms. Paris was also director of practice information and professional development at Davis Polk, working in intranet-based knowledge management. She is the author of *How to Draft for Corporate Finance* (Practicing Law Institute, 2000). She has a B.A. degree from the University of Illinois, an M.A. degree from the University of Texas, a J.D. from Stanford University, and an M.B.A. from Columbia University.

(Chapter 3)

Michael L. Pinedo is the Julius Schlesinger Professor of Operations Management and deputy chair of the department of information, operations, and management sciences at the Stern School of Business, New York University. He has previously taught at Columbia University, Instituto Venezolano de Investigaciones Cientificas (Caracas), and the Georgia Institute of Technology. Mr. Pinedo has worked extensively in industrial systems development, with a focus on planning and scheduling of production and service systems, for clients such as Philips Electronics, Siemens, and Merck. He is the author or coauthor/editor of several books on operations scheduling, queueing networks, and value creation in financial services, as well as editor of the Journal of Scheduling. He holds an Ir degree from the Delft University of Technology and M.S. and Ph.D. degrees from the University of California at Berkeley. *(Chapter 3)*

Richard C. Porter is a human resources consultant specializing in advising global companies on organizational issues. Experienced working with industry leaders in North America, Europe, Asia, South America, and Africa, he possesses particular expertise in multinational mergers, acquisitions, divestitures, and joint ventures. Most recently he was the global head of human resources for Young & Rubicam Advertising, an agency with operations in more than eighty countries. Previously Mr. Porter served in a number of international human resource appointments for Guinness and United Distillers Inc., part of the Diageo Group. He is an economics graduate of the University of Strathclyde and holds a master's qualification from the CIPD in London. Mr. Porter is an International Fellow at Tulane University's AB Freeman School of Business, regularly lectures at New York University's Stern School of Business, and has lectured at universities in Beijing and Cairo. He serves as human resources adviser to the National Foreign Trade Council. *(Chapter 7)*

Clifford A. Rathkopf, a partner at the Greenwich, Connecticut, law firm of Gilbride Tusa Last & Spellane, began his career as an antitrust litigator and has since concentrated in corporate, hi-tech, and intellectual and industrial property matters. He has represented the commercial interests of numerous clients from Europe and the Far East as well as a wide range of domestic clients, with much of his work focusing on acquisitions, licensing, and contract negotiations. Other areas of his practice include leasing, purchase and sale of real estate; creditor's rights in bankruptcy and distress situations, and commercial dispute resolution. Mr. Rathkopf graduated cum laude from Colgate University and received his J.D. cum laude from Columbia University Law School, where he was coeditor in chief of the *Journal of Transnational Law.* He studied at the International Court of Justice in the Hague and received his LL.M. degree in International Trade Law from Georgetown University, which included studies at Goethe Universität in Frankfurt am Main, Germany.

(Chapter 5)

Norman J. Resnicow, a partner at the New York law firm of Fox Horan & Camerini, has many years of cross-border transactional experience. He counsels inbound (non-U.S.) clients, primarily from Europe and Asia, on establishing and expanding their U.S. operations. His work encompasses a broad range of corporate and commercial transactions, including mergers and acquisitions; joint ventures and partnerships; distribution/marketing/licensing arrangements and disputes; executive employment and terminations; and real estate purchases, sales, and leases. A graduate of Yale College and Yale Law School, Mr. Resnicow was for nineteen years a partner at the world's largest international law firm. He now serves on the Committee on International Employment Law of the New York State Bar Association, previously was on its Committee on International Law, and is a member of its International Law section. Also a member of the International Law and Practice and Business Law sections of the American Bar Association, he has been a term member of the Council on Foreign Relations. Mr. Resnicow has lectured on international legal topics at New York University's Stern School of Business, the American Management Association, and the World Trade Institute.

(Chapter 5)

Arthur H. Rosenbloom, managing director of CFC Capital Corp. in New York, is a thirty plus-year veteran of the domestic and cross-border M&A marketplace, with client representations that include Continental Airlines, Hyatt Corp., and American Express. His contributions on investment banking topics have appeared in *The Harvard Business Review, Forbes, Business Week, Mergers and Acquisitions* magazine, and the *National Law Journal.* The coauthor of several books on international mergers and acquisitions, he is an adjunct professor of finance at the Stern School of Business at New York University. Mr. Rosenbloom holds B.A., M.A., and J.D. degrees from Bucknell University, Columbia University, and Cornell Law School, respectively.   ***(Chapter 1)***

Cynthia N. Wood is a principal in Wood Associates, a consulting firm specializing in change management, organizational development, international mergers and acquisitions, and executive training. Her clients have included international food and beverage companies, automobile manufacturers, paper bag manufacturers, institutions of higher education, and software companies. Dr. Wood has assisted clients in profiling their organizational cultures and understanding the implications for the successful acquisition of new business units. She has also developed plans for the post-merger integration of global businesses and assisted with the implementation of those plans. Dr. Wood has published extensively in the journals of the International Academy of Business Disciplines and the Society for the Advancement of Management. She received a Ph.D. from the University of Virginia and completed post-doctoral work at the Johns Hopkins University. She also studied at the University of Salamanca in Spain.   ***(Chapter 7)***

1 Due Diligence in the Global Economy

ARTHUR H. ROSENBLOOM

C ROSS-BORDER TRANSACTIONS are an integral feature of business in the twenty-first century. Expansion in the Asia-Pacific region as well as in North America, with NAFTA-incentivized trade by and among the United States, Canada, and Mexico, continues apace. Much the same may be said for the salutary effects of the economic cooperation among countries in the European Union. Latin American cross-border transactions abound, and U.S. investors await the emergence of a post-Castro era and opportunities to join the Canadian and European companies already transforming Cuba's trade. The trend is less pronounced in most of Africa, whose time for significant cross-border transactions is yet to come. On the whole, however, increasing numbers of cross-border transactions are likely to occur going forward. The purpose of this chapter and of the book itself is to suggest how effective due diligence can result in more thoughtfully planned and better executed transactions in an ever shrinking world.

These days, even small and middle-market firms regularly engage in cross-border transactions. As capital and technology move more frequently across borders and international trade agreements expand, cross-border deals are no longer the sole domain of corporate behemoths. Yet it's a sad fact of life that many deals fail to live up to the parties' expectations. *Mergerstat* reports that in the period 1992–2000, outbound mergers and acquisitions (those involving a U.S. buyer and a non-U.S. target) went

1

from 403 to 1,400, a 247 percent jump, and their total dollar value (where reported) rose from $14.05 billion to $136.75 billion, an 872 percent increase. In that same period, inbound M&A transactions (those involving a non-U.S. buyer and a U.S. target) soared from 167 to 1,248, a 647 percent rise, and their total value (where reported) went from $9.3 billion to $299.2 billion, an unprecedented 2,217 percent increase. While the number of such transactions decreased in 2001 and 2002 (but only to about 1997 levels), one may confidently predict a rebound in such transactions when economies and capital markets turn upward.

Given the huge increase in the number of cross-border M&A transactions that has characterized much of the past ten years, one might expect to hear of boardroom bliss and satisfied stockholders. Quite the contrary has been the case. A 1995 *Business Week*/Mercer Management study that echoed the results of many prior and subsequent studies found, in examining 150 M&A transactions worth over $500 million in the period January 1990 to July 1995, only 17 percent resulted in substantial shareholder returns to the investing party, with 30 percent resulting in a substantial erosion of shareholder returns to the investor. Results in cross-border transactions have been especially unattractive. A 1999 KPMG study of the top 700 cross-border M&A deals between 1996 and 1998 concluded that over 53 percent diminished the buyer's shareholder value.

Unsuccessful transactions, like dysfunctional families, go sour for many reasons, but high on the list in most surveys is the absence of thorough due diligence. Some experts argue that merger failure is not as pronounced among middle-market and small companies as in large ones (see the *Business Week*/Mercer Management study cited above), or, as Peter Peckar of international investment banking firm Houlihan Lokey Howard & Zukin asserts, that strategic alliances or joint ventures are likely to produce more attractive results than mergers.[1] What is crystal clear, however, is that good due diligence will cause thoughtful parties to back away from what are likely to be ill-starred unions or to identify, early on, problems in attractive deals so that they can be dealt with before or soon after the closing.

Sound transactional due diligence is a prerequisite to successful business deals in good times of rising expectations and in bad times when success may be more elusive. And it is particularly necessary in this postmillennial deal period, in which cyberspace, biotech, and other kinds of technology-driven companies are, more than ever, subjects of the transactional process. Determining the value and use of the intellectual property of postindustrial-era companies is dramatically more difficult than determining the value of the real property and hard assets of industrial-era companies. Many of the tried-and-true valuation yardsticks just don't apply to intellectual property.

What Is Due Diligence?

Transactional due diligence is the investigation by an investor or its advisers of the accurate and complete character of the target company's business. The target may be an acquisition candidate, a joint venture or strategic alliance partner, a prospective public offering registrant, or a company the investor is considering for minority interest private placement purposes. Due diligence must be linked to the investor's corporate strategy; in fact, the goal of much of the legal, financial, and operational due diligence is to determine whether a transaction with a given target is in the service of that strategy. Due diligence also includes investigating the target's legal status, from its proper legal authorization to do business to its actual or contingent liabilities and all points between. In addition, it includes analyzing the target's historical, current, and projected financial statements. It involves scrutinizing the target as a whole and its corporate, divisional, or subsidiary affiliates. When the investor and the target are in the same industry, transactional due diligence explores financial, operational, or managerial synergies between the investor and the target.

Transactional due diligence is not the exclusive province of the investor. Target companies should perform transactional due diligence on the investor, especially if the investor is offering consideration other than cash. Even in an all-cash transaction, a thoughtful target investigates the extent to which an alliance with the investor will assist it in growing its business, not to mention the critical question of whether, in an M&A or joint venture situation, corporate cultures can mesh. History's lesson is that transactions resulting in personality clashes or dramatically different styles of doing business (entrepreneurial versus highly structured companies, centralized versus decentralized, or the special culture wars that sometimes arise in cross-border deals) seldom produce attractive post-transaction outcomes.

No two due diligence efforts are alike, and for the practitioner each transaction presents novel issues. Due diligence may reveal that a Native American tribe claims title to the land under the target's principal facility, disclose questionable transfer payments between the target and its corporate affiliates, or unearth unfavorable information on the target's CEO. However, no solution can be provided unless the fundamental facts are discovered in due diligence.

Types of Due Diligence

Although due diligence practices are far from uniform around the world, they can be categorized roughly in two forms. What has been characterized as the "Anglo-Saxon" practice involves comprehensive legal and financial due diligence and significant disclosure before the signing of an agreement. The deal is embodied entirely in the documents, which set out in detail the rules governing the parties' rights and obligations. Contrast this with the practice in much of the rest of the world, which involves more modest preliminary legal and financial due diligence with correspondingly limited disclosure.

The goal among many non-Western transactors, for example, is to build trust between the parties, leading to provisional agreements. These provisional agreements are followed by more intensive due diligence, culminating in a final agreement embodying a business relationship in which the contractual documents form one of the constituent parts. Thus, U.S. parties involved in outbound transactions with companies in countries in which Anglo-Saxon-style due diligence is not practiced often must obtain the necessary information and assurances by means other than the highly documented, full-disclosure process to which they are accustomed in their home market. International deal makers must be flexible and sensitive to the differences between what is acceptable in a domestic deal and what is acceptable in certain cross-border deals.

Who Is Involved in Due Diligence?

The cast of characters in most due diligence efforts is likely to include company employees, the company's traditional professional advisers, and those hired for their expertise in certain legal, tax, accounting, and operational issues present in the target's home country. They include legal, financial, and operational professionals.

Legal pros. Because law has become highly specialized, today even midsized deals involve armies of corporate, tax, real estate, environmental, employee benefits, insurance, and other kinds of legal specialists. Although some of the due diligence legal work may be done in-house if the companies have sufficient legal staff, outside counsel is likely to be engaged in larger and more complex transactions. Over the years, business has been regulated increasingly by local and national governments as well as by treaty-created organizations like the European Union. As a result, regulatory resistance outside the United States can cause problems in what is, at least nominally, a purely domestic deal. These facts make lawyering an increasingly important part of the transactional due diligence scene.

Financial pros. In M&A and private placement due diligence, both the investor and the target typically rely on in-house personnel (CFOs and controllers) as well as their outside auditors. The underwriters and registrant in a cross-border public offering also use both in-house CPAs and outside CPA firms. One or both sides may use investment bankers and commercial banks, and other institutional personnel are certain to perform their own due diligence on the issuance of any debt required to fund the transaction.

Operational pros. The buyer must evaluate every material aspect of the target's business. Key operating personnel (in-house managers or outside consultants) must scrutinize the target's business and report their findings to the decision makers. The target's prospective ability to help the investor execute its strategy should infuse every aspect of the operational due diligence process. Operational due diligence includes investigating the target's intellectual property, its production (if a manufacturer), its sales and marketing efforts, its human resources, and the other operational issues described below. For financial investors, the problem of valuing these operations is magnified if the transaction represents the investor's first foray into the target's industry. Financial investors tend to be especially meticulous in their collection of independent financial data on the target's industry. They generate some of it internally and rely on outside advisers for the rest.

What Constitutes Legal Due Diligence?

Whether the transaction is domestic or international, due diligence must address certain fundamental legal issues. Among the basic corporate law issues are whether the target's debt and equity securities identified in the target's Certificate of Designation have been validly issued and whether the target is in good standing in the places in which it does business. Its tax compliance status in all such jurisdictions and whether it has good title to all of its assets should also be examined. Although the bona fides of all of these will surface as the target's representations and warranties and covenants in the purchase agreement, the ability to sue for breach of the agreement is cold comfort after the deal is done, when the funds have been expended and when the parties, comfortably or otherwise, must join as one to accomplish the common goals that brought them together in the first place.

Tax attorneys and accountants examine the target's tax practices, undertake the tax planning for the transaction itself, and consider post-deal tax planning. Lawyers also investigate whether the deal will raise antitrust questions. In this respect the cross-border deal may present interesting challenges, such as those the European Union's anti-monopoly group posed to the GE-Honeywell transaction, a nominally domestic U.S. transaction.

Legal due diligence requires careful attention to actual and threatened litigation. Such litigation can come from debt or equity security holders, tax authorities, customers, or suppliers, in the form of breach of contract, product liability, or breach of warranty claims, and the liability exposure and damage implications of all such matters should be carefully investigated. Due diligence of so-called lawyer's representation letters that describe such litigation is a must.

In this post-Enron age of increasing regulatory and judicial scrutiny, issues like allegations of improper behavior by corporate officers, directors, and employees (as in accusations in 2002 concerning misuse of company funds by executives of Tyco International Ltd., for example); workplace safety matters; employee benefits; potential equal opportunity violations; and increasingly significant, environmental regulations, may loom large. Second perhaps only to environmental concerns, pension and related issues have, over the past three decades, become an item of ever greater concern. Thus, ERISA lawyers are inevitably involved in due diligence. The list of legal specialists the above discussion presupposes is far from exhaustive.

Lawyering in cross-border due diligence involves considering all of the matters found in purely domestic transactions as well as those that arise from different or conflicting legal regimes operating in the countries in which the parties are domiciled. Selected examples in developed markets include rules that require minimum amounts of capital to be invested, requirements to purchase or manufacture in the target's country, and restrictions on acquiring assets in certain types of "national interest" industries (such as defense, telecommunications, or broadcasting). Many countries have foreign investment control laws, impose limits on foreign ownership, require restrictions on share transfers, or regulate the prices that companies can charge. Tariffs, duties, required government or workers' counsel approvals, and bilateral or multinational tax treaty implications are but a few of the elements involved in legal due diligence.

To this daunting list, add the legal issues that arise when targets are in emerging markets. These issues include questions about the enforceability of judgments and creditors' rights. Indeed, one investor recently abandoned a cross-border transaction because it was not able to obtain a security interest in the target's assets given the absence of a Uniform Commercial Code–type procedure in the target's home country. Contradictory laws and regulations as well as new laws (such as environmental ones) might affect how future business is conducted in an emerging market.

What Constitutes Financial Due Diligence?

Financial due diligence (leaving aside, for the purposes of this general overview discussion, the important related area of tax due diligence) involves considering a company's historical, current, and prospective operating results as disclosed in its historical, current, and projected financial statements, tax returns, backlog data, and other information. From these data, an income statement review can establish trends in revenues and profits, investor returns, and compound growth rates. Examination of the cost of sales; selling, general, and administrative (SG&A); extraordinary and nonrecurring expenses; interest; and other fixed charges and taxes can lead to a thoughtful profit margin analysis.

Financial due diligence also involves a balance sheet review, from cash to marketable securities, receivables, inventory, prepaid expenses, and other current assets, as well as the value of fixed assets. On the liability side, accounts payable, taxes, and debt obligations must be closely examined. Contingent liabilities such as those from special-purpose partnerships and the like that are usually "off balance sheet" require particular attention in due diligence. Price redetermination issues in government contracts, warranty or service guarantees, product liability issues, unfunded pension plans, equal opportunity employment issues, and the ubiquitous environmental issues require careful attention.

A review of the target firm's financing and capital structure is de rigueur. Issues to analyze include details of short-term and long-term borrowings, including maturities and acceleration clauses in debt agreements, the terms and conditions of equity securities (common and preferred), the percentages of debt and equity in the company's balance sheet, interest and fixed charges coverage ratios, and so on.

In many companies, cash flow is king. Therefore the target's sources-and-applications statement demands serious review to determine the ability of internally generated cash to finance the company's future growth. The company's capital budget and its projections require thoughtful scrutiny as well.

On "softer" but no less critical issues, financial due diligence involves examining the quality of the company's relationships with its lenders and an ultimate opinion concerning the reliability and credibility of its financial statements (such as the effectiveness of its internal controls and the quality of the accountants' work papers). These efforts are designed to forestall problems of "managed" or "puffed" earnings that could be the product of aggressive accounting practices such as cutbacks in discretionary expenses, inadequate compensation of key executives, withholding of payables during recent cutoff periods, and underaccruing for taxes.

As in cross-border legal due diligence, cross-border financial due diligence carries with it the overlay of different countries' rules—in this case different accounting and tax regimes. Reconciling the target's financial statements to U.S. generally accepted accounting principles (GAAP) may be difficult, and tax compliance may be less than punctilious, especially in emerging-market countries. There may be more than one set of accounting books. In addition, financial due diligence may need to consider the anomalies of financial statements that reflect the policies of former command economies, with their emphasis on asset size rather than bottom line results. In one deal, the investor discovered that the Eastern European target acquired redundant assets like lakeside villas to dampen earnings in order to avoid "upstreaming" profits to state agencies.

What Constitutes Operational Due Diligence?

Operational due diligence may involve consulting environmental experts on toxic tort exposure, actuaries on pension and profit-sharing matters, or insurance experts on risk management concerns.

Because operational due diligence varies dramatically from target to target, meaningful generalizations are difficult to make, but operational due diligence concerns likely to surface in most transactions include the following:

New product or new service creation. Due diligence requires understanding how the target firm creates the new products or services it sells. Is the process organized or random? Is there one "genius," the loss of whom will be materially adverse to the business, or is there a staff? Has the target skimped on R&D to inflate earnings? Is R&D responsive to customer needs? How good is the target's intellectual property: Is there real, defensible know-how? Does the target own the rights to the intellectual property it uses?

Markets. Is demand basic or created? Who buys the target's products or services (individuals, companies, governments)? Is the market growing or mature, and what is the target's market share? What factors affect demand (general business conditions, population changes, new products or services, energy availability, ecological considerations)? Is the market expandable? How is it segmented (for example, by customer type, product, geography, distribution channels, or pricing)? To what extent is the market seasonal or cyclic? One need look no further than the collapse of many dot-com companies to recognize the mistakes that even savvy financial investors can make if they skimp on market analysis.

In cross-border deals it is easy to overestimate market demand. The 90 percent market share of an Eastern European company before privatization may be sharply eroded in the postprivatization period, when it must compete against new and tough rivals, many of them from outside the country. Although hindsight is 20/20, one wonders about the assumptions the Daimler-Benz economic gurus made in 1998 about projected U.S. auto sales when they were negotiating the Chrysler deal.

Thoughtful due diligence allows companies to avoid costly mistakes in what may prove to be misguided notions of globalization. Thus, an employee benefits consulting firm catering to multinational corporations might think twice about expending time, money, and effort on a globalized acquisition, joint venture, or cross-marketing strategy if it turns out there is no consistency in the legal, tax, and accounting rules of the countries whose companies offer pension, profit sharing, or stock option plans, or if local affiliates of those multinational clients couldn't care less whether their employee benefits consulting firm was global. In such a situation it might be wisest simply to have offices of the consulting firm share leads, perhaps with a financial incentive to the referring office (and perhaps to the individual referrer) providing the lead, payable out of the fees generated by the office to whom the lead was referred.

Competition. Due diligence must ferret out the competition. Who are the competitors, and what market share do they have? On what basis is competition waged: price, service, quality, or something else? What is the market size now and prospectively? To what extent is the market subject to significant federal, state, and local regulation?

Sales. Who sells the company's products or services: Employees? Independent agents? The principals themselves? How is the sales force organized: Centrally? Regionally? How are salespeople compensated: salary, commission, or both?

People/organizational matters. How many employees are there, and what are their functions? Is there an adequate labor pool in the geographic areas in which the company operates? Are these areas likely to attract a trained workforce (given the transportation network, quality of schools, cultural and recreational opportunities, and so on)?

Over the years, human resources professionals have developed techniques to determine what sort of workforce an investor is acquiring in a target. They ask, are there unfilled positions in key slots? What's the morale like? They check for data on Friday/Monday absences, frequency and length of sick leave, worker turnover, poor safety reports, and strikes.

Due diligence must also address the nuts and bolts of pay. What are the terms of existing collective bargaining agreements? What are the benefit programs (vacation, sick leave, insurance, stock options)?

Examine the organization chart. Who are the senior managers, and who are the successors? Is there merit in considering the use of private investigators to uncover what may be embarrassing and costly disclosures concerning one or more of the company's senior managers? What are the career paths, and what is the retention outlook? What is the nature and size of management's compensation package, and, as in the case of the workforce, how does it compare within the region and within the industry?

People and organizational matters often are highly sensitive issues in cross-border deals. The cost of laying off redundant workers should be calculated as a component of the purchase price in those countries where terminated employees typically receive large settlements. When acquiring targets in former Soviet bloc countries, for example, investors have typically bid a modest purchase price to accommodate the extraordinarily high termination costs. In the final analysis, for both investors and targets, the bedeviling, sleep-depriving questions may be "Can we live with the managers on the other side of the bargaining table?" "Can we trust them?" "Is their corporate culture sufficiently similar to ours so that we can deal with the difficult issues that will necessarily attend our joining forces?" Double the importance of these issues in cross-border transactions.

Integrating Due Diligence Efforts

The boundaries dividing legal, financial, and operational due diligence are porous. Say, for example, that a toxic waste disposal problem affects a target firm in China. Due diligence on this issue properly involves the investor's legal counsel, because the investor must understand the consequences of civil or criminal liability, current or prospective, resulting from the problem. Financial professionals also must perform due diligence on this problem in order to measure the present and future economic costs of compliance. Furthermore, operational due diligence should focus on the extent to which environmental issues will impede day-to-day operations. Thus, an environmental issue flagged in legal due diligence, quantified in financial due diligence, and evaluated operationally in operational due diligence may affect the price at which the deal is struck, the structure of the transaction, and the contractual character of the representations and warranties, covenants and conditions to closing.

As to *price,* the environmental problem will affect the investment bank's pricing recommendation. Discounted cash flow analyses of the target will take the form of lower cash flow projections and terminal value computations and higher discount rates. And these factors will result in lower multiples in the banker's use of comparative company analysis.

The environmental risk unearthed in due diligence also will affect how the legal and financial experts *structure* the terms of the transaction. Faced with a material risk of this sort, the parties are likely to discuss escrows, milestone payments, earn-outs and installment sales with the right of setoff.

The same environmental risk also will affect the *terms* of the agreements between the parties. In particular, the scope of the target's environmental representations and warranties; covenants the target may be compelled to make as to the commencement of remediation between contract and closing; and an investor's condition to closing (typically a preliminary environmental investigation—a "Phase I" investigation in U.S. parlance), are all likely.

In the pages that follow we take you on a trip through the labyrinth of strategic planning, legal, operational, accounting and financial, tax, and people/organizational cross-border due diligence. We also describe new resources in investigative technology that can assist all professionals involved in the due diligence process. We hope you find the journey instructive and rewarding.

Chapter Notes

1. To the contrary, however, see Miller, Glenn, Jaspersen, and Yannis, "International Joint Ventures in Emerging Markets: Happy Marriages?" *IFC Discussion Paper* No. 29, World Bank/International Finance Corporation, 1999. See also Reuer and Leiblein, "Downside Risk Implications of Multinationality and International Joint Ventures," *Academy of Management Journal,* Vol. 43, No. 2, p. 203, 2000.

2 | Strategic Due Diligence

GEOFF CULLINAN
TOM HOLLAND

ALUE CREATION, the ultimate aim of a merger, acquisition, joint venture, or related type deal, is anything but certain. One in five such deals falls through after it's announced, due to either regulatory issues or a failure to resolve outstanding disagreements. Of those transactions that do close, one-half to three-quarters fail to create shareholder value (their earnings are less than their cost of capital), according to several studies by Harvard Business School and surveys of CFOs by Bain & Company. One of the main reasons is a failure to align strategic goals with the process of generating and executing transactions.

Cross-border transactions, involving companies based in different countries, often present mouthwatering opportunities for expansion into new markets. However, these deals also include regulatory and legal issues and complex cultural considerations, such as the need to understand foreign market dynamics, employee work styles, and managerial bias to integrate the companies successfully afterward. The merger involving Swedish Asea and Swiss Brown Boveri Inc. was a classic multicultural merging of equals. Yet the complexity of integrating these companies into engineering giant Asea Brown Boveri (ABB) extended well beyond internal business issues. For instance, ABB had to contend with strong national companies, governments, and striking unionized German workers, plus powerful and culturally different management comprised of five nationalities on the eight-person executive committee and nineteen nationalities among the 170 head-office employees.

Transactions that succeed—be they cross-border or within the same country—share a common element: The deals are closely aligned with the buyer's strategic purpose.

British American Tobacco (BAT), the world's second-largest tobacco company, understood the importance of aligning transactions with strategy when it purchased Toronto-based Rothmans, Canada's number-two tobacco company, in 1999. The acquisition involved weathering three major antitrust inquiries and combining operations in more than seventy countries. Despite this complexity, integration was largely completed within a year. BAT chairman Martin Broughton emphasizes, "You need absolute clarity ... and you must stick to your strategy, or you'll lose the troops."

To make sure two companies in a cross-border deal can achieve and maintain strategic alignment, you must conduct exhaustive strategic due diligence. Often called "commercial assessment" or "commercial review," strategic due diligence begins with a company's corporate, or strategic, planning. Hence, you must understand the strategic planning process to understand strategic due diligence.

Strategy Precedes Due Diligence

Transactions should be made only when they improve the strategic position of the investor's existing business or add to its core competencies. To probe the logic of a transaction, ask the following five questions:

1. *Strategy formulation:* Is a transaction (acquisition, joint venture, strategic alliance, minority interest stake) required to fulfill corporate or business unit strategy?
2. *Transaction target screen:* Who is the best candidate based on attractiveness and availability?
3. *Due diligence:* Does this particular deal meet the investor's strategic objectives?
4. *Target valuation:* Can we do the deal at the right price?
5. *Integration:* Can we execute our integration or restructuring plans postdeal to extract the full value?

Before trying to incorporate a cross-border deal into your strategy, therefore, you first must have a solid understanding of your current strategic position.

Reviewing Your Strategy

Corporations view strategic planning on two levels: from a corporate perspective and from a business-unit level. Corporate strategy is about being in the right portfolio of businesses, whereas business-unit strategy is about making a particular business the best in its industry. *Figure 2.1* illustrates this planning framework.

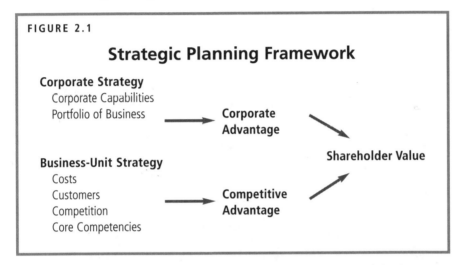

FIGURE 2.1

Strategic Planning Framework

Corporate Strategy
Corporate Capabilities
Portfolio of Business → **Corporate Advantage**

Shareholder Value

Business-Unit Strategy
Costs
Customers
Competition → **Competitive Advantage**
Core Competencies

During strategic planning, assess the strategic position of the business unit that you suspect would most benefit from a transaction involving external development through M&A, strategic alliance, or the like. Analyze the "four Cs"—costs, customers, competitors, and capabilities—to assess the full potential of a business.

Costs

First, analyze your business unit's strategic cost position relative to its competitors', and identify opportunities for cost reduction. Address the following questions:

Relative cost position. Do competitors have a cost advantage? Why are we (or they) performing above or below what we would expect, given our relative market position? What is our full potential cost position?

Experience curve. To what extent is the business unit using its experience curve to drive down unit costs? Where are we versus competitors? What will prices be five years from now?

Cost-sharing analysis. Is this business separate from another? How well can competitors in related businesses attack our business? Does the benefit of sharing costs with our other business units outweigh any lack of focus that sharing costs across multiple businesses would introduce?

Best demonstrated practices (BDPs). How low can we take our costs if we employ the best internal and external practices? How low can competitors take costs? (Benchmarking is a related tool in this analysis.)

Product-line profitability/cost allocation/activity-based costing. Which products and customers really make the money? Which ones should we drop?

Customers

Next, turn to customers to identify revenue- and profit-maximizing strategies.

Market overview and map. What is the market size? Is it growing? How is it broken down by geography, products, and segments? What is each competitor's market share?

Customer segmentation. Which parts of the market require different offerings? Are we fully penetrated in some segments and neglecting others? Can we adjust our offerings to grow sales or increase price realization? Which segments are financially attractive for us to invest in?

Distribution-channel analysis. What range of channels is possible for each product/service? Do some offer superior economics? Are we reaching our full potential in each?

Customer retention and loyalty. How can we identify the most profitable customers? How many more of them are there yet to reach? How do we increase our retention of our best customers? What is the profit impact of increasing retention by X percent?

Customer acquisition. How/where can we acquire profitable customers? What will it cost?

Competitors

Third, investigate opportunities to achieve differentiation and preempt competitor moves.

Competitive position overview. What is the business unit's market share/revenue and profit by geography, product, and segment? What are its strengths, weaknesses, opportunities, and threats (SWOT)?

Profit pool analysis. Are we (or others) getting our fair (or better) share of the industry's available profits? Where in the value chain is the profit concentrated? Can we move to capture more of it?

Competitive dynamic. How will competitors act or react to external events? To our strategic actions (such as a merger or acquisition)?

Relative performance. How do we and each competitor make the profits expected by the relative market share we have? Are we/they underperforming operationally? Is the business correctly defined?

Capabilities

The fourth, and often overlooked, "C"—capabilities—considers strategies that best fit with the business unit's core competencies.

Core competencies. What special skills or technologies does the business unit have that create differentiable customer value? How can it leverage its core competencies? What investments in technology and people will help build unique capabilities?

Make versus buy analysis. What products should the business unit make itself, and what products should it buy from another company?

Organizational structure. What organizational structure will enable the business unit to implement its strategy most effectively? How can all other aspects of the organization be aligned with the strategy (such as compensation, incentives, promotion, information flow, authority, and autonomy)?

The business unit strategic planning process outlined above should precede and inform any transaction. Meanwhile, corporate-level strategic planning will help management distinguish the portion of corporate growth that can be achieved organically from the areas where growth through acquisition makes sense.

Not all external growth strategies—that is, growth through acquisition—succeed. The misguided expansions of Gillette when it bought French pen maker Waterman and of Sears when it acquired Dean Witter illustrate the perils of making acquisitions based on a poorly thought through strategy. In the early 1980s Sears paid $6.7 billion for Dean Witter, based on the strategy of creating a one-stop financial supermarket for its department-store customer base. However, Sears soon found that there was limited cross-selling and cost-sharing potential between the two companies and that the capabilities required to operate a retail operation and financial services company were quite different. Sears refocused on its core retail operations by divesting Dean Witter just over a decade after the acquisition.

Strategic planning is obviously a crucial part of organic growth, but it is even more critical when undertaking external expansion, because strategic due diligence cannot occur unless a sound strategic plan is in place. Strategic planning is what you do to determine whether a transaction could help you achieve a goal. Strategic due diligence is what you do to determine whether a particular target could fulfill the strategic plan. For instance, as a part of its international expansion strategy, one of the world's largest consumer goods manufacturers decided to develop its own distribution system in Turkey. The high profile of major competitors, as well as the global ineffectiveness of the potential local partners, complicated the situation. The company's strategic planning, however, had focused on market sizing and retail models to estimate market potential and determine current demand. Market and competitor analysis had helped to estimate the scale of local opportunities in each region, as well as current regional distribution patterns and key distribution hubs. The analysis also defined hub distribution methods and how to capture market share. With all aspects of investigation pointing to an attractive strategic opportunity, the company had the basis from which to negotiate a major strategic alliance with the state monopoly to enter the market. Most of the strategic due diligence work had already been done in the strategic planning process.

Objectives identified through strategic planning can—and should—inform the conduct of due diligence in both domestic and cross-border transactions.

Achieving Value

As purchase multiples rise, the leeway to create value tends to diminish. Buyers have a much smaller margin of error, because high multiples are justifiable only with high growth and correspondingly high investor internal rates of return. Whereas a buyer, as the more proactive party in any transaction, might be happy to pay a multiple of 15 for a high-growth business, it won't for a more mature business. Such deals require rigorous purchase decisions and extraordinarily tight portfolio management.

Until 2000, an increasing amount of capital chasing a limited number of deals led to higher purchase multiples. *Figure 2.2* illustrates the economics of purchase multiples in transactions characterized by private equity investors, a small subset of the merger and acquisition universe.

By 2000, multiples had leveled off, and what makes a deal at a given multiple attractive has evolved again. Consider the changes over time: During the 1980s, buyers made great returns because they put up to 90 percent debt on companies they bought. But there was little growth during this period, and little multiple expansion. In the 1990s, lenders' reaction to the overleveraging of the 1980s as well as rising stock prices made deals for buyer's equity more attractive and debt-driven financial deals less popular. But there was to be another great call on debt: The 1990s' rising tide of entrepreneurship culminating in an explosion of ventures in e-commerce led to greater amounts of capital, and hence competition for a limited number of deals. This led to the greatest multiple expansion (up to infinite) of all time. *Figure 2.2* illustrates the pattern of an increasingly competitive environment. Multiples have since retrenched as investors realized that the growth aspirations of most dot-commers were unrealistic and the market for Internet stocks corrected.

Today, buyers should look to tried-and-true ways to enhance the value-creation potential of a transaction. Developing superior strategies for growth, improving performance, and identifying excellent opportunities are ways that transcend market fluctuations. This approach consistently brings acquirers, joint venturers, and other investors to more rigorous purchase decisions and to better portfolio management through strategic insight and enhanced operating capabilities. Such strategies should be formulated before due diligence begins. The due diligence process should, among other things, map the extent to which the prospective transaction does or does not enhance value creation for the parties.

Strategic due diligence may appear to add extra layers of time and money to transactions, but it occurs along with other forensic, accounting, legal, environmental, and actuarial due diligence. Strategic due diligence, as a percent of equity, is relatively inexpensive, usually coming to tens of basis points on the equity and a small fraction of the enterprise

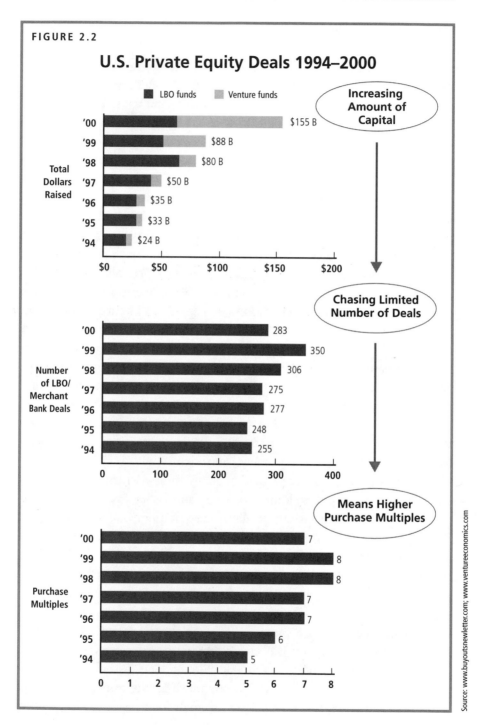

FIGURE 2.2

U.S. Private Equity Deals 1994–2000

value. And the investment pays off in spades. For instance, since 1996, Bain & Company has co-invested $60 million with its clients in seventy-two transactions in which Bain assisted with strategic due diligence. Of those, twenty-five transactions—about one-third of invested capital—have been realized or revalued, outperforming the market with a gross internal rate of return (IRR) of 67 percent. If Bain had invested that capital instead in the Standard and Poor's 500 index (and borrowed half the investment amount, as it did with its private equity investments), the firm would have realized a 20 percent return.

Compare these results with fifteen other private equity funds that invested $7.6 billion in 152 transactions that have been realized or revalued; this cluster of transactions yielded a 56 percent gross IRR. The bottom line? Buyout funds spend many times more on due diligence than their corporate counterparts, and they reap on average much higher returns. Given their lack of specific industry experience by which to test a target's projections, they build their own models and carefully evaluate the downside. They attach a price tag to risk and achieve a high level of confidence in the acquisition's value to them. What can we learn from buyout funds?

A small buyout group that had rolled up a U.S. construction equipment manufacturer into a new company approached a major private equity firm offering to sell the new company before it did an initial public offering (IPO). The private equity firm conducted a strategic review of the target company and tested the owners' forecast of 20 percent revenue growth. The team interviewed hundreds of end users, rental-fleet managers, and competitors to understand market trends. It also analyzed purchasing patterns for other types of heavy equipment to understand the effect of economic cycles on demand.

Two major flaws emerged in the owners' projections for the target company. First, a projected year-long recession in the construction industry during the next five years would result in sell-offs by rental fleets. As a result, increased sales of used equipment would depress new-equipment sales and prices for an estimated three-year period. Second, the owners had forecast that the U.S. market would grow to match European penetration levels—an assumption that turned out to be wrong, as strategic due diligence uncovered. The equity firm discovered that lower equipment-ownership levels in the United States were the result of a highly efficient, mature rental market, suggesting that organic growth in this sector would be severely limited. This situation contrasted with the absence of a rental market in Europe, which drove much higher equipment sales there.

As a result of this strategic due diligence, the private-equity group decided not to pursue the deal. The small buyout firm went ahead with its IPO. The company's share price stagnated near the IPO level for two and a half years. After earnings per share dropped 66 percent in one year, a strategic buyer acquired the company for a pittance.

Investors must recognize that economic cycles happen in different countries and in different industries at different times. For instance, it's important for a Canadian investor to have a handle on when the Italian construction industry might take a downturn if it seeks to do an Italian construction industry transaction.

Factoring in Cross-Border Complexities

The cross-border deal adds an extra layer of complexity: lack of familiarity with foreign markets. A complex combination of legal, economic, and cultural factors drives potential market penetration levels for any product by country. It would be naïve to assume, for example, that just because the United States has 99 percent penetration of Internet applications, the same potential exists in France. Yet it's harder in cross-border deals to peel away such assumptions and grasp different market dynamics to understand the true potential value of a cross-border deal.

Such complexity existed when a U.S. health and fitness club sought to roll out its concept in Europe. Although the U.S. company was unfamiliar with European markets, strategic due diligence helped it assess the attractiveness of the markets and ease of entry into key European countries. Extensive research and interviews quantified size, growth, demographics, and spending trends in each market. Further efforts assessed the level of consolidation within each country, rental/property costs, the cost of leisure-sector assets, the number of large operators, and the number of available targets.

Strategic planning showed that the European market had high growth prospects, that supply was fragmented, and that the players were local or regional. Part of the strategic due diligence thus focused on identifying and assessing potential targets to create a pan-European club. Face-to-face interviews with leading targets in priority markets determined the availability of each target, its level of fit with the buyer, and the economics of club operations in each country.

After the benefits of a number of targets were identified and quantified, it became clear that the U.S. company could also improve the target's postdeal profitability by applying its best practices (better operating systems and more effective marketing) from the U.S. market to existing European players. Note, however (as many have failed to), that for industry investors, the driver of successful expansion is strategic fit. Deals justifiable only because they appear capable of generating operating efficiencies should be viewed warily.

Identifying Your Strategic Rationale

As we have made clear, the chances for transactional success dramatically improve when the target's business is aligned with the buyer's strategic goals. Discussed below are five principal strategic rationales for transactions: active investing, scale, adjacency, scope, and transformation. Each rationale should be evaluated as part of the corporate strategic planning process and the results used as guidelines to determine the attractiveness of a target.

Active Investing

Leveraged buyout companies and private equity firms engage in "active investing." Unless the private equity investor has previously invested in a company in the industry, this form of investing involves acquiring a company and running it more efficiently and profitably as a stand-alone firm, with no operational integration. Typically, these transactions improve performance through financial engineering, incentive compensation, management changes, and stripping out costs. Private equity player Bain Capital's purchase in 1990 and restructuring of Gartner Group illustrates the power of "squeezing the lemon." With its operations fine-tuned, Gartner became a premier broker of computer-industry information. According to Chris Zook's *Profit from the Core: Growth Strategy in an Era of Turbulence,* (Harvard Business School Press, 2001), Gartner expanded its margins from 10 percent to 30 percent before Bain Capital resold Gartner to Dun & Bradstreet in 1993. Active investing can, and often does, add value; however, it is truly the domain of leveraged buyout and private equity firms. For strategic investors, a more persuasive fit is needed.

Scale

The most common strategic rationale is to expand scale. Scale doesn't mean simply getting big. The goal is to use scale in specific elements of a business to become more competitive. For instance, if materials costs are a significant profit driver, reducing costs through volume discounts will be a useful consequence of scale. If customer acquisition is critical, channel scale (domination of a distribution channel to gain both distribution power and cost reduction via bulk shipping or fleet maintenance) will be critical. Getting scale-based initiatives right requires the correct business and market definition. Setting initiatives can be tricky because, over time, the definition of scale in an industry can change dramatically.

For example, the mergers of Pfizer and Warner-Lambert and of SmithKline Beecham (SKB) and Glaxo Wellcome were responses to a sea change in the internationalization of the pharmaceutical industry. For decades, pharmaceuticals were national or regional businesses. Regulatory processes were unique to each country, and such barriers made drug introduction to foreign markets difficult. Distribution and regulatory costs needed to be spread over as many local markets as possible. Today, many of those barriers have been lowered, while drug-development costs have risen dramatically. Jan Leschly, retired CEO of SKB, said it directly in the May–June 2000 *Harvard Business Review:* "What really drives revenues in the drug business is R&D." Research and development can and should be spread across the entire global market, leveraging drug discovery and commercialization to more countries, more products, and more diseases.

Adjacency

Another strategic rationale prompting transactions is expansion into highly related, or *adjacent,* businesses. This rationale can mean expanding a business to new locations, developing new products in existing markets, or providing products or services addressed to higher growth markets or to new customers. Experience has shown that the additions should be closely related to the investor's existing business. In Zook's *Profit from the Core*, he and coauthor James Allen provide empirical evidence that acquisitions of closely related businesses drove some of the most dramatic stories of sustained, profitable growth in the 1990s: Emerson, GE, Charles Schwab, and Reuters, to name a few. Travelers Insurance's acquisition of Citicorp gave the merged companies, renamed Citigroup, a complete range of financial services products to cross-sell to their combined customers across a broad range of global markets.

Scope

Broadening a company's scope is closely related to adjacency expansion, but instead of simply buying a related business, the serial investor is engaged in buying expertise to accelerate or substitute for existing new business development or R&D. This serial transaction model has been successfully employed in a number of industries, such as financial services (for example, GE Capital), Internet hardware (Cisco), and chip manufacturing (Intel). For these firms and companies like them, organic development is often too expensive, too slow, or too diluting of their focus on existing businesses.

Transformation

Companies can use external expansion to redefine a business. This is an appropriate strategy when an organization's capabilities and resources very suddenly grow stale, for example, due to a major technological change. In such instances, a firm cannot quickly shore up its technology or knowledge by making internal investments and incremental adjustments. When telecommunications equipment provider Nortel Networks embarked on a strategic shift toward becoming a provider of Internet infrastructure, it transformed its business model through a series of acquisitions. From January 1997 through the end of 2001, the company made nineteen major acquisitions, including Bay Networks, a competitor of market leader Cisco Systems. The mergers refocused Nortel from supplying switches for traditional voice communication networks to supplying technology for the Internet as well. It undertook mergers and acquisitions strategically to make what then CEO John Roth called Nortel's "right-angle turn." Hard hit in the 2001 technology downturn, Nortel Networks nonetheless became and remains Cisco's closest rival.

Sometimes a bold strategic acquisition can redefine an entire industry, changing the boundaries of competition and forcing rivals to reevaluate their business models. This is the highest risk rationale. In the early 1900s such mergers created the likes of General Motors and DuPont, and their marks on respective industry competition have endured. More recently, the AOL/Time Warner merger has tried to rewrite the rules for communication and entertainment. But the new model remains unproven.

Managers overseeing transactions face different problems based on the strategic rationale of the deal. Thus, financial and scale deals, which often attempt to squeeze more efficiency out of targets, differ from deals attempting to enhance the scope of new technologies or products. "If you acquire a company because your industry has excess capacity, you have to figure out quickly which plants to close and which people to lay off," writes Joseph L. Bower, a professor at Harvard Business School, in the March 2001 issue of the Harvard Business Review. "If, on the other hand, you acquire a company because it is developing a hot new technology, your challenge is to hold on to the acquisition's best engineers."

Dynamic companies treat strategic planning as a work in progress, not a one-time event. In response to a company's ever-evolving strategic focus, the company may approach future transactions based on different strategic rationales. The London-based Grand Met is a classic example. It completed a successful hostile buyout of Pillsbury, owner of Burger King, in early 1989 for $5.7 billion. Grand Met's adjacency-focused strategy was to become the world leader in food, drink, and retailing, based on the premise that it could capitalize on synergies among these sectors. In 1997 Grand Met merged with Guinness. The combined entity, now known as Diageo, realized that projected operating synergies between food and drink products might have been overrated and decided to focus primarily on drinks. Diageo has since begun divesting its food holdings and targeting liquor and beverage acquisitions to further increase its scale in that area, exemplified by its purchase of a piece of Seagram, and divestiture of Pillsbury.

Even a single acquisition may provide more than one strategic benefit. For instance, when a private equity firm married an Italian vending machine company with a similar one in Scandinavia, it derived benefits

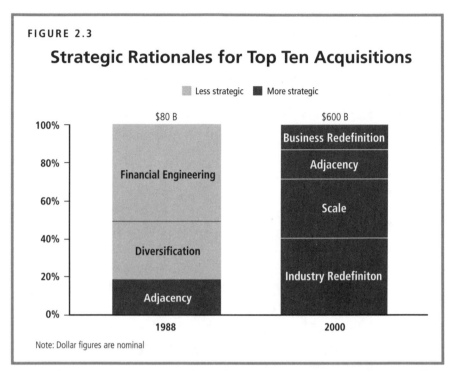

FIGURE 2.3

Strategic Rationales for Top Ten Acquisitions

Less strategic   More strategic

by combining production and purchasing (to maximize scale) as well as by implementing one company's best-management practices in the other (to broaden scope by acquisition of management expertise).

It should come as no surprise, then, that the popularity of different types of deals shifts over time. As *Figure 2.3* illustrates, the share of financial engineering and diversification deals in the top ten mergers by price tag has shrunk in recent years, while transactions based on scale and industry redefinition have ballooned.

In 1988 fewer than 20 percent of the top ten mergers by price tag reported were highly strategic. This was the era of LBO takeovers such as RJR Nabisco/KKR and Federated/Campeau. In 2000, the era of transformational mergers such as AOL/Time Warner and scale mergers like Glaxo Wellcome/SKB, all of the top ten mergers were strategic. (Acquisitions in 2000 include "announced" deals, such as the GE/ Honeywell merger, which subsequently fell through for antitrust reasons.) While deal volume declined in 2001, deal rationales remained highly strategic.

Undertaking Thorough Due Diligence

Once your strategic planning produces a sound rationale for pursuing a cross-border deal, you must undertake a thorough commercial review of each target you identify. The commercial review, or strategic due diligence, process identifies the drivers of earnings to establish whether the target is a good investment. The rigorous analysis evaluates the stand-alone cash flow value of a deal. It addresses the four key aspects of business attractiveness:

1   Market analysis
2   Competitive positioning
3   Customer evaluation
4   Company analysis

As discussed previously, however, good strategic transactions add sig-

---

FIGURE 2.4

Critical Due Diligence Activities

Output	Market Analysis	Competitive Positioning	Customer Evaluation	Company Analysis
Market Definition/Sizing	●			
Industry Dynamics	●	●	●	
Industry Trends	●			
Competitor Market Map	●	●		
Competitor Dynamics/Profit		●		
Competitor Benchmarking		●		●
Customer Analysis		●	●	
Impact of Input Costs				●
Cost Reduction Opportunities				●
Internal BDP Opportunities				●
Growth Opportunities	●		●	

nificantly to the combined entity's value over and above the target's stand-alone value. Due diligence also helps uncover prospects for making operating improvements and assesses the potential for market redefinition.

Figure 2.4 shows the analytical activities that underlie each of the four key steps in commercial review.

Market Definition

In market definition, you first identify the target's industry and the stages of the value chain in which the target operates. Second, you determine whether the target's products fit into one business or whether they should be treated as distinct product categories. Third, it's necessary to establish whether the size of the market should be seen as local, regional, or global.

Industry Dynamics and Trends

One must always be aware of industry dynamics and trends. Investors often define a target's business synergies by the extent to which the target company shares production costs and customers with the acquirer. They inquire whether the target's products are sold to the same customers and whether the production and distribution processes share costs. Cross-border issues add another dimension to the analysis. Principal geographic concerns include whether customers are local, regional, or global and whether they can be shared across specific geographies. For example, can producing globally unearth cost advantages? Is the product cheap to transport, and are there significant economies of scale across regions? The matrix in *Figure 2.5* illustrates these issues.

In the following example, a potential acquirer investigated a global building-materials firm as a target. As part of strategic due diligence, it assessed whether it should consider the European market as a single market or as a number of separate markets. This business definition not only established the target's relative market position in Europe but also formed the basis of an investigation into potential cross-border synergies that would result from an acquisition.

Upon investigation, the acquirer discovered that customers and distribution channels in the European countries were very different, and it needed to view these factors, and hence its business units, separately. On

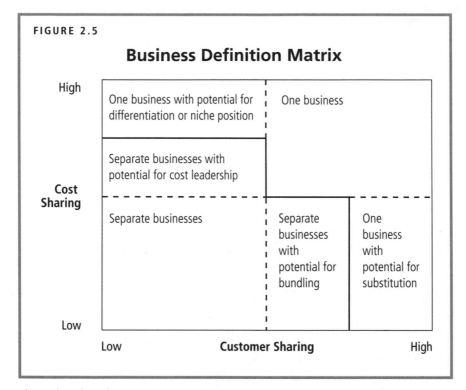

FIGURE 2.5

Business Definition Matrix

the other hand, as transportation was a small proportion of total costs, the European market offered opportunities for significant cost sharing among both the acquirer's and the target's business units. This market definition suggested that the acquirer should view the competitive landscape at a country level, but view production, and hence synergies, at a pan-European level. On a pan-European basis, the target, the number-one player, appeared to have a market share of only about 20 percent in a highly fragmented market. When viewed at a country level, however, the target was clearly a dominant player, with market share of 50 to 80 percent in most of its markets.

Market due diligence also requires determining trends in *how* the market behaves. The forces that affect industry dynamics include the following:

◆ competition (pricing, tactics, consolidation, orderly behavior);
◆ distribution channels (direct versus brokers/third parties); and
◆ fundamental shifts (new technologies, replacement/substitution).

Competitor Market Map

A market map of competitors helps determine the size of each market segment; which segments are attainable (for example, government contracting may be off-limits to foreign firms); and the market share of companies within each sector. In addition, market maps can be broken down by distribution channel and customer type to establish the target's advantage within each subsector of the market. This breakdown can help identify specific threats that other players may pose that are not captured in a less differentiated overview of the market.

Competitor Dynamics

Competitor dynamics involves evaluating whether industry rivalry is passive or aggressive, understanding competitors' strategies, and determining the basis of each player's strategy, including the following factors:

♦ value proposition (price, service, breadth of offering, quality);
♦ strategic initiatives (channel/product focus, growth initiatives); and
♦ strengths and weaknesses (level of proprietary processes, level of vertical integration, structural advantages/disadvantages).

In the example of the building-products manufacturer described earlier, other competitors had gradually eroded its U.K. market by targeting specific distribution channels. To identify the cause of this market share decline, the company constructed a market map, segment by segment, which uncovered an aggressive competitor. This competitor had built a strong position targeting the market's specification channel and whose competitive advantage hinged on its focus on the top 100 architects/specifiers. Due diligence enabled the company to identify the reason for its loss of market share, and, through interviews with leading specifiers, develop defensive solutions that allowed the company to stem further volume losses.

Competitor Benchmarking

You can determine the target's position versus its competitors by comparing its cost of goods, operating costs, and returns on assets and capital against the industry's best companies. Benchmarking is often based on a combination of information a competitor publishes—such as annual reports, press releases, and price lists—and interviews or site visits to discuss data that are not publicly available. The ability to benchmark competitors also depends on geography: In certain countries, for example, privately owned companies must file detailed financials, but in other countries they may release only very limited figures. Benchmarking helps the acquirer identify areas of potential improvement for the target.

During customer interviews the building-products company learned that certain foreign competitors were able to sell similar products at 20 to 30 percent lower prices than its potential target and still achieve typical industry margins. Self-evidently, the competition had lower operating costs than the target's. But which costs? Because many of the competitors were privately owned, the acquirer could not obtain detailed financials to define their components of cost. However, through interviews with raw material suppliers, the acquirer established that raw materials costs (approximately 70 percent of costs) were probably similar to the target's given the similar scale of competitors. On further analysis, the acquirer discovered that competitors used the same machines as the target, thus leading to the conclusion that the competitors' cost advantage lay outside the manufacturing process.

The acquirer looked hard at selling, general, and administrative (SG&A) costs and concluded that the target's problem lay in maintaining a similar level of sales expenditure per each U.K. customer regardless of profitability. This analysis identified a problem—and suggested a solution. Through profitability analyses, the acquirer could reduce the target's number of unprofitable customers and introduce a new pricing structure to weed out cherry-pickers. The target would thereby enjoy margins comparable to those of its competitors, who targeted only customers from whom they could obtain respectable margins. As the acquirer found, analyzing customer segments often helps pinpoint profit-enhancing opportunities.

Customer Analysis, Input Costs, and Price Elasticity

Assess the target's relationship with its customers and measure how price affects demand—in other words, the company's price elasticity. Increases in input costs can have a major impact on a firm's cash flow that cannot be passed on to the customers without reducing sales. To assess customer price elasticity, establish the historical impact of price changes on key inputs by investigating their relationship to margins. Cross–border price elasticity issues are important to understand—especially the local industry norms for price and cost adjustments based on raw materials price increases.

For example, in a recent transaction, a company selling consumable products to heavy industries faced a surge in the price of a critical raw material at the same time that the underlying markets were declining for the first time in years. From customer and management interviews it soon became clear that in the United States there was a tacit understanding that these costs temporarily could be passed on to customers. European customers, however, were far less likely to be so accommodating. The quid pro quo in the United States was that in periods of weaker input prices, such customers would receive price cuts, whereas European customers exerted far less pressure on their suppliers in such situations.

Due diligence not only evaluates the potential for cost reductions, it also establishes the likely timing of when (if at all) such savings might be achievable and how customers will react to the prices costs dictate. To attain the right picture of price elasticity companies need to benchmark costs internally, across the target's plants or units, and thoughtfully evaluate the benefits of achieving best demonstrated practices (BDPs) throughout the acquired or merged company and its offerings.

Growth Opportunities

The last part of cross-border strategic due diligence focuses on the target's growth opportunities, often the greatest generator of value. Determining these opportunities is one of the hardest aspects of due diligence to execute. Eager to maximize price and terms, target management too often makes "hockey stick"–shaped profit projections that greatly exceed the company's historical performance. Many targets project growth from regions where they only recently have established a presence. For example, a small U.K.-based supplier to the leading electronics companies realized that to serve the global market, it had to establish new operations in Mexico, Central Europe, and China in addition to its existing plants in the United Kingdom and the United States. The supplier, which we'll call TechCo, accomplished this expansion quickly through a series of acquisitions and joint ventures, at the same time executing a management buyout.

The revenue from the first of TechCo's acquisitions increased TechCo's apparent growth rates and raised expectations, which were raised further due to a bidding war between potential investors in the management buyout. Two years after management bought TechCo, its revenue had turned flat, and the company was struggling to maintain its debt repayment schedule, a problem exacerbated by the declining high-tech markets. The cause of TechCo's poor performance was that both the management team and the investors had underestimated the complexity of globalizing operations as well as the regional market share required to compete effectively in different markets.

Hindsight is a marvelous thing, but it seems clear that more effective strategic due diligence would have questioned TechCo's ability to match its customers' fast growth rates by understanding the source of that growth and the operational complexity of transforming a regional firm into a global leader. Better due diligence could have thrown cold water on the red-hot projections.

A target's future cash flows must be established based on realistic assumptions and converted into a more concrete value through the use of discounted cash flow and comparative company analysis. In this regard, number crunching based on unrealistic assumptions is a recipe for disaster. Consider the case of a leading LBO firm contemplating a $400 million acquisition of a major value-added reseller of personal computers and networking products. At a four-times-earnings multiple, the deal looked great. Management projected future growth from increased hardware sales and a significant expansion of its service business, which it planned to enhance by introducing higher-margin services like systems integration and outsourcing.

There was only one problem: The target's five-year revenue and profitability forecast was hopelessly unrealistic. A more penetrating analysis revealed that the economics of direct versus value-added PC sales favored the direct-sales channel, a sure sign that the target's hardware business was about to decline. Second, interviews showed that few large customers perceived value-added resellers to be capable of delivering a full range of services. The target's existing customers had no intention of extending the range of services they bought, giving the target no prospect of generating sufficient incremental margin to offset the decline in hardware sales. In fact, the survival of the whole value-added reselling sector was under serious threat. The LBO firm walked away from the deal.

The next year, the value of the target's public competitors declined more than 5 percent. Another purchaser eventually bought the target company for $100 million, a 75 percent drop in value.

Cross-Border Complications

Blaise Pascal said, "There are truths on this side of the Pyrenees which are falsehoods on the other." And Duncan Angwin, from Warwick Business School in Coventry, England, asserts that we can today replace "Pyrenees" with any national border to better understand the complexities of cross-border transactions. As *Figure 2.6* shows, these fall into three categories: peculiarities of local markets, cultural differences, and regulatory and legal issues. These factors affect the firm's stand-alone value and become increasingly important when evaluating the strategic rationale of a deal.

Peculiarities of local markets. A variety of factors, from climate to the dominance of local players, drive customer trends in a market. One classic example may be the popularity of sport utility vehicles (SUVs) in the U.S. automobile market, compared with a much lower penetration of such vehicles in Europe. There are many reasons why this is true, not the least of which is substantially lower fuel prices in the United States.

Cultural differences. Different styles of doing business often make a market for the same product vary from country to country. Also, cultural peculiarities often dictate the organizational structure of the target company (such as hierarchical organizational structures in Japan).

FIGURE 2.6

Cross-Border Complexities

Peculiarities of Local Markets	Cultural Differences	Regulatory/ Legal Issues
Different sales channels Different purchasing patterns	Ways of doing business Organizational structures Local politics	Labor laws Tax implications Antitrust laws Financial/operational reporting requirements

Some cultural differences can be overcome; others cannot. Due diligence can determine the extent to which change can or cannot occur smoothly within a firm or market, a theme Chapter 7 develops further. For purposes of this chapter, it is sufficient to point out that in assessing whether a target is likely to satisfy corporate strategy, cultural compatibility issues should be considered.

Regulatory issues. The high-profile attempted takeover of Honeywell by GE illustrates the complexities arising from regulatory differences across regions. As it was a U.S.-to-U.S. takeover, GE appeared convinced that once the U.S. Department of Justice approved the $41 billion proposed merger, the deal was as good as done. The European Commission, however, had a different opinion, and the combined companies' sales in Europe gave the EC jurisdiction. Legal considerations of this sort are further highlighted in Chapter 5, but a rigorous corporate strategic planning process should anticipate such issues early on.

Key Factors in Evaluating Strategic Rationales

Strategic rationales lie on a continuum, from deals that play by the historical rules of merger transactions and valuation (like any classic LBO scenario) to those that stretch the rules (like the Travelers-Citicorp merger that aimed at scale benefits, adjacency expansion, and product scope all at once) to those that transform these rules (like the AOL/Time Warner deal, which sought to redefine the media industry). With more complex rationales—such as business or industry redefinition—more work is required to determine the right price. *Figure 2.7* illustrates the value considerations for each type of deal. These considerations include stand-alone cash flow, cost of integration, economies of scale to be achieved, revenue and customer synergies, and value of the option to compete in new businesses.

Although due diligence is most commonly associated with a target's stand-alone cash value, it also provides the insights to understand the potential synergies and scale benefits that may be fundamental to the strategic rationale. Without in-depth strategic due diligence, a thoughtful acquirer will find it difficult to determine whether its vision of redefining an industry can become a reality. Extensive due diligence should therefore form the basis of any investigation into a transaction's desirability and real value.

FIGURE 2.7

Strategic Rationales

Value Considerations	Play by the rules				Transform the rules	
	Active Investing	Scale	Agency Expansion	Scope	Redefining Business Models	Redefining Industries
Stand-alone cash flow	●	●	●	●	●	●
Cost of integration		●	●	●	●	●
Scale economies		●	●	●	●	●
Revenue and customer synergies			●	●	●	●
Value of business options					●	●

By definition, a deal will take place if the buyer prices the target at an equal or higher value than the target values itself. To get a return on a transaction, the buyer must believe either that the target is undervalued or that more effective management or strategic fit will increase its value— or that of the combined entity. To avoid the pitfall of buyer hubris that has caused untold numbers of deals to fail, the buyer must rigorously test whether it can realistically trim costs and enhance revenue sufficiently to make the deal worthwhile. In more strategic investing, the buyer must test its potential to add value to the stand-alone company and the ability to translate perceived strategic advantages into profit. The primary role of strategic due diligence is to test whether and how quickly these opportunities can become bottom-line realities and what price, therefore, is justified.

Due Diligence for Scale-Driven Transactions

After discounting future cash flows to determine net present value of a stand-alone business, a buyer in a scale-driven transaction needs to value the benefits of combining the target's operations with its own. Failure to do so is likely to doom a deal. In cross-border due diligence, use the framework described above to test whether the benefits of scale are easy to translate across borders. It's important to check your assumptions—especially the ones that drive the biggest benefits—by doing the following:

- ◆ Define similarities/differences
- ◆ Identify overlap of shared customers, costs, and competitors
- ◆ Quantify level of expected scale economies, such as improved plant utilization and sales force
- ◆ Calculate the cost of achieving such economies
- ◆ Estimate the experience curve (the rate of decrease in product cost per unit based on combined volumes produced by the merged companies)

One U.S. specialty retailer attempted to grow throughout Europe by expanding its existing format into European markets to obtain a competitive edge through superior purchasing scale and a retail concept proven in the United States. But the ambitious rollout flopped, because the company did not properly recognize the differences in markets from country to country. A more thorough due diligence effort would have spotted competition from high–end department stores in the United Kingdom, small-shop retailers in Germany, and established "hypermarkets" in France. The U.S. retailer soon found that it could not exploit its big-box format, so successful on its home turf. The out-of-town specialty retail concept was relatively unfamiliar to European consumers and failed to catch on.

The economics were also different in Europe. For instance, U.K. property costs are relatively high compared with U.S. costs. Large out-of-town locations were difficult to find and required high traffic to generate profit. The U.S. retailer quickly tried to adapt by changing its product portfolio to rival local competition and meet local consumer tastes, a strategy that failed to realize the hoped-for synergies, like common purchasing, that had driven its original case for expansion.

Careful strategic due diligence could have informed the U.S. company, before it rolled out its big-box format into Europe, whether market differences were consistent with its concept. The company's failure to test the assumptions behind its original investment thesis prevented it from understanding the local consumer, store economics, and competition.

Deals based on scale benefits must explicitly identify and quantify expected economies. The first step is to determine which aspects of scale really count—in other words, what allows the company to take advantage of merging revenue and earnings streams? Different businesses achieve the benefits of scale differently. Some, such as automotive companies, gain it from global scale, while supermarkets gain it from regional or local scale. Others, like medical product manufacturers, get it from scale within a distribution channel. In sectors such as cosmetics, profitability is only partly linked to scale because branding has a stronger impact on margins.

To achieve scale benefits, the merged businesses must be similar enough to share some costs. In 1995, Rexam's new chief executive, Rolf Börjesson, envisioned transforming the U.K. company from a conglomerate of unrelated, cyclical, low-value-added businesses into the world's leading consumer packaging producer, through acquisitions. The first transaction closed in 1999, when Rexam purchased Sweden's PLM, Europe's largest beverage-can manufacturer. PLM provided opportunities for cost reduction through shared European manufacturing facilities. In 2000, Rexam boldly purchased American National Can (ANC), making Rexam the world's largest can maker. When Rexam acquired ANC, Börjesson focused his due diligence on making certain that ANC's processes were similar and that the two companies could share customers. The scale achieved through the ANC acquisition brought further cost savings and superior U.S. process technology to Europe while opening up the U.S. market for Rexam.

To become an international leader in the industry, Börjesson has planned to create a packaging conglomerate of sufficient scale to attract investors' attention. Börjesson and his team are building a position from which Rexam can trade business units with other companies to pursue the most efficient global mix of packaging operations and businesses.

Börjesson knew he would have a hard time convincing the market he could overcome the significant challenges these deals created. Part of Rexam's due diligence therefore included significant postmerger integration planning to consider the likely difficulties that combining the operations would generate. Differences in management and manufacturing style in Europe and America combined to make unlikely an easy cross-border integration of eleven major company sites. Another issue was the ongoing investigation from the European Union's monopolies commission, which constantly changed the playing field. Börjesson and his team developed a plan to integrate the companies quickly and establish a uniform strategy to avoid uncertainty during the transition. He also immediately rebranded the company and put in place a senior management team to provide clear direction to all members of the organization.

To earn early shareholder support, Börjesson focused on making a success of each acquisition rather than trumpeting Rexam's long-term strategy. "Give them some detail before the deal, and lots after," he says. He picked acquisitions he believed could produce results quickly. "I ask, 'Can we have all the savings on the bottom line in three years?' "

After an acquirer understands how to capitalize on scale, it needs to predict the financial impact of combining the companies to understand the premium the acquirer would be willing to pay. For instance, the Rexam synergies from two acquisitions were estimated at $49 million to $56 million. At a 10.7 to 10.8 multiple, the capitalized value of these synergies reached $530 million to $600 million. By the end of 2001, Rexam had already captured $46 million in savings, or 82 percent of its high-end goal.

Over time, as a company produces a certain product, the average unit cost usually falls because the company gets better and better at producing it, resulting in lowered prices to customers because of those productivity gains. This relationship is captured by industry-experience curves.

Companies use experience curves to develop pricing strategies, improve performance, and assess commercial prospects. In due diligence, a company calculates its own and the target's cost-experience curve and projects an experience curve for the combined entity. For each function the acquirer must ask the following: Where can I save on head count? How many employees should be offered severance or redeployed? Which plants, distribution centers, or stores can be closed, and which activities can be moved to more efficient locations? What contracts can be renegotiated at advantageous rates? What savings will these changes yield, net of lost sales, closure, and severance costs?

Further questions relate to the balance sheet: What capital equipment or property can the combined company sell as consolidation progresses? Can inventory reduction free up cash? Will scale-related revenue benefits result from a broadened product mix or a more effective advertising budget? A cash-flow model, constructed from answers to these questions, will more reliably predict value than industry acquisition multiples or comparisons with top-performing companies. If the due diligence of a transaction aimed to produce cost efficiencies suggests that such savings will be modest, the acquirer might well ask whether this is a deal worth doing.

Due Diligence for Adjacency-Driven Transactions

A transaction provides the maximum cost savings when the target's products and services are similar to those of the acquirer. Incremental revenue from such a transaction, which aims to make one plus one equal more than two, is more elusive to obtain than many people think. Due diligence uses the tools of market definition and customer evaluation to test whether such benefits will occur if a deal goes through.

To help sales grow from existing customers and products, a company usually needs to change its customers' behaviors. This is no simple task. For example, additional revenue may depend on cross-selling new products or persuading consumers to buy bundles of goods or higher-priced brands and services. These objectives are tough to achieve at a time when sales forces, brands, and pricing also may be changing. The key to correctly valuing incremental revenue involves rigorously testing whether the new entity's combined offerings would hold more appeal for customers than separate, stand-alone offerings. Test adjacency by asking the following:

Cross-selling
♦ Which customers purchase each product?
♦ Do they purchase products in a bundle?
♦ What are customers' buying criteria?

Cost of achieving benefits of adjacency
♦ How much will it cost to retrain the sales force?
♦ How much must we invest in information technology?

The adjacency expansion of the U.K.–based bookseller W. H. Smith illustrates these perils. Facing competition in its core markets, the distributor and retailer (with approximately 1,000 stores, including traveler, convenience, music, and book stores, and $3.5 billion in sales) decided to launch a do-it-yourself chain; add new product lines such as toys, typewriters, and gifts, as well as music through its bookstores; and look for international growth opportunities. One part of this strategy involved buying a United States–based music retailer, The Wall. After losing $310 million in 1996, W. H. Smith decided to refocus on its core business. Among the many reasons for this return to its core business was W. H. Smith's inability to effectively cross-sell some of the new product lines.

A recent acquisition by a leading private equity group in Europe illustrates the many benefits of creating a pan-European player in markets that were once dominated by large, nationally focused enterprises. As in many European industries, multiple regional players dominated the coffee vending machine market, which presented extremely attractive opportunities for consolidation. Recognizing this opportunity, a private equity firm acquired the number-two European competitor and then sought to buy the number-one player to create a strong European position. The strategic rationale of the deal was to provide buyers a one-stop shop for coffee vending needs.

The rationale presumed that combining the highly complementary products of the two companies would provide significant cross-selling opportunities to a customer base seeking to consolidate suppliers. Furthermore, consolidation within the vending services industry would provide the opportunity for common platforms and standards. These platforms would reduce the service costs for customers and create large savings opportunities in production for the manufacturers. Such benefits would accrue in addition to the significant cost savings available through sales of redundant plants and overhead consolidation.

The due diligence focused on the benefits of cross-selling and the ability to consolidate operations and achieve cost savings. There were concerns that instead of cross-buying benefits, existing customers might reduce their combined purchases and shift some volume to other suppliers in an effort to maintain multiple sources. However, extensive customer interviews demonstrated that the combined company not only would retain its volumes but also would grow them due to the products' complementary features, thereby proving the original thesis. A detailed review of SG&A and production also conclusively demonstrated the opportunities for significant consolidation.

Due Diligence for Scope-Driven Transactions

Transactions can allow companies to add new capabilities or scope. Some companies, most notably fast-growing technology outfits like Cisco, Microsoft, and Intel, have used acquisitions as a principal source of growth. They target companies with capabilities that would be too expensive to replicate, too slow to develop internally, or too diluting of managers' focus on their existing businesses. To quantify the expected profit implications from the additional scope, the potential buyer must do the following:

♦ Identify capabilities sought
♦ Compare the value of revenue enhancement and cost savings to costs and benefits of organic growth
♦ Determine whether the employees and company can successfully be integrated
♦ Calculate the cost of integration, including the cost of retaining key employees.

For these transactions, the potential for cost savings or revenue growth is an important factor in the valuation, but the make-or-break issue is whether a target has high-quality employees who can be integrated into the buyer's organization.

Transactions based on scope often are more complex than other strategic deals. A scope-based acquisition requires something more than simply extending the acquirer's core competencies.

For example, an industrial conglomerate that produced automobile and aerospace parts considered buying an industrial hydraulics manufacturer to widen the scope of its product offerings. Management wanted to use the target employees' skills to enter the lucrative aerohydraulics market. The acquirer interviewed major customers, technical engineers, and industry experts during the due diligence process. The investigation determined that the skills needed to produce aerohydraulic parts were very different from those needed to produce industrial hydraulic components. In this case, the commercial review found that the strategic rationale of the acquisition, namely scope, was flawed, and so prevented a potentially costly mistake.

Due Diligence for Transformation-Driven Transactions

Economic, technology, or industry changes may require a company to alter its business fundamentally. Transactions based on changing the combined entity's business are often based on a vision that's difficult to quantify. As a result, they are risky and hard to justify. Here, due diligence is essential to establish the risks of trying to redefine the industry. The key tools applied for this type of commercial review are customer and competitor interviews to carefully test whether a new business model can be applied to the market in question. In implementing these tools, companies must do the following:

◆ Focus on possible outcomes (scenario analysis)
◆ Test customer acceptance and cost and revenue synergies for each scenario to develop probable outcomes
◆ Determine market size, expected growth, competitive position, and customer acceptance of new markets

A clear example cited earlier in this chapter of an attempt to redefine an industry comes from one of the highest-profile mergers of recent years, the AOL/Time Warner merger. AOL/Time Warner aimed to take a lead in redefining the way people buy media offerings. The company made a bold, long-term strategic move that, as was noted, has yet to prove itself but has certainly shaken up the music industry.

In transformation transactions, executives are wise to address soft issues, such as corporate culture, head-on. A Bain & Company study of twenty-one high-performance business turnarounds shows that a fact-based approach to solving soft issues works for businesses driving transformational change. The study found three constants of corporate transformation that yielded high returns: The most successful transformers focused on results, not the process of change; they replaced key senior executives, not departments wholesale; and they implemented multiple moves quickly and simultaneously.

In business, as in life, the personalities of the people involved are critical for success. The due diligence process must include an evaluation of the capabilities of current management. If the acquirer deems them unlikely to expand the company to achieve the necessary returns, it may need to replace them, or coach them. The potential acquirer may rather drop the deal entirely or approach it differently.

Assessing Your Findings

Cross-border issues often complicate the due diligence process, reducing the potential to realize the value sought. Many cross-border peculiarities, such as market dynamics, local competitors, and local consumer tastes, are as straightforward to quantify as they are in a domestic deal. However, the risk of cultural differences between two firms can affect the value. Although it is difficult to accurately quantify such risks, acquirers must evaluate them. Nonquantifiable barriers associated with a deal represent an execution risk that acquirers must consider and mitigate through an effective implementation plan.

From a cross-border perspective, therefore, the probability that a deal will succeed depends primarily on two factors: the quantifiable value of the deal and the level of cultural barriers or execution risk. *Figure 2.8* below shows how these factors affect the likelihood of any particular deal succeeding.

A deal with high quantifiable value and few cultural barriers will have the highest chance of success. Conversely, a deal that is likely to generate little value and has many cultural barriers is very likely to fail. Generally, acquirers prefer transactions that fall into the "high value/low barriers" segment. If there is a clear strategic rationale to the deal, there may be little alternative to selecting a target that will involve significant cross-border issues. A clear example of such a deal was the attempted GE takeover of Honeywell. It would be naïve to assume that Jack Welch was unaware of the potential European opposition to the deal. However, the enormous strategic benefits of the deal made it a risk worth taking. As he took ownership of the merger process, he said, "My neck is on the line."

Significant cross-border issues should not deter buyers from considering a merger or acquisition. A private equity firm that owned a U.K./U.S. industrial products manufacturer was considering an acquisition of a U.K./E.U. company. Significant cross-border issues included the cultural differences between the entrepreneurial U.S. management team and the European division management team; fundamental differences in

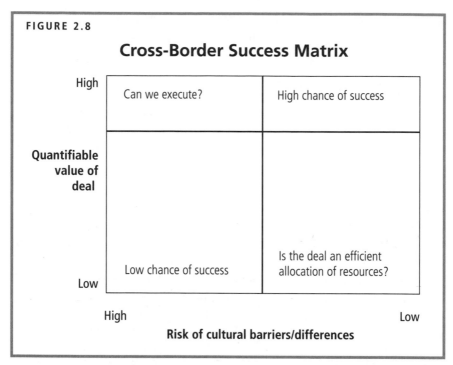

FIGURE 2.8

Cross-Border Success Matrix

	High	
Quantifiable value of deal	Can we execute?	High chance of success
	Low chance of success	Is the deal an efficient allocation of resources?
	Low	

High   Low

Risk of cultural barriers/differences

market dynamics (for example, distributor-based sales in the United States versus direct sales in Europe); and different capabilities and sector strengths. The strategic benefits included synergies in the U.K. operations, product portfolio enhancement, regional branding, scale benefits through purchasing/production rationalization, and internal benchmarking. These issues placed the deal in the "high value/high risk" box. The buyer did not walk away. By addressing the risks, it was confident it would realize synergies. For instance, the parties addressed and resolved branding issues and established the future strategy of the firm.

Figure 2.8 also underscores the possibility that a deal with very few cross-border complications can still fail to add much value to the acquirer. Companies that either are more risk averse or have a portfolio gap may still be willing to undertake such deals. They accept a lower return in exchange for the reduced risk that the relatively straightforward deal offers. Of course, the price of a deal is likely to take this into account, so the returns may be no easier to achieve.

Creating value through M&A transactions has always been an uncertain business. Information that increases the level of confidence in value creation is extremely valuable. The added complexities of cross-border deals accentuate the need for a comprehensive strategic due diligence driven by the acquirer's need to understand the key issues that could affect the specific deal. A comprehensive review in the context of the acquirer's corporate strategy helps it understand the stand-alone value of the deal, the potential for improvements through active investing, and the potential to add value through strategic rationales unique to the acquirer.

The authors would like to acknowledge the support of Bain colleagues John Billowits, Katie Smith Milway, Robin Stopford, and Christian Strobel in writing this chapter.

Cross-Border Strategic Due Diligence

EVERY TRANSACTION IS UNIQUE and requires a customized approach. However, the following questions provide a guide to the types of issues generally encountered. **Questions in bold refer to those specific to cross-border deals.**

GENERAL
1. Market Analysis
- ❏ What is the target's key market (market definition)?
- ❏ What are the underlying trends in the target's market?
- ❏ How will these trends affect the growth and profitability of that market?

2. Competitive Position
- ❏ Which competitors participate in the target's market?
- ❏ What is the target's size and growth relative to the competitors in the market?
- ❏ How has the competition developed over time?
- ❏ How do the competitive dynamics vary by distribution channel?

3. Customer Evaluation
- ❏ Who are the target's customers?
- ❏ What are the key trends in the customers' markets?
- ❏ What are the key criteria for gaining and retaining new customers?
- ❏ How does the target meet the customer retention criteria?
- ❏ How profitable are the different customer segments?

4. Cost Evaluation
- ❏ What is your cost position relative to the target's?
- ❏ Who are your least profitable customers, and how much are they costing you?
- ❏ How much further can competitors drive down costs?
- ❏ What costs can you truly share with your target?
- ❏ How much further can you drive down costs on your own? As a merged entity?

5. Company Analysis
- ❏ How does the target's profitability compare to the profitability of its competitors?

❏ How sensitive are the target's margins to input costs?

ACTIVE INVESTING (What is the firm's full potential?)
1. Market Analysis
❏ Are there any opportunities for the target to influence the market structure?

2. Competitive Position
❏ Are there any opportunities to increase the target's market share?
❏ Are there any threats to the target's position?

3. Customer Evaluation
❏ Is there an opportunity to weed out unprofitable customers?
❏ Is there an opportunity to trade up customers to higher-value-added products/services?

4. Company Analysis
❏ Are there any opportunities to improve profitability (cost reduction opportunities, revenue enhancement)?
❏ Can you achieve these improvements (timing to full potential)?

STRATEGIC RATIONALE
❏ **What are the expected costs of integrating the two firms?**
❏ Do the quantifiable strategic benefits associated with the acquisition outweigh the costs?

1. Scale
❏ Does the target participate in the same market as you?
❏ How will the transaction improve the competitive position of the combined entities in the related markets?
❏ What are the potential scale economies of the transaction?
❏ What are the specific cost-reduction opportunities, and how quickly can they be achieved?
❏ Do you share customers/customer types with the target?
❏ **What are the similarities/differences of the markets in the different countries?**
❏ **Are competitors local, regional, or global?**
❏ **Are scale economies relevant on a local, regional, or global basis?**
❏ **Is there customer sharing between countries?**

2. Adjacency

❏ Is the transaction highly related to your corporate strategy?
❏ How large is the potential to cross-sell the target's products with yours?
❏ How similar are the buying criteria for the two products?
❏ Which roles will overlap in the combined companies?
❏ What is the potential for cost savings in the combined companies?
❏ **Are opportunities for cross-selling transferable across borders?**

3. Scope

❏ Does the target possess the capabilities you seek?
❏ Will the new capabilities significantly improve your profitability?
❏ How does the cost of acquiring the capabilities from the target compare to the cost of building them internally?
❏ Can the capabilities be retained postacquisition?
❏ **Are the capabilities transferable across borders?**

4. Transformation

❏ What is the underlying potential for transforming the industry? Will customers accept the transformation of the industry?
❏ How will the integration of the target aid the transformation of the industry?
❏ How will the transformed industry benefit the combined companies?
❏ **Are the benefits of the transformation local, regional, or global?**

3 | Operational Due Diligence

LINDA D. ARRINGTON
NELSON M. FRAIMAN
CAROLYN E.C. PARIS
MICHAEL L. PINEDO

D UE DILIGENCE BEGAN as a precautionary measure for securities underwriters. Although it is now a regular part of deal making, and a substantive exercise, due diligence often still tends to be heavily weighted toward legal and financial aspects of the target company. [1]

As a result, the typical staffing of a "deal team" with corporate legal and financial executives and their outside advisers means that operational due diligence is often focused on balance sheet assets and their most easily documented qualities, such as location, appraised value, age, condition, and capacity. The key members of the deal team are not always equipped to grapple with the less tangible but no less critical aspects of operations, like process, work flow, and quality control.

Mapping these qualities of a target company is not as simple as locating records in a file cabinet or its virtual equivalent; companies' policies and practices regarding operations analysis and documentation vary. Hence, what is really important to know about the target probably can't be found in documents in a data room. For this reason, dealing with critical questions such as "How good is this business, and does it fit with ours?" requires the involvement of line-operating professionals.

If the acquirer has no line-operating professionals with the expertise to perform due diligence on the target's operations, that in itself might be a warning sign: Most successful deals involve a target that is engaged in the acquirer's core business or a closely related business. In a *Harvard Business Review* roundtable, Mackey McDonald of VF Corporation commented,

> In our business, we find that if we venture too far from our core com-
> petencies, the risk isn't worth it. Many of the companies we buy are run
> by entrepreneurs who generally know a lot more about why they're sell-
> ing than we know about why they're selling. We like to stick to our core
> businesses so if we run into problems, we have the resources and know-
> how to resolve them.[2]

Operational due diligence is often given short shrift, due to real or perceived time constraints. Even when performed well by the persons having the right expertise, it is too often not integrated within the over-all management of the deal process. Thus, teams of specialists are field-ed to "sign off" on the areas of their expertise, but their findings aren't always cross-checked. More important, the operational questions relat-ing to postmerger integration don't surface.

Although a checklist approach (which often, not coincidentally, cor-responds to prospectus requirements) is a good way to manage a com-plex information-gathering process under time pressure, it won't, by itself, yield answers to the most important questions. Instead of relying on responses to a list of unrelated questions parceled out to specialist teams, due diligence that focuses on development of a post-transaction integration plan, which is itself premised on clearly defined so-called value drivers, is most likely to be useful in answering the ultimate ques-tions: Should we do this deal? And if so, how much should we pay? When due diligence is not approached in this way, the postdeal integra-tion team at best duplicates the due diligence effort or may find itself car-rying out the due diligence that should have taken place before the deal was finalized—often with poor outcomes.

Operational Due Diligence in the Cross-Border Context

In U.S. domestic transactions, both parties typically share an under-standing about the need for and scope and depth of due diligence. But due diligence concepts don't always cross borders easily. In cross-border transactions, there may be little due diligence performed beyond the bare bones required to establish the legal structure and financial terms of the deal.

As in some domestic deals, this may be because the parties feel they already have a good grasp of each other's businesses or because the deal is being struck principally on the basis of a strategic vision that does not accord much weight to details of execution. In a cross-border deal, it may also be because one or more of the parties is used to operating in a business culture that emphasizes relationships and trust rather than full disclosure and close scrutiny. In such cases, operational due diligence is not deemed a priority, and, if performed, takes place after a long period of confidence building.

Designing Due Diligence from a Strategic Perspective

The nature and scope of operational due diligence for a given transaction should be determined by management's goal in pursuing the deal. Typical articulations of such a goal might be:

♦ to enter a new market or otherwise expand territorial scope or market share in existing territories;

♦ to share and leverage complementary products, skills, and knowledge across the conjoined territories; or

♦ to exploit synergies arising from scale or scope efficiencies.

Interestingly, it is not always clear that top management has as a stated goal to increase shareholder value. *World Class Transactions: Insights into Creating Shareholder Value Through Mergers and Acquisitions* (KPMG, 2001) reports that, based on a survey of larger global deals completed between 1997 and 1999, reasons stated for pursuing M&A opportunities were to increase market share (29 percent), to enter new geographic markets (28 percent), to maximize shareholder value (23 percent), and other (20 percent). KPMG found no correlation between the stated objective of the transaction and the success of the deal in terms of creating shareholder value.

Too often, focus seems to be on the top line, not on the bottom line. But an unstated rationale for any transaction, including one across borders, must be that the deal will end up being profitable to the acquirer, or provide a defensive or survival strategy (in other words, eat or be eaten).

The trend toward growth through cross-border deals is particularly strong in those industries that see inevitable consolidation due to global pressures and technological changes affecting the fundamental business proposition. In many businesses, managing global production efficiently is most easily accomplished when the business has a critical mass of volume. Most of the growth in international production has been via cross-border M&A, not through greenfield production, in large part due to the perceived need for speed. Or a business, such as financial services or pharmaceuticals research, may be so dependent on large-scale information technology infrastructure—networks, databases, and the associated systems engineering or statistical analyses—that the related investments can be supported only by an enterprise of significant size. Merging permits companies to share the costs of critical systems infrastructure and innovation.

Too often overlooked, however, are the transaction overhead costs that may take several years to work through the system, jeopardizing productivity and profits in the interim. In the rush to complete a strategic merger, parties have overlooked critical liabilities or made overoptimistic assumptions about the cost, the time required, and even the feasibility of the theoretical integration plan.

Well-executed operational due diligence allows the parties to determine how the combined enterprise will conduct its business to maximize earnings. Such due diligence is required in order to assess whether the hoped-for transaction benefits can be realized, and, if so, in what way, in what time frame, and at what cost. Operational due diligence should answer the question: Does the combination result in economies, efficiencies, and synergies that make the company a more profitable, more competitive enterprise than it was predeal, without incurring large incremental investments or unacceptable risks along the way?

Validating and Integrating Other Due Diligence Efforts

Well-executed operational due diligence by line-operating managers will integrate a number of other aspects of due diligence that might otherwise tend to be reviewed in isolation and signed off on by area experts. Areas of operational due diligence that should dovetail with HR, finance, accounting, IT, legal (including intellectual property, environmental, and insurance), and strategic due diligence include the following:

♦ Workforce needs, staffing assumptions and practices, recruitment and training

♦ Environmental matters, other potential liabilities arising from the company's operations

♦ Cross-border risks and issues (exchange and currency risks, tax burdens, and political risks broadly defined to include human rights concerns)

♦ Other macro-level issues, such as shifts in methods of production, changes in demand, or vulnerabilities such as exposure to uncertainties in the supply of power, labor, or raw materials

♦ Information systems

♦ Insurance

♦ Proprietary business know-how and intellectual property matters

♦ The cost-accounting bases for operating profitability

♦ Projected capital expenditure needs

A thorough operational due diligence exercise can validate assumptions or documentary findings regarding these and other important business matters, or it can highlight areas of concern.

Serving as the Foundation for the Integration Plan

Operational due diligence should provide the intelligence needed to develop the postdeal integration plan. Experience has shown that a merger is more likely to succeed if the combined entity shows incremental revenues and profits—not just cost-cutting—shortly after closing, and that a key to achieving this sort of success is having a detailed integration plan (and the team to implement it) in place and ready for execution at closing. The only way to get to an integration plan at closing is to have worked through all the operational issues during the due diligence process prior to closing.

Serving in Support of Deal Strategy and Pricing

If operational due diligence has been carried out and translated into an integration plan, the resulting conclusions should have made their way into the financial projections. These projections for the combined company form the basis for the pricing and structuring of the deal and, of course, for any related financing. Therefore, operational due diligence, carried through to the relevant conclusions about the integration and subsequent operations of the combined entity, should come into play to support the negotiation strategy and pricing.

To summarize, operational due diligence should not be a pro forma exercise of "kicking the tires" but rather should serve as a prudent reality check on strategic vision and global ambition and reduce unpleasant surprises. Operational due diligence should accomplish the following:

♦ Validate (or not) the value proposition for the transaction

♦ Validate (or not) the findings gleaned from legal and financial due diligence

♦ Provide a realistic basis for the preparation of financial projections, and thus aid in developing negotiating strategy and pricing for the deal

♦ Form the basis of a detailed integration plan, ideally one that will be in place at closing.

In a cross-border transaction, there is even more reason to emphasize strong operational due diligence. For example, the parties may mistakenly believe they have a good understanding of one another's businesses. This may be because of something as fundamental as a language problem or something less obvious. People may be speaking the same language formally but from a different frame of reference, so that misunderstandings are subtle and pervasive. Further, when communicating cross-culturally, it is sometimes quite difficult to pose hard and probing questions in a way that elicits a constructive response; it is quite easy to make the other party uncomfortable, angry, or defensive, and it is easiest of all to defer, and assume the details will be worked out later.

If the communication is potentially more difficult in the cross-border context, the reasons to nail down details are more compelling. In addition to the usual problems with workforce integration, management must consider language barriers and differences in work and communication styles. In manufacturing, measurements and engineering standards might differ. Where engineering is embodied in physical plants, re-engineering for compatible platforms may be required at large cost. Something as superficial as optimum packaging size and design can be quite important and can vary significantly country to country. Services or products developed for one market may require rethinking in the context of a new cross-border market and possible redesign. Mundane aspects of life such as the relative size of housing, what people eat and wear, and how people communicate may have implications for product mix and design. And, in addition, managing communications across time zones is often difficult. (One of the participants in a conversation across ten or twelve time zones is likely to be tired.)

What Should Operational Due Diligence Cover?

Properly framed and executed, operational due diligence can help the parties generate a mutual understanding of the key business processes from the ground up. It encompasses the following subjects:

♦ The processes that create value, including products and services, market positioning and brand, sales and distribution, and customers; manufacturing or other production of goods/services; and procurement of supplies, supply-chain management, and external infrastructure requirements

♦ Information, communications, and general systems support of the value-creation processes

♦ People, training, and corporate culture (including management structure and labor relations)

Designing an appropriate operational due diligence program starts with a clear definition of the acquisition rationale: What is the strategy underlying the transaction? (For a thorough discussion of strategy, see Chapter 2.) All aspects of operations require review, but key drivers of revenue growth and improved profitability for the combined enterprise merit special focus.

Three principal kinds of businesses may be the subject of operational due diligence:

1 Manufacturing: extracting or transforming tangible goods for sale (for example, the automotive industry)

2 Services, including retail sales: providing professional or other services (for example, transportation), and goods and services sold at retail (such as financial services and specialty apparel retailers)

3 Information and communications: the media and information industries (content creation), telecommunications, and the software industry

Many businesses contain elements of more than one of these types of industries, but it is helpful to consider characteristics of prototypical businesses in order to understand how operational due diligence should be conducted for each, as illustrated in *Table 3.1*.

TABLE 3.1

Due Diligence Focus by Industry

Type of Industry	Operational Due Diligence Emphasis
Manufacturing/extraction	Physical plant/process, supply chain
Services/retail; networks (e.g., transportation/communication)	Systems, including supply chain
Content creation; design-driven retail/manufacturing; professional services	People; intellectual capital/ intellectual property

Mapping the Value-Creation Process

In cross-border operational due diligence, it's important to chart the processes that create value. Such a chart should map supply chain, facilities, personnel, and products and services produced against sales, distribution, and marketing channels for the combined enterprise. The big-picture questions include: (1) products and services, market positioning and brand, sales and distribution, and customers; (2) manufacturing or other production of goods/services; and (3) procurement of supplies, supply-chain management, and possible related reconfiguration of distribution processes; external infrastructure requirements; and system cash needs.

Products and Services, Market Positioning and Brand, Sales and Distribution, and Customers

Starting with the customers first, where are they and how will the combined enterprise meet their needs? What is the product mix, and what are the brand and pricing dynamics? Are products of the combined enterprise competing with one another? At what stages are the products in the product life cycle in each of the relevant markets? What is the competitive picture in each of the targeted markets? What will be the dynamics between country managers versus centralized management in terms of marketing strategy?

From a pure operations perspective, it may seem counterintuitive to work from the customer back through production into procurement. But cross-border deals often fail because the parties never defined exactly what the products, services, customers, and markets of the combined enterprise would be. In "A CEO Roundtable on Making Mergers Succeed" (*Harvard Business Review,* May–June 2000), Tig Krekel, former president and CEO of Hughes Space and Communications, said, "In the drive to complete a deal, it's easy to lose sight of the concerns of customers. There's almost never any detailed analysis in due diligence of how the customers will react or of the pros and cons of the deal from their point of view."

Some of the most prominent cross-border deals of recent years have struggled over the issue of brand. The failure to get a firm grip on brand management was a problem for BMW when it bought Rover, and it has also been an issue for DaimlerChrysler. BMW planned to use the Rover brand to expand into new market segments and grow volume, but the plan was never achieved. BMW tried and failed to bring Rover up to the BMW perceived standard of quality. For DaimlerChrysler, Chrysler did not turn out to be a successful design or marketing platform for small cars, part of the value that Daimler-Benz sought in acquiring Chrysler. There were also problems with product positioning. In each of these cases, product lines of the two companies actually competed (BMW X5 with Land Rover Discovery and Range Rover; BMW 3 with Rover 75; Mercedes-Benz M class with Jeep Grand Cherokee).

The United Kingdom's Marks & Spencer likewise struggled with the Brooks Brothers brand and associated pricing and sourcing decisions after it acquired the U.S. company in 1988. Brooks Brothers had classic brand positioning and a tradition of quality. It was dependable and represented good value for high-quality wardrobe basics that lasted season to season. Not cutting-edge fashion, Brooks Brothers clothes were private label, manufactured in their own factories, or by stable long-term suppliers. Marks & Spencer brought in competitive bidding and disrupted these long-term supply relationships. In addition, in an attempt to compete both with Polo (Ralph Lauren's more fashion-forward rendering of the same Ivy League styles) and with mass marketers selling American basics (such as The Gap, Banana Republic, and J. Crew), Brooks Brothers alienated its traditional clientele and entered a more crowded, and probably overextended, marketplace. Brooks Brothers also may have confused customers, with the mix of clearly lesser-quality goods competing on price points, and to some extent on fashion, with middle-market merchandisers. In late 2001, Brooks Brothers was sold for less than one-third of the price Marks & Spencer had paid thirteen years earlier.

In terms of designing operational due diligence, the message is clear: Before you can analyze productive capacity and the associated engineering and sourcing questions, you must have a firm grasp of what the post-deal company is going to be producing and how it is going to attract customers and compete.

Consider the following: "Fine Papers" was a family-run paper business in Germany. Founded in the early 1800s, it had two mills and produced high quality paper for the German domestic market. The company's paper had a reputation as being the best for art books, annual reports, and fine catalogs, and its clients were household names. The family had just completed a large capital investment in a state-of-the-art paper machine when it decided to sell its business. It approached the U.S.-based wood and paper company that had been its long-term supplier of pulp. The U.S. company was amenable to a quiet, friendly deal that would provide an entrée to the coated paper market in Europe. The deal was concluded on the basis of a valuation analysis. There was no operational due diligence, not even a visit to the mills.

Once the acquirer started running the business, management made some interesting discoveries, among them that the company, with over 400,000 tons of coated paper output and 2,500 employees, was hemorrhaging cash. The mills' operating efficiencies were below industry standards, with each stage of production from paper production to coating running at different speeds, creating built-in bottlenecks. In addition, as the company shifted runs on its lines to meet different orders, it was oscillating between an acidic pH treatment and a neutral pH treatment on the same line. At the end of the production cycle the company was producing five different paper grades.

At the heart of the problem was the company's market niche and product mix. It produced its paper—admittedly of the finest quality—to meet very small volume requirements, while competitors were specializing in fewer grades over much larger volumes. The U.S. acquirer had failed to understand the market in which the paper company operated.

In doing the deal, it had not followed its own guidelines for approaching an acquisition. After the U.S. company spent several years improving productivity and financial efficiency, it sold the paper company, which was no longer viewed as a strategic fit.

Manufacturing or Other Production of Goods/Services

How well is the combined enterprise, consisting of existing personnel, plant, and other facilities, equipped to meet the needs of the projected market? Based on the company's market strategy and sales projections, is there overcapacity, and if so, where and how should capacity be reduced? Or is there a need for capacity expansion? Are there logistical hurdles (such as transport costs and production quotas, lack of available real estate, lack of skilled labor), legal or regulatory inhibitions (costs of downsizing, inability to obtain licenses for expanded production), or cultural or systems issues creating barriers to integration or rationalization of production?

In the retail and services sector, the location of outlets and related staffing are key parts of any integration plan, and thus key elements of operational due diligence. Are there unprofitable locations? How will a migration to a unified marketing strategy be accomplished in physical terms? How realistic is it to expect that multiple outlets in nearby locations will be eliminated, and in what time frame?

For an industry like telecommunications, operational due diligence means working through the details of technological, infrastructure, and regulatory problems and weighing these against projected subscriber demand. Buildout costs are high, and figuring out how many customers the company will have and how much they will be willing to pay can be difficult. Observers noted that Deutsche Telekom's offer price for VoiceStream was very high on a per-subscriber basis, suggesting the company was paying a premium to make up for deals it had previously lost out on: Deutsche Telekom had earlier failed in its attempt to buy Sprint and had lost out to Olivetti for Telecom Italia.

In another high-priced deal Vodafone paid over $14,000 per Mannesmann customer, in a business where customers are notoriously fickle. Vodafone's acquisitions since 1995 have made it the world's largest operator of mobile phone services, with Mannesmann the largest of its acquisitions. Getting control of such a huge enterprise is a clear management challenge, and the pricing environment ever more competitive. At the same time, sales growth is slowing, and important uses of wireless, principally Internet and other data transmission, are some years off. To reduce some of the cross-border management challenges, Vodafone's involvement in the U.S. wireless market is through a 45 percent stake in Verizon's wireless business. Vodafone's strategy has been to be the first and the biggest with new services as the technology develops. Its game plan features reduced infrastructure costs as a percentage of sales, and volume purchases eliciting the lowest possible prices from suppliers. One advantage is Vodafone's great brand name, which conveys the essence of the business and crosses many linguistic and geographic boundaries.

In other information industries, it may be harder to define the value-creating business as one transcending cultural borders. Also, maintaining the right level of autonomy for management in a specific cultural milieu may turn out to be difficult. Consider, for example, the difficulties that non-U.S. companies (Matsushita, Sony) have had as owners of Hollywood studios.

Procurement of Supplies and Supply-Chain Management: Possible Related Reconfiguration of Distribution Processes, External Infrastructure Requirements, and System Cash Needs

For manufacturing and retail, analyze the supply chain closely, and review cross-border and other risks, as well as how relative wage costs interact with timing factors and shipping costs. Supply-chain management efficiencies, particularly in combining reconfigured distribution processes, often present at least a theoretical benefit of growth through cross-border deals—but can they be realized? Managing global production necessarily requires a continuing reassessment of these factors, which makes them factors to address in due diligence.

All businesses depend on external support infrastructure—communications capabilities, air and other transport, water, fuels, and utilities. Operational due diligence should include a review of production dependencies on these services and facilities, and suggest where backup and redundancies should be constructed.

Finally, the review of the supply chain and resource needs can include a global tie to the system's cash needs, highlighting the criticality of the combined company's treasury function.

Systems and Know-How Support of the Value-Creation Process

Another area of operational due diligence concerns the systems and know-how support of the production or other value-creation process. Historically, management information systems have focused on financial accounting and the corporate record-keeping practices necessary to back up financial accounting (payables and receivables, employee records, and so on). Now, however, it is generally recognized that a firm's know-how, however embodied, is likely to be one of its most valuable assets. This category of business assets includes not only intellectual property, as formally defined to include patents, copyrights, trademarks and trade names, and trade secrets, but also operating procedures, standards, and product/services know-how.

Many of these assets are not recognized for financial accounting purposes, and many are not legally protected as registerable "intellectual property" or in contract rights. Nonetheless, their value can be enormous. The value of the intellectual capital that turns raw materials into finished goods, a group of educated people into a professional firm, storefronts and finished goods into a branded retailer, or a group of airplane leases and landing rights into an airline must be considered integral to any transaction. Operational due diligence, not bounded by financial accounting concepts or legal constructs, can catalog this valuable know-how, and help answer such questions as the following: What are the processes and technologies in this company that create value? Does the company have rights to the know-how it is using? If it has them under license, what leverage does the licensor have?

Is a given process or technology transferable? How must a process or technology be tailored to local needs in the cross-border context? How easy or hard would it be for competitors to duplicate the process or technology? This set of questions can have an important impact on the form of a transaction. On the one hand, a particular technology or process might not work in another country because of differing technological or social constraints. This might argue for teaming up with a foreign partner with local expertise. On the other hand, you would not want to conclude an international alliance or joint venture on a basis that permitted your partner to take your know-how and become your competitor.

Does the company have an R&D capability (which could include a customer list or an R&D database), transaction system, or computer-based algorithmic capability—such as a scheduling system—that is a significant asset? If so, how will the asset be protected, deployed, and scaled going forward?

Scaling R&D expenditures over an expanded product and geographical market base, in response to downward pressures on drug prices, is the driver for much M&A activity in the pharmaceutical business (notable examples include Upjohn/Pharmacia/Monsanto, Glaxo Wellcome/SmithKline Beecham, and Zeneca/Astra). In the May–June 2000 *Harvard Business Review,* Jan Leschly, former CEO of SmithKline Beecham, stated:

> … There are enormous opportunities in the new technologies now being developed. When we looked at merging with Glaxo, for example, we were talking about synergies in R&D. By merging the two organizations, we probably could save in the neighborhood of $500 million. That's $500 million more a year we could reinvest in the R&D itself, and that's where the merger's real benefit would be.
>
> In terms of improving growth, though, I'd have to say that we have been much more successful at acquiring products and technologies than at acquiring companies. We have a venture capital fund that invests in start-up biotechnology companies whose products and services we then buy. We invest small amounts—half a million dollars here and a million there—and we put our people on the boards. Once the companies get going, we can decide whether to buy them out completely or not. With large acquisitions, you're buying an awful lot of problems along with the products and technologies they bring.

Information technology implementations pose questions at two levels. The first is principally technical: What systems are in place? What will it take to get them to work together? What are the specific issues for system integration: hardware, software, technical staff, languages? How much will integration cost, and how long will it take? Are there intermediate solutions, or can we expect productivity lags during the integration period?

At a second level, information technology should be viewed as a tool in the enterprise's overall management and production system. It should be thought of as supporting value creation and corporate strategy, not as an end in itself. Where should the combined enterprise be headed in terms of IT deployment—in other words, what are the database needs, network needs, manufacturing-support and decision-support needs, or other intelligent agent systems needs? How will financial accounting be supported, and how will knowledge sharing be accommodated? IT due diligence that comes from an operational perspective can be a useful complement to work undertaken by experts focused solely on more micro issues, such as systems compatibility.

People, Training, and Corporate Culture

The inquiry into the "people dimension" is emerging as one of the most important in domestic and cross-border deals alike. (This topic is the focus of Chapter 7; we cover it here briefly as it relates to operational considerations.) At one level, the questions are quite concrete. They include such items as: How are people organized to do the work? Where do they work, and how is their work day structured? How will different workforces interact after the integration? Where are there opportunities to reduce the workforce, if that is part of the strategic plan? How costly will that be in terms of hard costs such as severance and other benefits payments, and what are the intangibles associated with a reduction in force, such as low morale, voluntary departures, and lower productivity among the remaining employees? How are recruitment and training accomplished now, and what will be required in the future? Seen in conjunction with a facilities analysis, these questions may be difficult to resolve but are susceptible to a rather straightforward analysis.

Corporate culture raises a more difficult and intangible set of issues. Some commentators have noted that corporate culture may be more important than national culture in determining how well the combined enterprise works. Corporate culture is embodied in the characteristics of top management, but while the issue of top management roles has always received significant attention, the corporate culture issue is far more pervasive. The relative compatibility of corporate cultures determines the degree of friction in the system after closing and affects the quality of the transaction process pre- and post-closing.

Corporate or business culture is defined by many small behaviors, all of which together add up to how the people in the enterprise work together. How do they dress in the office? What methods of communication are favored? Do they tend to be formal or informal? What is the attitude toward sharing (or hoarding) knowledge within the company? What are the roles of labor and management in the enterprise? Are workers at each level encouraged to show initiative or instead rewarded for keeping their heads down and not asking questions? Do work processes tend to be fluid and open, or are they rigidly defined and rule-bound? What will be the effects if the existing workforce does not like changes that are likely to be implemented?

Corporate culture problems crop up even in a domestic context. For example, consider the acquisition of Snapple, an entrepreneurial company with an unconventional marketing strategy, by the more conservative Quaker Oats. Blending disparate corporate cultures also has been difficult in high-profile service industry mergers, such as Morgan Stanley/Dean Witter, PriceWaterhouse/Coopers&Lybrand, and Citibank/Salomon SmithBarney under the Traveler's umbrella. Different salary scales (as between "commercial bankers" and "investment bankers," for example, or among different groups of bankers) and a history of competition are especially likely to incite friction between merged workforces. Differing salary scales and corporate culture issues generally have been noted as major problems for DaimlerChrysler, for example.

In the cross-border context, the people part of the equation is extremely important, because the corporate cultures of the parties may operate within disparate background cultures. For example, is the background business culture one that accords a significant amount of weight to written contracts, or do long-term business relationships depend more on personal or family trust and connections? How much is written down? Do companies typically share information with outsiders, such as lenders and investors, or do they tend to be secretive? If written rules and procedures exist, are they likely to be followed most of the time, ignored most of the time, or somewhere in between? What is the general business community's attitude toward financial accounting standards, taxation, and regulatory compliance? What are general practices and attitudes with respect to customer service and product warranties (for example, something as seemingly trivial as the right to refunds and exchanges)? What is the background understanding about the basic social contract with employees?

Does the background culture value change and fast response or stability and the status quo? One U.S. executive noted a difference in how his managers and the managers in a French subsidiary might tend to react to falling prices—the U.S. managers looking immediately for ways to cut costs, and the French managers likely to move with more deliberation in the belief that prices may well recover.

Which are the most important questions among these depends in part on the type of industry. In manufacturing, labor/management issues typically come to the fore and are intricately bound up with production analysis. In services, in particular in retail, design and marketing are critical parts of the product delivery. Understanding for a given market the way of life and how customers value different product and service attributes is key: Is staff up to the task and sufficiently sensitive to cross-cultural issues? Will employees be able to spot potentially costly and embarrassing mistakes before they occur? For service firms, will the personnel of the combined enterprise be able to present an identifiable and consistent face to the public, appropriately tailored to the customers' needs?

Is the "people" value of the target likely to remain with the surviving company or walk out the door? This is obviously a key question in professional and financial services firms. The CSFB acquisition of DLJ attracted negative commentary when several of DLJ's star producers went elsewhere. CSFB agreed to high levels of guaranteed compensation in order to keep others, arrangements that had to be undone when the industry hit hard times.

Staff retention also has been an issue in high-tech industries, where keeping the contributors at the firm and happy with the work environment is critical to success. Even in manufacturing, design and engineering executives may be very important to the success of the combined business. The loss of some key executives at the time of the merger probably did not help in the DaimlerChrysler situation, for one. Even if a workforce rationalization program is successful in retaining desired workers, these very workers may suffer from low morale as their teams are disbanded and reorganized or as they are asked to pick up more work. Typically, these are the employees who have the greatest opportunities for obtaining positions elsewhere.

In the content-creation industries, will the creative, design, and editorial staff stay put and stay productive under a new regime? Will their work product translate successfully in new marketing environments, and will they be able to work with others from a different cultural milieu to good effect?

Managing corporate culture issues is one of the biggest challenges in cross-border deals. It may have a bearing on choosing the best structure for executing a cross-border strategy. In some countries and regions, it is easier to team up with a local alliance or joint venture partner than to try to master the cultural issues; Western executives often take this approach in Japan. Translating a global vision into profitable enterprises worldwide is difficult. For example, Merrill Lynch bought Yamaichi Securities, a large Japanese brokerage house, in 1998, when Yamaichi was in financial difficulties. By 2002, indications were that Merrill had decided to reduce its commitment to the retail end of that business, having closed some twenty of twenty-eight branches in Japan.

What Can Go Wrong

The typical scenario for a cross-border deal that goes wrong involves partners who feel under pressure to merge to address some vulnerability or who entertain a global strategic vision that is short on detail. A company considers its declining profitability and seeks to cut per-unit costs by growing volume. Or perhaps a company feels it must merge to avoid becoming the target of an unsolicited takeover. In problem cases, the transaction often represents not organic growth but instead dramatic repositioning that is supposed to cure the ills of the combining companies. For companies that feel they have run out of options, there aren't likely to be many other potential partners to consider, and having found each other, the parties may become more interested in running upside scenarios than in conducting in-depth due diligence.

When Japan's Bridgestone sought to gain a foothold in the North American market with its 1998 acquisition of Firestone, what it got, according to the *New York Times* article "Cross-Border Mergers May Face Unexpected Hurdles" (May 8, 1998), were "five old factories with outdated equipment and employees who wouldn't accept" the extended work schedule that Bridgestone demanded (twelve hours a day for three or four days in the week). Only after years of losses—including two years of a strike—did Bridgestone/Firestone win acceptance of the work schedule. The strike and quality control problems at the plant where the strike occurred have been cited in connection with the Ford Explorer/Firestone liability situation.

Automotive woes. BMW wanted to expand its presence into larger markets without losing its brand image, so in 1994 it bought Rover, with the idea of bringing it upmarket. No substantial due diligence was conducted, and no investment bank was engaged to handle the deal. The new owners of Rover failed to see the danger signs. Once inside, BMW found "run-down production plants, overstaffing, low productivity, poor quality and increasing costs as the British pound rose in value" ("DCX, BMW-Rover: Parallels Abound," *Automotive News*, March 19, 2001). Meanwhile, the new BMW SUV, the X5, was cannibalizing sales of the Land Rover Discovery and the Range Rover. BMW was slow to react, relying on Rover's old management team. It wasn't until 1998 that BMW sent a turnaround team to England. Ultimately, shareholders lost their patience, and the board fired the BMW executive who had constructed the deal. After putting billions into the Rover business, BMW sold Rover Cars for the nominal sum of £10 in 2000; Land Rover was sold to Ford.

Daimler-Benz also wanted to become a global player in the automotive world. So it sought as a merger partner the mass-market brand of Chrysler. Again, no meaningful due diligence was performed, and Goldman Sachs was brought in only to make the deal happen. "There was no due diligence," said Juergen Hubbert, DaimlerChrysler board member for Mercedes-Benz and Smart, in an interview with *Automotive News Europe*. Daimler's management was impressed by Chrysler's profits and projections but failed to notice brand and design weaknesses, excess inventories, and increasing reliance on incentives to sell cars. There was no detailed support prepared or required for earnings forecasts, while at the macro level, Chrysler was facing industry overcapacity and tough competition, leading to eroding margins and possible volume reductions, in an industry where worker layoffs are very expensive and retiree costs are high.

The initial idea was of complementary product mix, but executives soon found a mismatch, as Chrysler pursued a more upscale market with, for example, the PT Cruiser. Logistically, there were problems in integrating the operations and extracting operational synergies due to their different drive concepts. Mercedes uses rear-wheel drive and Chrysler front-wheel drive. Component sharing was limited and platform sharing almost impossible. In *Taken for a Ride: How Daimler-Benz Drove Off with Chrysler* (HarperBusiness, 2001), Bill Vlasic and Bradley Stertz reported:

> DaimlerChrysler could save big money if the two sides shared mechanical underpinnings—the "platforms"—on Mercedes and Chrysler cars. But that, the Daimler executives argued, was out of the question. Any platform sharing would dilute the sanctity of the Mercedes brand. Mercedes charged premium prices for its cars, and racked up big profits, precisely because its platforms were unique. Engines could be shared. Transmissions, air-conditioning units, axles, and airbags could be shared. But never platforms. "A Mercedes has to be only a Mercedes." Image was a major component of Mercedes' allure.

In fact, when Daimler-Benz was faced with the decision to convert a plant for $30 million or build a new one for $100 million, the M-class Mercedes SUV was built on a Grand Cherokee line at Chrysler's plant in Graz, Austria.

As in the BMW/Rover situation, DaimlerChrysler's brand strategy was flawed. The new DaimlerChrysler cannibalized its own product line, as the Mercedes M class collided with the Jeep Grand Cherokee, affecting one of Chrysler's most profitable product lines. Chrysler was supposed to pick up the small-car segment, but the Chrysler brand didn't fit the small-car image. Management did not realize this until some months after the deal closed, leaving DaimlerChrysler looking for a new partner to develop the small-car segment. Neither Daimler-Benz nor Chrysler could successfully engineer for emerging markets.

There were significant pay and compensation disparities in DaimlerChrysler; the Chrysler chairman came into the deal with an annual compensation many times that of his German counterpart. In general, American salaries were much higher, but the Daimler-Benz travel and entertainment expense policies were more generous. The differentials in salaries created friction, while the lavish T&E irked Chrysler cost cutters. German executives were willing to relocate to Michigan, but very few American executives were willing to move to Stuttgart. More generally, there was a classic corporate culture mismatch, with the Daimler-Benz style characterized by formality and hierarchy. All the German executives spoke English, but almost none of the American executives spoke German. Key "change agent" executives left Chrysler at the time of the merger. The time difference led to the German side of the business being "ahead" of the Americans, every day.

What were the rationales for the deal? Chrysler was very weak internationally and topped out in production, so the Daimler-Benz distribution network in Europe and elsewhere outside the United States was attractive. Chrysler offered Daimler-Benz logistical and service support in the United States, as well as, in theory, a down-market branding platform. Combining purchasing, R&D, and eventually vehicle development was supposed to generate $3 billion in annual cost savings. The expressed basis of the deal was a merger of equals, and there were to be dual headquarters. But control ended up with Daimler, and Daimler-Benz head Juergen Schrempp acknowledged that his intent all along had been to own and control Chrysler as a division of Daimler, which embittered the already confused and disappointed Chrysler workforce. Less than two years into the deal, as the American economy weakened, Chrysler was embroiled in a bloody incentives war to maintain market share and run its shifts, resulting in losses of hundreds of millions of dollars and putting Daimler-Benz in a loss position. By the time Daimler-Benz placed a German executive in charge of the Chrysler division, the story was one of massive layoffs and plant idlings, with negative effects on DaimlerChrysler's stock price.

Media misfires. The Matsushita/MCA deal was also concept-driven but not well thought through. In 1990, Matsushita Electric Industrial bought MCA, the owner of Universal Studios, and in 1995 sold it to Seagram for roughly the price it had paid (in dollar terms; the sale price was far less in yen terms). Matsushita had thought of the acquisition as a means by which to get a lock on content for electronic media equipment like videocassette recorders and high-definition television sets. But theoretical synergies between content production and entertainment equipment manufacturing did not materialize. Cultural and management issues played a part as well. The film industry is idiosyncratic and volatile in its investment yields, with big winners in the portfolio making up for the losers. And there's a strong emphasis on deal making in each project. This up-and-down, talent-driven, entrepreneurial business is very different from the line manufacturing of consumer goods at which Matsushita excelled.

Vivendi's 2000 acquisition of Universal from Seagram raised questions about whether there was a plan that would generate new profits or only a grand scheme to own media businesses worldwide. Vivendi also was engaged in the media distribution channel through the acquisition of pay-television company Canal Plus in France and was said to be looking at significant cross-marketing opportunities. By latter 2002 it was uncertain whether Vivendi's management would be able to hold together its various media and communications properties in a way that generates incremental profits. Note that content producers generally want to see their material placed with as many distributors at each level of distribution as possible, so distributing its content through its distribution channels alone seemed risky. The sale of content in a single distribution channel became the subject of a U.S. investigation into the recording industry's proposed online music distribution businesses. In addition, Vivendi was reporting a significant credit squeeze that cast doubt on its media business strategy.

In another cross-border media play, Madrid-based Terra Networks SA bought Lycos, the U.S.-based Web search service, in the fall of 2000. Terra had the dominant position as ISP/portal in Spain and much of Latin America. Terra's hope was that via Lycos it could expand its market reach to include Hispanic households in the United States, Asia, and Europe. But the person originally chosen to be CEO, and in particular to add value to Terra's Spanish/Latin American access business, did not speak Spanish and had lived and worked in the Boston area almost his entire life. Beyond the management difficulties, it is unclear that the rationale for the deal had developed into a concrete action plan at the time of closing. A year later, the business was still running at a loss.

Deals That Got It Right

Of course, many cross-border transactions work out well. Volkswagen's acquisitions of Audi, SEAT, and Skoda are viewed as successes. With these acquisitions, Volkswagen was able to execute a common platform for becoming Europe's biggest automaker.

GE Capital has bought unprofitable Japanese finance companies at low prices and has achieved success in integrating them. In general, its acquisition strategy has been to find small companies and methodically bring them into the GE fold.

Tyco International achieved most of its growth from acquisitions. Dennis Kozlowski, Tyco's then CEO (later ousted and indicted for sales-tax evasion), said at an analyst presentation in February 2001, "Our deals are fed from the bottom up. ... Corporate only negotiates deals. Operations people take ownership of the deal, making sure it goes smoothly." In Tyco's approach, corporate executives developed the deals, while manufacturing and sales employees scouted the competition for potential targets and then determined how they could integrate the target into their business. Tyco's key to integration was to move fast. Kozlowski points out, "We move very, very fast on this front. That way everyone can focus on growth and not worry about more layoffs, and anxiety within the organization doesn't fester."

Royal Ahold owns supermarkets in Europe, Asia, Latin America, and the United States, as well as food service businesses in the United States. In an industry known for thin margins, Ahold became profitable as it grew through acquisitions. In April 2001, *CFO Magazine* attributed Royal Ahold's success to its disciplined approach to the operations side of the acquisition equation:

> ... Ahold makes sure it maximizes the know-how of local management, relying on local managers to determine their own product assortment, pricing policies, and store formats, while also having them take responsibility for human resources and real estate. On a global basis, meanwhile, its supermarkets jointly procure, source, and deliver products, and work from standardized IT networks.

Even Ahold stumbled when it took its formula to Asia, however, facing punishing competition from both the local street stalls ("wet markets") still favored in Asia and hypermarkets run by Carrefour, Casino, and Tesco. Still now, in Asia, the grocery store does not seem the favored venue for food shopping. The lesson here is that even a winning operations strategy won't do the trick if the market isn't receptive.

In the real world, it's not likely that a typical deal will permit comprehensive operational due diligence into every aspect of the target and/or the combined enterprise. Therefore, as covered in Chapter 2, a pre-established rationale for the proposed transaction—a strategy that examines products, markets, synergies, or complementarity—will allow operational due diligence to focus on the kinds of issues that can best test whether the transaction makes sense. The results of such a focused effort will ensure that management has the information it needs to make appropriate decisions in directing or terminating negotiations or in restructuring the deal. If the deal goes forward to closing, the integration team, armed with these data, will be prepared to address the issues presenting the greatest downside risk and upside potential.

Chapter Notes

1. Deloitte and Touche/Deloitte Consulting, "Solving the Merger Mystery: Maximizing the Payoff of Mergers and Acquisitions," indicates that focus areas of due diligence are financial review and analysis (39%), operational review and analysis (35%), legal review and analysis (35%), and other (2%) (540 companies responding to a survey regarding M&A activity for 1995–1999).
2. *Harvard Business Review*, May-June 2000, "A CEO Roundtable on Making Mergers Succeed."
3. "Many Big Cross-Border Mergers Don't Make Returns Expected," *Bloomberg Markets*, April 2001.

Author's note regarding sources: The references in this chapter to various public companies and the descriptions of particular transactions involving those companies or their M&A activities generally are based entirely on publicly-available press reports and other publicly-available sources, not listed here due to space limitations, but which the authors acknowledge and are happy to provide upon request.

Cross-Border Operational Due Diligence

BELOW IS A SUGGESTED CHECKLIST for operational due diligence from a strategic and integrated perspective. It incorporates most of the points noted in this chapter as checklist items. As a generic checklist it will be over-inclusive for some deals or industries and underinclusive for others. However, by adapting it you can design an operational due diligence useful to your deal and integration teams.

FRAMEWORK FOR OPERATIONAL DUE DILIGENCE INQUIRY

1. Deal rationale
❏ Identify rationale for the transaction (e.g., markets, territories, products and product development, other strategies for revenue growth, strategies for cost savings).

2. Concrete goal
❏ What concrete goals are expected to be met, and over what time frame? How will achievement of those goals be measured?

3. Preliminary plan for achieving goals
❏ Specifically, what is the preliminary plan for achieving the goals outlined above?

4. Drivers of value creation
❏ Based on the above, what is the preliminary view regarding the drivers of value creation for the transaction?

5. Most significant hurdles: preliminary view
❏ What is the preliminary view of the biggest hurdles to achieving the goals set for the transaction?

6. Key due diligence
❏ Are there aspects of due diligence, including operational due diligence, that are especially critical to the plan for the combined enterprise?

7. Integration plan
❏ How will the due diligence process be developed into an integration plan? Are the people and processes in place to make sure there is a seamless transition from due diligence to integration?

8. Negotiation and pricing strategy

❏ How will information and analyses generated through the due diligence process be taken into account in the negotiation and pricing strategies? As the deal negotiations proceed, will due diligence be appropriately retargeted along the way? Are the people and processes in place to make sure that these things happen?

9. Macro framework for due diligence

❏ What are the deal team's key assumptions about macro economic and demographic factors that should frame operational due diligence? These include world economic growth; trade growth; and population growth, age profile, income levels, and other demographic assumptions in the relevant jurisdictions.

10. Economic factors affecting the relevant jurisdictions

❏ What are the assumptions about economic factors affecting the relevant jurisdictions: foreign exchange rates, currency exchange regulations, and fiscal and monetary policies, including taxation and import-export?

11. Political factors

❏ What are the assumptions regarding macro-level political/environmental/ecological factors, such as political stability, potential human rights issues, environmental or health issues, and community or social development obligations?

ANALYSIS OF THE VALUE-CREATION PROCESS

Undertake the following analysis for the target company as well as for the combined enterprise.

A. The Operations Overview Map

1. ❏ **On one or more maps,** chart the supply chain, facilities, personnel, and products and services produced against sales, distribution, and marketing.

2. ❏ **On these maps,** analyze the following:
   ◆ Markets, including new markets, for products/services
   ◆ Competitive positioning
   ◆ Distribution channels
   ◆ Marketing strategies

- Operations and technology strategies
- Sales/service outlets
- Planned production
- Supply and transportation synergies and vulnerabilities
- Political and macroeconomic trends and vulnerabilities
- Personnel overlap and shortfall
- Flow of funds and financing needs, both operating and capital expenditures; analyze currency requirements and foreign exchange and exchange control risk, as well as taxation and transfer pricing issues (see also Chapter 6).

B. Sales, Distribution, and Marketing; Customer Relationship Management; Channel Management

3. Product analysis

❏ Describe the company's products/services. Break down into relevant categories and describe territorial markets. Describe uses of the products and assess the qualities of the products against those of competitors, including product substitution. Consider the following factors:
- Price
- Quality
- Service
- Availability/sales formats
- Design/engineering features and standards
- Sales terms (right to return, credit terms, charge-backs, warranties)
- After-sales service, upgrade, follow-on, etc.

❏ Which of the above are most important to customers in the various markets? In which of the above does the company enjoy an advantage, and is that advantage sustainable or natural, or is it marginal and temporary (can be copied or eroded)?

❏ At what stage of the product life cycle are the various products in their various markets?

❏ Do any of the products of the combined enterprise compete with one another? What is the proposed approach to this problem where it exists?

❏ Are there any known negative qualities associated with the product, such as health risks, product liability risks, or negative environmental or social qualities?

4. Market analysis: demand

❑ How is demand generated, and on what does the level of demand depend? For example, is demand dependent on general economic conditions or conditions in a specific industry? Is it seasonal or cyclical? Is product substitution or technological obsolescence a major risk in terms of basic demand? To what extent can the company control demand? What are the biggest drivers of changes in demand?

5. Market analysis: competitors

❑ Describe the competitive situation by product/market and its effect on product design, product mix, marketing and positioning, and pricing.

6. Market analysis: customers (and end users)

❑ What is the market, and who are the company's customers? If customers are not end users, this analysis should be done for direct customers and at each stage of the distribution chain all the way to end users. Break down along all relevant categories (for business: industry, size, profitability, outlook; for retail: national, cultural, income level, lifestyle choices, other demographic features), including geographic. For each major category of customer (end user), assess prospects and indicate the most significant macro trends that could affect demand. Indicate whether customer (end user) relationships tend to be long term, one-off, or something in between. Is there dependence on one or just a few customers?

7. Customer data

❑ What level of information is available and useful, on a realistic basis, about customers (and end users, if different) and the market? How much of that information is being gathered now? How much of the gathered information is, or should be, analyzed for marketing or product design and positioning purposes? What are the implications for IT needs, in terms of capture of customer data in a database, data mining, and customer relationship management?

8. Using product/market data to identify synergies (cost reduction, rationalization, product extensions)

❑ Map existing products and services to existing customers/markets. Are there obvious overlaps? Are there obvious product or market extensions? What are the implications for production rationalization, cost reduction through efficiencies over a greater base, design and production for product extensions?

9. Pricing

❑ Describe price levels and pricing strategies on a product-by-product or product category basis, and broken down by geographic market and selling format.

❑ What are the major external factors on price levels—for example, market structure, changes in demand? To what extent can cost increases (and which cost increases) be passed on to customers in the form of increased prices? If there is an RFP or bidding process that is typical for the company in selling, describe the typical other parties and the dynamics of the process.

10. Management of pricing and marketing

❑ How are pricing and marketing strategies determined and to be determined going forward? In particular, are there country/local managers? If so, how is their role reconciled with that of product/marketing managers and with centralized corporate policy on these issues? How are profit centers determined, and how much of a role does profit-center analysis play in executive compensation? (See, in particular, Chapter 7.) Are the cost and price assumptions in the deal model consistent with the realities in the various jurisdictions?

11. Advertising and promotion

❑ What leads up to the point of sale? How do people come to be customers/clients? Describe all marketing channels and all sales or new-business materials. Describe other promotional activities. For all marketing and promotional initiatives and expenditures, how is their reach and effectiveness measured? What is the cost? What cost/yield figures are available or can be generated?

12. Distribution generally

❑ Describe product distribution or delivery of service generally. Where and how does this occur?

13. End-user sales and service outlets

❑ Map by products or product category the physical locations of end user sales outlets/service centers. Indicate sale format, relevant pricing information, and volume figures. Indicate where sales are direct; by franchisee through wholesale-retail or other multistage distribution chain; or by way of some other arrangement.

14. End-user remote sales
❏ How much selling occurs remotely—by phone, mail, or computer? Describe how this works and present volume figures and product/customer information. Indicate where sales are direct; by franchisee; through a wholesale-retail or other multistage distribution chain; or by some other arrangement.

15. Point of sale analysis
❏ What exactly happens at the point of sale? In terms of display, product packaging, and pricing, describe the point of sale. Describe the point of sale in terms of human (or other, such as online) interaction. If people are providing a service or assisting at the point of sale, describe how they interact with customers, the level of staff, the type of interaction with customers (on-off versus ongoing and personalized), staff turnover, the level of training, and quality control.

16. Inventory analysis
❏ Analyze inventory levels and mix. What are the levels of stock-outs, substitutions, and back orders? What is inventory turn at each level and by product/product category? What is the analysis at each level of fast-moving, slow-moving, and obsolescent inventory?

17. Wholesale comparable analysis
❏ If the company makes a significant amount of sales on a wholesale or other mediated basis, prepare an analysis comparable to that above regarding the point of sale, sales volume by product, and so on.

18. Sales and distribution analysis
❏ Based on the above, and as relevant, chart the company's sales through distribution channels, indicating markup or other cost at each level and the associated method/timing of transport. Does this analysis suggest possible cost-reduction and efficiency moves, such as the following:
  ◆ Elimination or consolidation of duplicated or overlapping sales/service outlets
  ◆ Elimination or consolidation of duplicated or inefficient distribution paths
  ◆ Use of centralized warehousing
  ◆ Creation of additional distribution centers
  ◆ Negotiation of better transport contracts or integration of the transportation function.

19. Possible weaknesses or anomalies
❏ Is the distribution system subject to channel stuffing or "field ware-housing"? What portions of sales are made on consignment or on approval? What is the experience with returns and charge-backs? What are the possible effects of FIFO/LIFO/average basis accounting as used by the company and others in the chain of distribution, such as retailers—for example, what are the dynamics or pressures relating to inventory management in different price scenarios?

20. Sales force analysis
❏ How are people involved in making sales? Who employs them, or are they independent agents/distributors? From the company's point of view, how are they organized (by product, by region, and so on), and how are they compensated (salary, commission, and so on)?

21. Channel management
❏ What are the sales channels? Is there real or potential channel conflict, and is it being managed? Does company organization maximize sales overall, or are business units competing with each other for the same business? Describe any existing areas of channel conflict, and describe the effect of the proposed transaction in terms of channel conflict.

22. Systems analysis of sales and distribution
❏ What is the state of systems support of product or service delivery? Consider physical and logistical aspects such as the following:
  ◆ The order-processing and order-fulfillment process from a systems perspective. Are there possibilities for automation or for enhanced support of sales personnel? Are sales data fully exploited for marketing purposes, including customer relationship management? What are the implications for IT support of this function?
  ◆ The state of inventory delivery to or availability at point of sale: Is that inventory sufficient, and is the product mix correct? If the company sells through a retailer or other agent, is inventory management executed in a coordinated fashion resulting in optimal product delivery and sell-through?
  ◆ Are the logistical aspects of product transport and delivery optimized by actively managing scheduling?
  ◆ Are the logistical aspects of inventory storage and handling optimized by use of coding, warehouse management, standardization of materials and packaging, and so on?

◆ How does information about sales make its way back into the inventory ordering and management system? How does it make its way back into product design and marketing? How frequently and on what basis?

◆ Are there opportunities for rationalization of the sales and distribution system, such as streamlined order processing; smarter coding and packaging; improved tracking; use of computerized stock picking and automated packaging; improved IT-based scheduling systems, including loading dock scheduling and the like; integration of scheduling systems with those of transporters; tighter design of inventory management by use of current sales data and automatic or rapid replenishment/redirection strategies?

23. System flexibility and responsiveness

❏ How much flexibility and responsiveness is built into the sales and distribution system, and can it be increased (at what cost)? How sophisticated is the company's rapid replenishment capability, how far back into the production process does it go, and what is the customer's ability to change or cancel orders? How does the company deal with unhappy customers or those who change their minds after order fulfillment has been completed? What is the IT support for the above?

24. Outsourcing

❏ If aspects of sales/distributions have been outsourced, describe. What are the benefits and possible negative aspects of this outsourcing?

25. After-sale

❏ What are the company's responsibilities after sale?

❏ What are the company's policies on returns or exchanges?

❏ What are the company's policies on warranties? What is the associated pricing, if any? What is the company's experience? Assess the cost of warranties to the company, and analyze the warranty reserve, if any.

❏ If the company provides after-sale service, what are the terms and pricing? How well is it performed? If there are call centers, are they staffed and organized to optimize response against cost, using queuing theory, IT support at the phone level, and knowledge management tools to assist personnel? Analyze these systems and their cost.

If service is at the customer's location, how is availability and training of personnel managed?

❏ How is customer satisfaction measured? Be specific.

26. Brand management

❏ By product or product category, describe the company's branding strategy or other corporate identity as it is intended to be perceived by the public, including customers. How is the company's brand managed across product categories and across borders? Is there a corporate brand that serves as an umbrella across subsidiary brands? Comment on how the branding strategy is or is not reflected in various communications channels, including online and intracompany. Comment on how consistent the branding strategy is with the corporate culture, and if there is a mismatch, how that is managed. Do any of the aspects of the proposed transaction pose a challenge in terms of managing brand?

27. Brand and product design and positioning

❏ How is the company's branding strategy translated into product or service design and engineering and product positioning, including pricing? Does branding strategy and market information get communicated effectively to R&D, engineering, and design professionals? Is it adequately communicated to sales personnel and others who interact with the public, including customer service call centers and the like?

28. Outside consultants and advertising agencies

❏ Describe the company's relationships with corporate image consultants, PR firms, and advertising agencies around the world. Are any firms or individuals especially important in this regard? Does the company do most of the global coordination in-house, or do outsiders handle it?

29. Value of the brand

❏ What is the estimated value of the brand? Does the proposed transaction pose any threat of diluting brand value?

30. Implications for the integration plan

❏ Do any of the above points suggest potential cost savings through streamlining of the sales and distribution channels, or potential product or market extensions, product repositioning, or different or additional branding and marketing strategies?

31. Implications for projections, negotiation, and pricing

❏ How strongly does the information regarding customers, products, and markets support deal assumptions about projected revenues? In particular, if revenue growth for certain product lines is assumed, does the information gathered point to clear paths—through product or market extensions, acquisition of new customers, or higher sustainable price points—through which the increase in revenues can be achieved? Discuss the implications for deal negotiation and pricing.

C. Extraction, Manufacturing, or Other Production of Goods and Services

Assuming the target's market and planned products/services have been defined above, assess in general how well the existing manufacturing or other production system is set up to profitably meet market demands (giving effect to possible divestitures for antitrust or other reasons). As relevant, answer the following questions on a physical site and/or process or process-unit basis.

32. Geographic map of production capacity

❏ Review the map of productive capacity against customer needs on a geographic basis. Indicate overall industry capacity for the relevant markets. Tie product sales estimates arrived at above to production capacity.

33. Process and process unit

❏ Describe the process of production or provision of services at a schematic/technical/engineering level. Categorize the work in terms of work flow as special order, batch process, line process, or continuous flow. Analyze the critical inputs into the production process: capital investment, know-how, plant design or specialized machinery, skilled labor, pool of available labor. Is the company's use of these inputs consistent with industry norms? Better? Worse?

34. Process flow analysis

❏ Within a physical plant or between physical plants, and including approval processes, transport stages, and all other stages of the production process as relevant, chart process flow for production on a critical path or other comparable basis, with special attention to the following:
- ◆ How production tends to relate to production schedules, and how production schedules relate to sales forecasts, specific orders, and so on

- ◆ Defective production, excess production, returned goods, and warranty claims
- ◆ Idle time and downtime, for all reasons (differentiate among reasons)
- ◆ Waste and scrap
- ◆ At all points in the process, damaged or obsolete stock/inventory
- ◆ Absenteeism, accidents, grievances, overtime, employee turnover (see Chapter 7)
- ◆ Whether design and ongoing production reflect sophisticated operations management tools, such as economic production order quantities, time and motion studies, queuing theory, and so on
- ◆ Capacity/throughput mismatches creating bottlenecks
- ◆ Bottlenecks due to approval requirements or other management processes (especially where approval from a different location or time zone is required)
- ◆ Excess inventory buildups (with associated working capital cost)
- ◆ Critical inventory and spare parts requirements management against lead times (where disruption in supply will result in immediate stoppage)
- ◆ Flexibility for product changes (for example, setup time required, batch size, potential to reorder custom steps toward the end of the production process)
- ◆ Associated IT or other information-based or automated support of the process, such as tracking

35. Outsourcing
❑ Is some of the production outsourced? If so, describe the extent to which the company can control execution against specifications, and how quality control is managed, particularly in light of timing considerations. Assess the pluses and minuses of the outsourcing arrangements. Are there potential environmental liabilities, social obligations, or other costs, liabilities, and risks associated with the production outsourcing?

36. Risk analysis based on process flow
❑ Identify the most significant risks associated with the process flow, and their impact on the business. Are backups, work-arounds, or replacements available? Is insurance coverage for the risk available on a cost-effective basis? What risks cannot be either mitigated or insured against?

37. Review of physical plant
❏ Describe in detail the physical plant and facilities of the company:
- ◆ Type
- ◆ Location
- ◆ Size/capacity/throughput measures
- ◆ Measures of utilization, including as a percentage of capacity
- ◆ Level of downtime, exclusive of scheduled maintenance
- ◆ Scheduled maintenance and associated downtime
- ◆ Quality of output
- ◆ Age, original cost, and method of depreciation
- ◆ Depreciated (book) value
- ◆ Market (appraised) value
- ◆ If leased, terms of lease
- ◆ Remaining useful life
- ◆ Adequacy of warehousing/storage
- ◆ Associated environmental facilities
- ◆ Social obligations (housing, medical, family care, schools, roads, parks, other)
- ◆ Facilities related to social obligations (medical or day-care facilities, other)
- ◆ Materials handling methods (pallets, conveyors, forklifts, trucks, vacuum or magnetic lifting or moving devices)
- ◆ Proximity to transport
- ◆ Utilities infrastructure support
- ◆ Climate and natural hazards (flood, volcano, earthquake, tornado, hurricane, rain, snow)
- ◆ Building code and zoning
- ◆ Real estate taxes and other fixed costs
- ◆ State of title (including leasehold title); liens and condemnation proceedings
- ◆ Insurance coverage
- ◆ Safety and security features
- ◆ Maintenance costs; capital improvements

38. Review of machinery and equipment
❏ List and describe principal machinery, noting the following:
- ◆ Age, original cost, and method of depreciation
- ◆ Depreciated (book) value
- ◆ Market (appraised) value
- ◆ If leased, terms of lease

◆ Remaining useful life
◆ Maintenance
◆ Health and safety issues
◆ Auxiliary equipment—tools, patterns, materials handling equipment

39. Quality of technology
❏ Describe the technology used in overall terms: Is the company an industry leader in advanced, high-quality technology? Is its applied technology the most modern? What is the risk of rapid obsolescence? How does the technology used rank in terms of production efficiency (inventory, utilities, workers needed, maintenance requirements, periodic capital improvements)? Is there a rival technology being utilized or upcoming that will create competitive difficulties for the company or render its technology obsolete?

40. Quality control
❏ What is the company's quality control structure? Are the company's facilities ISO-compliant? What specific quality control measures are used (Total Quality Management, Statistical Control Processes, Six Sigma, and so on), and what is the management structure for dealing with quality control problems?

41. Review of engineering platforms and standards
❏ Describe in detail the engineering platforms and standards used in production. If it is assumed that the production process will be spread among different facilities in order to optimize capacity utilization, have the underlying assumptions been identified and checked out— engineering platforms, measurements and standards, languages used by engineers, and so on? How long will it take for manuals, processes, and standards to be written down and harmonized to enable dispersed production? How will conflicts that arise in this process be resolved?

42. Analysis of capacity on a combined basis
❏ What does the analysis of process flow suggest about excess, duplicate, or inadequate capacity at one or more points of production? Analyze desirable production capacity, after smoothing within the system, against expected sales volume.

43. Excess capacity
❏ If there is excess capacity, how should the determination to reduce

capacity be made, and what is the plan for disposition or shutdown? What would be the financial consequences (on an accounting and cash basis) of disposition or shutdown?

44. Additional capacity
❏ If the analysis suggests that additional capacity is required, where would it be located, and what would it consist of? How long would it take to get online? What are the costs? Are there regulatory or other barriers to the planned expansion?

45. Production cost structure analysis
❏ If the analysis suggests the need for investments to improve the production cost structure, quantify the cost of those improvements, taking into account the time required to effect the changes. Weigh these against the expected operating cost reductions.

46. Tie production to cost accounting
❏ What are the company's policies for cost accounting? Are these consistent with industry norms? Tie these to the process flow analysis above, and reconcile for each company in the transaction. What is the relationship between fixed and variable costs, the break-even point, and the relation of volume to the break-even point? What are the effects of idle capacity and volume variances? Is the company's production process satisfactorily profitable on a cost accounting basis? What is the range for gross margin (by product or product category as relevant) based on the price assumptions made in the projections and supported by the marketing analysis above? (See Chapter 4.)

D. Procurement and Supply-Chain Management; External Infrastructure Requirements

47. Raw materials, intermediate inventory, and supplies needs
❏ Analyze the company's need for raw materials, intermediate inventory, and supplies, based on the market and capacity analyses above. Based on the process analysis above, describe critical items and associated lead times.

48. Cost of raw materials, intermediate inventory, and supplies
❏ Do raw material, intermediate inventory, or supplies needs represent a vulnerability to price volatility or constricted supply? Track the percentage relation of these components of production to price levels for finished goods, and for each category describe future price trends

and market conditions. Assess how much risk the company is taking with respect to these inputs to the production process.

49. Supplier analysis
- ❏ Describe suppliers by category of product and volume. Where are they located? Are they stable financially? Are there multiple suppliers for specific needs, or backup suppliers? Which suppliers are dependent on the company's business, and to what extent? On which suppliers is the company dependent?

50. The procurement system
- ❏ What is the procurement system?
  - ◆ How centrally managed is it?
  - ◆ Does it balance cost savings and efficiency with design and quality control?
  - ◆ To what extent does the company use a formal purchasing manual, based on order quantities, up-to-date vendor evaluation files (covering delivery and quality information), and a formal program for reviewing the value and quality of purchased materials ? What procedures are used in procurement? How are costs compared, and how is purchase approval given?
  - ◆ What are the circumstances in which goods may be returned or result in charge-backs? How flexible is the procurement system in dealing with changes in customer orders or fluctuations in sales?
  - ◆ Does consolidation or streamlining of procurement represent future potential cost savings? If so, quantify.

51. Long-term contracts
- ❏ If there are long-term contracts, describe the process for reaching agreement on them, their status, and in what circumstances they would be favorable and unfavorable to the company.

52. Utilities and other infrastructure support
- ❏ Analyze the company's need for utilities (including water supply) and other infrastructure support, such as transportation and communication. Are these facilities all available on an assured basis, or can backup be arranged if there is a problem? Are there potential cost savings here, or does infrastructure represent a vulnerability to price volatility or constricted supply?

53. Support for facility expansion
- ❏ If there is a decision to expand the facility, are sufficient supplies of the following available at the selected location?

- ◆ Manpower with the right skill levels
- ◆ Utilities, transportation, communication, and other infrastructure support
- ◆ Raw materials and supplies on a secure and cost-effective basis
- ◆ Real estate at appropriate pricing with appropriate zoning

54. Supply-chain analysis
❑ Analyze the logistics of the supply chain in light of rationalized production capacity. Are there potential cost savings in the supply-chain structure, such as streamlined order processing; smarter coding and packaging; improved tracking; computerized stock-picking; automated packaging, improved IT-based scheduling systems, including loading dock scheduling and the like; integration of scheduling systems with those of transporters; tighter design of inventory management by use of current sales/production data; and automatic or rapid reordering/redirection strategies?

55. Supply-chain risk analysis
❑ Are there vulnerabilities in the supply chain—to shipping disruption, transportation price volatility, currency risks—and, if so, are there available work-arounds, or are these risks inherent to the production process?

56. Collapsing the supply chain
❑ Are there potential efficiencies in combining the company's supply chain to the point of production/shipping with the distribution/sale to customers?

ANALYSIS OF INFORMATION, TECHNOLOGY, COMMUNICATIONS, AND GENERAL SYSTEMS SUPPORT OF THE VALUE-CREATION PROCESS; INTELLECTUAL CAPITAL AND INTELLECTUAL PROPERTY

1. Traditional MIS
❑ Describe the management information systems of the company as they relate to traditional MIS functions: payroll, benefits, payables, receivables, cost accounting, and financial accounting generally. What is the target company's hardware configuration for data processing and for networking? What is the target's software platform—vendors, operating systems, database management system, programming environments, and software applications—and how integrated is it across company units, both functionally and geographically?

2. Integration for MIS

❏ What does an integration plan for traditional MIS look like? Can priorities be applied, and are there any items that do not really need to be integrated? What is a realistic time frame for MIS integration, and how can functions be maintained with minimal disruption for that period?

3. ERP

❏ Does the company have an ERP system or other partially or fully integrated IT system? Which one? Describe implementation, vendor, contracts.

4. Other valuable IT systems and assets

❏ Does the company have other valuable systems or processes that are IT-based, such as:

◆ Online order or transaction processing
◆ Online search, tracking, or other information-retrieval systems
◆ Knowledge-sharing systems, such as a firm intranet or other groupware
◆ Engineering platforms such as computer-assisted design systems
◆ Computer-based scheduling or routing systems
◆ Document production systems that go beyond general office needs
◆ Special mathematical or engineering data-modeling or data-processing support, such as that required for minerals extraction
◆ Decision support systems
◆ Robotics
◆ Sensing, feedback, and control mechanisms in extraction or production
◆ Large database support of, for example, customer relationship management or R&D

5. System assessment; IT personnel and budget

❏ For any of the items above that are fundamental to the business, a full-scale assessment of hardware (data storage, processing, and network) and software adequacy, scalability, and robustness of the systems is required. While a Web-based catalog transaction-processing system is not very arcane at this point, the transaction-processing needs of a typical bank would be a quite substantial IT function. Security and backup are both very important to most of these types of systems, as is error-free ordinary operation. For all such systems: What level of personnel support is required? What are ongoing maintenance costs? How long to obsolescence? Are there multiple systems, and should some standardization be imposed? How is procurement managed?

6. Ownership; vendor relationships

❏ Does the company own the rights to its IT systems, or are some aspects of the systems operated under license? What is the company's position in terms of vendor lock-in? How vulnerable is it to forced and round-robin upgrades and price increases? Are some aspects of the company's IT systems proprietary to it, and if so, are these proprietary aspects treated as confidential or otherwise as protected as they can be from duplication by competitors, including departing employees?

7. Outsourcing

❏ Are any of the company's IT functions outsourced? Describe the arrangements, the vendor (including the vendor's stability), and the backup and recovery systems. Describe the pros and cons of the arrangements.

8. Systems risk analysis of the IT systems

❏ Describe the systems risk inherent in the company's IT infrastructure and such issues as redundancy, backup, and disaster recovery. How well does the system recover from ordinary system crashes, and how often do these occur? What is the tolerance for IT failure in terms of the company's operations?

9. Intellectual property and know-how; licensing

❏ What intellectual property underlies the company's value-generating processes? Describe these, including processes or branding concepts that might not be written down or that might not fall within a legal definition of intellectual property. Describe all licensing agreements and their terms.

10. Ownership of intellectual property

❏ Does the company have the right to use all of its important know-how? What is the risk of infringement claims? How much of the company's valuable know-how is proprietary to the company, and of that, how much is entitled to legal protection and under what rubric—e.g., trademark and trade name, patent, copyright, trade secrets? Has the company taken all appropriate steps to protect its rights in its intellectual property? In answering this question, be sure to examine the cross-border implications (in what countries are the company's intellectual properties protected, and so on).

11. Product development and innovation

❏ Assess the company's general product development and product innovation experience and strengths in design, engineering, and general creativity and responsiveness.

12. Cross-border implications

❏ For each aspect of the constituent companies' important know-how that it is assumed will be applied cross-border after closing: Must such know-how be tailored to local needs and conditions? Will the know-how retain its protected character if transplanted to the new site? How easy will it be for competitors in the new territory to copy the know-how?

13. R&D generally

❏ How important is R&D to the company and to competitors? How does the company's R&D budget compare to that of comparable companies, as a percentage of sales and against other measures? How successful is the company at turning R&D into valuable products/services over a reasonable period of time? How integrated is the company's R&D effort with its marketing strategy (or how relevant is its marketing strategy to its R&D effort)?

14. R&D facilities and capabilities

❏ Describe in detail the R&D facilities, capabilities, and directions of the company, and define areas of overlap or obvious areas of extension for the combined enterprise. Are there opportunities for cost reduction or important new initiatives in the combined R&D functions?

15. IT and intellectual property/know-how overview

❏ Of all of the company's IT-based systems and other know-how noted above, are some elements so valuable that they constitute a critical aspect of the value proposition? If so, are they fully understood, and is their legal status and confidentiality protected as fully as possible? Can the associated systems and know-how be successfully scaled and deployed across borders in the combined enterprise?

16. IT systems overview

❏ What knowledge and information requirements of the combined enterprise cannot be met through combination and integration of the existing information systems? What are the budget and timetable for these, and can they be grafted onto the more basic IT infrastructure?

PEOPLE ANALYSIS: MANAGEMENT STRUCTURE, LABOR RELATIONS, CORPORATE CULTURE, RECRUITMENT AND TRAINING, AS RELATED TO OPERATIONS

(*See also Chapter 7.*)

A. Management Structure from an Operational Perspective

1. Management structure and lines of reporting
- ❏ Document the official lines of reporting, and comment on management communications formats that do not coincide with the formal structure.

2. Management structure and business units
- ❏ How does management structure translate into operational/production functions, entities, or units such as:
  - ◆ Factories/mines/other facilities for extraction/production (manufacturing)
  - ◆ Professional and production offices and studios (professional services firms, media)
  - ◆ Networks and systems (transportation, communication)
  - ◆ Sales outlets and customer service centers
  - ◆ Corporate office; corporate-wide systems such as accounting and finance, legal, information systems, procurement, brand management and marketing, engineering, R&D, and quality control

3. Management operations across borders
- ❏ Are there country/regional managers? How autonomous is the country manager, and how do country manager roles integrate corporate-wide decision making? Are there matrix management structures or other processes in place to coordinate country practices and policies within a global strategy?

4. Identifying key personnel (nonmanagement) from an operational perspective
- ❏ Which nonmanagement categories of personnel are key from an operational perspective? Consider the following:
  - ◆ Creative
    - —Writers and editors (media)
    - —Designers (retail/manufacturing)
    - —Marketing

◆ Scientists and engineers
—Systems and operations engineers (airlines, other transportation, telecommunications)
—Doctors and other health professionals and researchers (pharmaceuticals, health care)
—Design engineers (automotive, other manufacturing)
—Software engineers, electrical engineers (information technology)
—Mining, construction, mechanical, or other engineers (extraction, construction, manufacturing)
◆ Finance/legal/other professionals
—Lawyers, accountants, consultants
—Bankers
—Pilots (for an airline)
◆ Sales and customer-relationship management
—Sales and marketing personnel
◆ Skilled and unskilled production labor
—Office staff (for a professional services firm, for example)
—Factory skilled and unskilled workers (manufacturing firm)
❏ For the target and the combined company, rank the relevant categories, and set forth the analysis and implications for integration strategy:
◆ Are there individuals or teams in this category so essential that losing them after closing would negate the value of the deal? Those people can take the value of the business with them or become competitors (for example, key bankers leaving after a bank is acquired, star sales managers leaving a marketing and distribution firm, a key creative team leaving an advertising agency, the most productive software engineers leaving a software development firm).
◆ Is one category of personnel so essential that managing that group as a whole is a key element of the deal (for example, airline pilots for an airline, doctors for a health care organization)?
◆ Are replacement personnel available?
◆ Will there be personnel redundancies postdeal? How will these be dealt with?
❏ For existing personnel, consider in general terms their numbers, location, work performed, compensation, and terms of employment (including union or other contracts).

B. Operational Questions across Categories of Personnel

5. Workers and planned strategic initiatives

❏ Review all categories of workers in light of strategic initiatives for the combined company. Will strategic redirection or reengineering of processes render some workers unneeded, or will new categories of workers be required?

6. Recruitment and training

❏ How are workers recruited and trained? Is recruitment and training appropriately geared to operational needs?

7. Workers and process review

❏ What are the general terms of employment as they relate to process design and other operations matters, such as shift length, vacation expectations, and flexibility in learning new skills and being rotated into different jobs? Will these need to be reconciled between the companies after closing, or reconfigured in order to implement new process designs, and if so, how?

8. Workforce integration

❏ Will there be integration of workforces? If so, what impediments are there to smooth integration (such as language barriers)?

9. Workforce reduction

❏ If a workforce reduction is contemplated, how will that be executed, keeping in mind the need to retain motivated staff? How much will it cost—soft costs as well as hard costs?

10. New hires

❏ If the combined enterprise plans relocation or expansion, or if new facilities or lines of business are planned, will new employees be required, and are they available?

11. Social obligations

❏ Does the company have social obligations to its workers, such as requirements to provide or fund housing, schooling, or medical services? What is the basic infrastructure available to employees to meet these needs? How do these obligations potentially affect operations?

C. Corporate Culture and Operations

Compare the corporate cultures of the parties to the transaction in terms that seem most useful to the deal structure and to developing an integration plan from an operational perspective.

12. General aspects of corporate culture

❏ Some markers or attributes that might be considered in terms of how employees work together might be these:

♦ Relative rankings of jobs as perceived in the companies, importance of formal hierarchy

♦ Formality, style of dress, office configuration, open doors or closed doors

13. Communications formats

❏ What are the formats for various types of communications, such as:

♦ Meetings scheduled in advance with/without prepared agendas

♦ Impromptu meetings

♦ Memos, e-mails, voice mails

♦ Formal reporting lines versus back channels

♦ Formal committees versus "kitchen cabinets"

♦ Collaborative work

14. IT support for communications

❏ Is there adequate IT support for IT-based intra-company communications (for example, e-mail, an intranet, or other groupware is important for intracompany communications, quality control and promulgation of standards, and collaborative design and engineering)?

15. Knowledge sharing and knowledge management

❏ What is the attitude about information in the enterprise: Is it shared, or do individuals tend to keep their knowledge to themselves? If knowledge is shared, is that solely through informal means or by way of formal training formats? What are the implications for IT support of knowledge sharing and transference (for example, for worker training and rotation)?

16. Company approaches to systems design

❏ Are employees rewarded for exercising initiative or for acquiescence in management instruction? How free do employees feel to question their superiors? How comfortable are managers with questions or challenges from those they supervise?

17. Documentation of systems design

❏ Are work processes and practices fluid and open, or do they tend to be rigidly defined and rule bound? Do work processes and practices tend to be documented, or is there more of an oral tradition?

18. Conflict resolution and change management in integration planning and systems design

❏ How do employees react to things that they don't agree with? Do they have a forum for discussing and resolving issues with management, or will dissatisfaction show up in other ways? Are people more or less comfortable with group or consensus decision making in comparison to individual leadership? How important is it that groups validate leaders' decisions? What is the mechanism for creating "buy-in," and has this process been considered in integration planning at a practical level?

19. Life-balance issues in operations planning

❏ How permissible is it to acknowledge the importance of family or personal life, and how flexible is the company in accommodating the family and personal lives of their employees?

D. Background Culture Questions Affecting Operations

20. Language

❏ What is the dominant language used for spoken and written communications, within the company and with suppliers, customers, and investors? Are there enough persons with multilingual capabilities to bridge the language gaps?

21. How things really get done?

❏ Does the background culture accord a significant amount of weight to long-term contracts, or are the most important relationships or aspects of relationships likely to be undocumented? A related question: How are business agreements reached? Are key decision makers interested in and patient with lengthy and detailed negotiations? Or do they rely more on establishing personal bonds with their correspondents? Do people enjoy haggling, or do they avoid it?

22. Importance of documentation and record keeping

❏ Are things generally written down or otherwise recorded and kept? How important is record keeping and the memorialization of events and decisions? How important are formal and written inquiries and justifications? To what extent is arbitrariness accepted?

23. Transparency to outsiders

❏ Do companies routinely share information with outsiders, such as lenders, investors, or the press, or is information closely held? What types of information are shared with vendors, suppliers, and customers, and on what terms?

24. Involvement of equity owners

❏ Does the ownership structure of the company have an impact on operational decisions—for example, has common ownership resulted in favorable or unfavorable business relationships with vendors and suppliers or customers? Is the background culture one in which professional management is given a great deal of leeway day to day or one in which equity owners are likely to be involved in operational issues?

25. Attitude toward rules and protocol

❏ Do people tend to follow written rules and procedures to the letter or take a more relaxed attitude? Do they feel it is appropriate to question or override formal rules and procedures when circumstances are out of the ordinary?

26. Attitudes toward accounting standards, taxation, and regulatory compliance

❏ What is the company's attitude toward these requirements?

27. The basis of customer relationships

❏ How would you characterize typical business-to-business transactions and business-to-consumer transactions? For example, is there more emphasis on a branded or otherwise consistent corporate identity or on local/personal relationships? In what circumstances are purchasers entitled to refunds and exchanges? What are the most effective channels for marketing and product/company communication?

28. Social contract with workers

❏ What is the background understanding about the social contract with workers? Among government, the family, and business, who bears the costs of various risks to workers: unemployment, health, family care, retirement, need for retraining? What are the long-term obligations assumed by a company when it hires an employee?

29. Attitude toward change

❏ Is change and rapid response valued, or do people tend to value tradition, the status quo, and stability?

4 | Financial and Accounting Due Diligence

JORGE M. DIAZ

INANCIAL DUE DILIGENCE and accounting due diligence are closely related. Financial due diligence is the process by which the investor determines whether the investment in the target makes business or financial sense. Financial due diligence includes corroborating, by independent third party data, the financial information the target provides. The financial due diligence process is the only opportunity the investor may have to evaluate the target's current economic viability and future prospects and the capital demands required to realize the deal's goals. Unrealistic expectations, inappropriate or incomplete due diligence procedures, or inadequate research relating to a target will cause any transaction to fail, regardless of size or complexity.

Accounting due diligence, although similar to financial due diligence, is more closely directed at the truthfulness and completeness of the target's accounting information. Accounting due diligence procedures should include tests of the reasonableness of accounting judgments and estimates presented by target company management. In an effort to maximize earnings and to enhance the target company's financial position, perhaps for the purposes of the contemplated transaction, the accounting procedures at the target company may be aggressive. Therefore, the investor's due diligence team may have to step up its efforts. In performing accounting due diligence, the procedures should concentrate on the internal controls imposed on the target's accounting

101

systems and information, the accuracy of the information processed, the correct application of accounting principles, the generation of estimates and accruals, and other similar factors.

When preparing for a cross-border deal, the target's senior management may be tempted to put undue pressure on middle management to make budgets, to meet revenue goals, or to achieve certain expectations. Middle management may even consider violating existing company policies and procedures to achieve these goals. Even the most ethical of organizations is susceptible to management efforts to manipulate the numbers if unrealistic goals and expectations are imposed on the company's employees. Often the pressure is not documented, but rather is expressed privately.

To detect and account for this problem, due diligence is vital—and should include as much contact as possible with as many members of the target's management and employees as possible. Without proper due diligence, investors who are eager to close a deal may make hasty decisions, which will unequivocally end in financial disaster. More often than not, decisions to invest in deals that ultimately fail are based on factors neither financially sound nor justifiable.

Typical of such mistakes are deals made solely to beat a competitor to a deal or to control a particular market without considering the financial and reputational risks. In fact, a deal made for the sole purpose of market share expansion generally results in substantial costs and possible losses to the investor. Investing in a company solely to beat a competitor in achieving a presence in a particular market very often may be outright wrong for economic and financial reasons. Thorough due diligence helps investors avoid these mistakes.

The two parties in a cross-border deal should be wary of committing any of the following common mistakes:

1   Having no clear strategy, which leads to general turmoil
2   Attempting to blend and merge different cultures
3   Making destructive changes to an existing positive work environment
4   Losing key talent, which leads to restructuring
5   Ignoring employee-related issues, which leads to employee disgruntlement
6   Failing to deliver on stated goals

7 Allowing chaos to reign during the often stressful stages leading up to and following completion of the deal

In this chapter, a number of these common mistakes are considered as they relate to the performance of financial and accounting due diligence.

Addressing All Aspects—Whether Large or Small

Financial and accounting due diligence should address all aspects of the target company's business and operations, for even the smallest of indicators may lead to serious issues requiring further investigation. Under no circumstances should an investor ignore issues of potential concern during due diligence. From time to time, what appear to be minor issues will turn into major problems requiring the expansion of due diligence and additional consultation with target management.

For example, in an acquisition of an overseas cable service provider, the investor's due diligence team requested that target company management provide a detailed budget for the purchase of property and equipment. At first, the investor's due diligence team perceived this to be a small request. Target management, however, could not produce such a budget, and the explanation provided suggested that management simply bought what was believed to be necessary at the time. As a result of additional investigation, the financial due diligence team discovered that the target company had

♦ no total company budget, not even a capital acquisitions budget, and that no financial plans had been presented to the board of directors for review and approval;

♦ no plan or strategy for capital acquisitions;

♦ no research relating to the requirements for expansion to penetrate the competition's market;

♦ no plans for the financing of the necessary purchases; and

♦ no analysis of the relationship between the potential benefits of expansion and the costs associated with such expansion.

In essence, the target had no idea of its position versus its competition, and no knowledge of the requirements to expand and maintain its market position, a point that proved to be critical to the acquisition. Once the due diligence team prepared an analysis of the capital require-

ments and of the benefits associated with the target's expansion requirements, the investor abandoned the proposed acquisition. The absence of
budgets and planning information also revealed the inadequacies of the
target's management.

In performing due diligence on a non-U.S. target in the airline industry, an investor requested information about the carrier's principal routes
and customers served. The target provided many types of information
relating to revenue passenger miles (RPMs) by geographic segment,
including an analysis reflecting the volume increases by segment, but not
by city pair or route. RPMs represent a critical indicator in determining
an airline's revenues and profitability. Generally, RPM growth should
reflect an airline's capabilities and indicate the potential to increase market share. However, because the prospective investor was headquartered
in the United States, it considered the target's route system vital. Once
it obtained the details, the due diligence team noted that approximately
20 percent of the target's traffic was derived from flights to and from
Cuba, a country with whom U.S. companies are prohibited from trans-
acting business. Thus, the airline's growth projections and objectives had
to be adjusted to reflect an additional growth factor of 20 percent, which
translated into a revised growth of approximately 35 percent for the airline to be a profitable investment. Given this high hurdle, the investor's
due diligence team concluded that the target would not be able to generate sufficient RPM growth to justify the investment.

Financial Due Diligence Procedures

Financial due diligence procedures begin in the planning phase and are
not concluded until the transaction is closed. The reliability of the figures, analysis, account balances, reports, and other financial information
is only as good as the people and systems responsible for preparing and
producing such information. The entire due diligence process, much like
an audit in accordance with generally accepted auditing standards, is
based on trust. The level of trust varies based on the target's (and its
management team's) background and financial status. For example, a
U.S. public company whose shares or debt are registered with the
Securities and Exchange Commission is expected to produce more reliable financial information than a typical privately held company would.

Depending on the sophistication of the target's management team, the scope of the procedures should be either expanded or narrowed.

Planning for due diligence is critical to the execution of the due diligence program. Planning includes defining the scope of the work and the conclusions to be reached. Testing the target management's assertions is initiated during the background evaluation and assessment process, particularly by the initial evaluation of the target's internal controls.

Thus, financial due diligence procedures vary depending on the quality of the target's personnel and systems. The due diligence team should be prepared to adjust the scope of its work to adapt to new developments and additional information. The due diligence team members should hold frequent meetings to focus on the most important issues uncovered, as soon as such issues are detected.

During the preliminary phase of one cross-border transaction in the banking industry, the due diligence team noted the following:

♦ The target company management team lacked direct knowledge of its own operations.

♦ The management team members did not work in concert, and corporate goals were secondary to individual goals.

♦ The target's data processing systems did not serve their intended purposes and were outdated and unreliable.

♦ Environmental controls affecting the data processing systems were not enforced and, for the most part, did not exist.

♦ Management team members did not have access to all of the available financial information.

♦ Company employees did not have adequate experience or training.

♦ The company's senior management team failed to provide leadership, goals, objectives, benchmarks, and compensation incentives, thus creating an atmosphere of individualism, arrogance, and self-preservation.

Given these findings, the due diligence team expanded the procedures to test the reliability of the target's financial and accounting information. The team concluded that target management's inexperience and lack of knowledge would require far-reaching procedures to test and verify the information supplied.

How to Verify the Numbers

Due diligence in any type of transaction is the responsibility of the investor's management team. While authority to make decisions may be delegated and shared with independent financial professionals, the investor must assume ultimate responsibility for the transaction, because the investor is responsible for funding the transaction, thus bearing the highest risk of loss. In other words, responsibility for financial due diligence cannot be shifted wholesale to third-party professionals.

The form of the investment affects how due diligence is performed. If the transaction is structured as an asset purchase, the level and scope of the procedures will vary from those found in the share purchase, because the risks assumed in the asset investment or acquisition relate only to the known items. In a share acquisition, the investor assumes all of the risks, for both disclosed and undisclosed assets and liabilities.

Asset purchases. For an acquisition of assets and liabilities, the reliability of the numbers relates only to the information applicable to the assets acquired and liabilities assumed. Unlike the purchase of shares, the purchase of assets and liabilities restricts financial due diligence to the information applicable to the selected items.

Verifying the information applicable to selected assets and liabilities is simpler and much more direct than in the case of a share purchase. Depending on the type of assets and liabilities being acquired, the principal procedures should include the following, which are not necessarily presented in order of importance:

1　The acquisition team should clearly identify the assets to be acquired and liabilities to be assumed and determine the extent of the due diligence procedures to be performed.

2　The due diligence team's procedures should be adjusted to avoid duplicating efforts.

3　The accuracy of information should be verified through the following:

◆　Physical observation of the assets, such as physical cash counts, observation and counts of investment securities, physical counts of inventory, and physical observation of property and equipment. For example, in performing physical inspections of existing inventories, the inventory should be stratified to understand the composition of the items. Valuable items should be identified, and more sample items from the higher-priced categories should be selected. Minimal counts should be made of the less-valuable items. Any missing items in the higher-priced categories should be extrapolated to the total inventory to determine the potential error and possible adjustment to be recorded.

♦ Confirmation of the existence of assets held by other parties.

♦ Review of documents from third parties providing evidence of the existence of the assets, such as bank statements, safekeeping statements, broker advice, warehouse receipts, shipping documents, and similar third-party-generated documents.

♦ Review of work done by other professionals, including the target's independent certified public accountants, applicable to the assets acquired.

♦ Examination of communications from applicable regulatory agencies to ensure that all relevant issues are analyzed and pursued.

♦ Review of documentation supplied by the target, including board and board committee meeting minutes, paying particular attention to the approval of significant purchases and investments in major asset categories.

4 For liabilities assumed, procedures similar to those performed for the purchase of assets should be considered, including the following:

♦ Confirm outstanding payable balances directly with vendors and other providers and suppliers.

♦ Perform a search for unrecorded liabilities, including a review of the payments made subsequent to the cutoff date, evaluation of adequacy of accruals recorded as of the cutoff date, and inquiries of senior management about the existence of unpaid or unrecorded invoices.

♦ Review minutes of the meetings of the board of directors and its committees to evaluate the existence of major purchase commitments, legal contingencies, or other regulatory issues.

♦ Contact the target's outside legal counsel to determine if any contingencies or unasserted claims exist, and in particular review all lawyer representation letters relating to existing or threatened litigation.

♦ Review the target's income tax returns and communications from the relevant regulatory agencies to determine if any unrecorded income or other tax liabilities exist. In this procedure, the acquisition team may elect to contact the target's existing independent accountants or other professionals and inquire about the target's compliance with existing laws and regulations.

5 Evaluate the results of the procedures performed and coordinate with other members of the due diligence team to ensure that the findings are evaluated thoroughly and consistently to minimize the possibility of duplicate efforts. Any and all issues noted should be investigated and resolved. (Consideration should be given to performing certain procedures summarized below under the section entitled Share purchases as well.)

Share purchases. The due diligence procedures applicable to share purchases include all of those described above for the purchase of assets and liabilities, as well as the following:

♦ Obtain a list of the financial reports produced by the management and systems of the target.

♦ Obtain copies of any financial analytical summaries and trend analyses prepared for internal use.

♦ Review the information presented and prepare summaries, paying specific attention to the consistency of the information provided. For example, an increase in inventory with a decrease in sales should provoke questions about whether the recorded value of the inventory is realizable and about the target's customer base, marketing efforts, and product mix.

♦ Consult with the tax and legal due diligence teams to ensure that all of the required corporate and tax filings have been made. Using this information, perform whatever procedures may be needed to determine whether any contingent liabilities or exposures exist.

♦ Circulate confirmation requests with the target's lawyers to determine whether any asserted or unasserted claims exist. Using the results of the confirmations, determine the reasonableness of the litigation accruals recorded by target management.

♦ Consult with other professionals as needed to determine whether any actuarial liabilities on pension and profit-sharing and other benefit programs exist that have not been recorded by the target company.

♦ If any groups of employees are represented by unions, review the status of labor contracts to determine the need for any additional labor cost accruals. Discuss with the appropriate management team members the company's intentions relating to renewal of the labor agreements.

♦ Discuss the existence of any stock options or grants with senior management, and determine the financial and accounting ramifications.

The amount of due diligence work to be done in a share acquisition or investment obviously depends on the circumstances. The due diligence team, in conjunction with the investor's management team, must decide on issues such as timing of the transaction, level of risk to be assumed, and the detail of work to be performed. Prioritizing the objectives is critical to the success of the work to be performed. At times, due diligence teams may become too involved with the details without evaluating the "big-picture" issues. An effective investor team will identify major risk areas and direct its efforts to such areas. Real-world time constraints may require that the work be done quickly and that certain non-material areas not be tested at all.

Inbound Transactions

Inbound transactions (between a non-U.S. investor and a U.S. target) are often complicated by the differences in disclosure practices. In one sense, inbound transactions may be simpler to complete because of the full disclosure characteristics of U.S. financial and legal practices and the frequency with which American companies engage in cross-border deals. Conversely, the need to jump through greater regulatory hoops in the United States (such as environmental scrutiny and Securities and Exchange Commission clearance) than in some other places or to document that process more fully may sometimes make such transactions more complex and time-consuming than in an outbound deal. Non-U.S. investors from limited-disclosure countries may balk at doing transactions in full-disclosure countries like the United States.

As explained earlier, most experts consider the reliability and availability of financial information in the United States to be better than in other countries. However, inbound investors should not be overly confident and should exercise healthy levels of professional skepticism. The procedures to be performed in any transaction should consider the target's internal controls system and other factors affecting its operations.

Under no circumstances should "complete the checklist" due diligence be a substitute for old-fashioned common sense and good judgment. This is especially important in outbound deals (between a U.S. investor and a non-U.S. target), as discussed in the sections that follow.

Outbound Transactions in Developed Countries

Financial due diligence for outbound transactions in developed countries is similar to that for inbound transactions, as described above. Developed countries' financial and economic systems are often as sophisticated as the systems in the United States. The levels of human and capital resources are similar to those found in the United States. Accordingly, the due diligence procedures to be performed to test the reliability, accuracy, and completeness of the financial information are often similar to those performed for inbound transactions. However, differences exist between generally accepted accounting principles (GAAP) in the United States and GAAP in other countries. To illustrate this point and demonstrate the need to understand the sometimes marked differences in outcome between U.S. and non-U.S. approaches, here is an outline of certain major differences between U.S. and Colombian GAAP:

ASSET REAPPRAISALS

Colombian GAAP. Reappraisals of property, plant, equipment, and investments are made periodically and recorded in compensation accounts, which are shown in the asset caption "Asset reappraisals" and in the stockholders' equity caption "Surplus from reappraisals of assets." The asset reappraisal for property, plant, and equipment is determined on the basis of the difference between appraisals of such assets and inflation-adjusted net book values.

At the close of each period the inflation-adjusted cost of investments in the equity of subsidiaries must be readjusted to their market or equity value (net book value), either by write-downs charged to income or by reappraisals recorded in the reappraisal accounts. Equity value is determined on the basis of the target's recent financial statements. Market values are determined on the basis of the average quoted price on the Colombian stock exchanges in the month of the transaction's closing.

U.S. GAAP. U.S. GAAP allows no asset reappraisals.

BASIC FINANCIAL STATEMENTS

Colombian GAAP. Until 1993, Colombian GAAP required a statement of changes in financial position as one of the general-purpose financial statements. Beginning on January 1, 1994, the statement of cash flows is required in addition to the statement of changes in financial position.

U S. GAAP. Companies must include a statement of cash flows instead of a statement of changes in financial position. The primary disclosure and presentation requirements concerning the statement of cash flows are:
    —disclosure is focused on cash and cash equivalents;
    —cash flows must be classified into operating, investing, and financing activities; and
    —the presentation of cash flow information using the direct method—by major classes of operating cash receipts and disbursements (that is, customers, suppliers, and employees)—is encouraged, but use of the indirect method involving a reconciliation between net income and net operating cash flows is permitted.

DEFERRED TAXES

Colombian GAAP. The effect on income taxes resulting from the recognition of revenues, costs, and expenses for financial accounting in periods different from those recognized for tax accounting is recorded as deferred taxes. In measuring the deferred asset or deferred tax liability, the company must use the "deferred method." Normally, no deferred taxes are recognized for loss carryforwards.

U.S. GAAP. The following are the basic principles of accounting for income taxes:
    —A deferred tax liability or asset is recognized for the estimated future tax effects attributable to temporary differences and carryforwards.
    —The measurement of current and deferred tax liabilities and assets is based on provisions of existing tax law; the effects of future changes in tax laws or rates are not anticipated, but enacted changes in future tax rates are reflected in tax expense in the period of enactment.
    —The measurements of deferred tax assets is reduced, if necessary, by the amount of any tax benefits that, based on available evidence, are not expected to be realized.

INFLATION ACCOUNTING

Colombian GAAP. Accounting for the effects of inflation has been required and regulated by Colombian law since January 1, 1992. The balances of nonmonetary assets and liabilities, equity, and profit and loss accounts must be adjusted in accordance with changes in the country's general consumer price index. However, nonmonetary assets and liabilities and equity accounts are not adjusted to reflect the effects of inflation prior to January 1, 1992. Also, prior-year financial statements presented for comparative purposes are not restated in terms of the purchasing power of the currency of the latest year presented.

U.S. GAAP. Financial statements are prepared in accordance with the historical cost convention.

PENSIONS

Colombian GAAP. Liability for pensions under Colombian labor law is unfunded and shared with government agencies and with certain private pension funds. The liability is determined on the basis of annual independent actuarial studies. Amortization of deferred pension costs and payments made to pensioners is charged to income. Companies are liable for separation payments and other benefits to employees under certain conditions specified by labor laws. Companies follow the practice of providing for these indemnities through charges to operations.

U S. GAAP. Pension liability is determined based on actuarial studies, including factors such as age, years of service, compensation in the years immediately before retirement, interest rates, mortality, and other factors. The amount reflected in the balance sheet is the net amount of the plan's assets.

PRIOR PERIOD ADJUSTMENTS

Colombian GAAP. Prior period adjustments are charged to income in the year the adjustment is made.

U.S. GAAP. Prior period adjustments are charged to the opening balance of retained earnings and excluded from the determination of net income for the current period if they result from the following:

—Correction of an error in the financial statements of a prior period, or

—Adjustments that result from realization of income tax benefits of pre-acquisition operating loss carryforwards of purchased subsidiaries.

Additionally, if financial statements are presented for one of the years being corrected, restated financial statements are required.

REVENUE RECOGNITION

Colombian GAAP. Revenues are recorded on the accrual basis, except that interest income earned by financial institutions is not accrued on commercial loans that are more than six months past due or on consumer loans that are more than three months past due. Interest on such over-due loans is credited to income when collected.

The Colombian Superintendency of Banking has set specific rules for the valuation of loans by area and risk factors, on the basis of which allowances for loan losses are recorded and updated periodically.

U.S. GAAP. Revenues, other than income from trusts and other fiduciary activities, are included in results of operations as they accrue. An allowance for loan losses is provided on the basis of management's estimate of the losses in the loan portfolio, based on historical loan loss experience and evaluations of specific loans.

Given the differences noted above, which are comparable to differences existing between the United States and other developed countries in Latin America and elsewhere throughout the world, investors should be aware of the effects of the differences and adjust due diligence procedures accordingly. Clearly, the complexity of accounting principles and disclosure requirements applied in other countries will present unexpected challenges and require additional time and resources. Based on the restatement of the target's financials to U.S. GAAP, an investor may discover a very different company than the one appearing on the face of the target's originally provided financial statements.

Outbound Transactions in Emerging Markets

Financial due diligence of a target in an emerging market is complicated. One of the critical but often ignored issues is the control major families exercise in the economies of emerging-market countries. U.S. investors may encounter difficulties even in hiring professionals, given the real or perceived conflicts of interest between those professionals and the "leading family" clients they often represent. Moreover, certain individuals and families exert significant influence in the conduct of business and the development of the country's economic and legal systems. In certain Latin American countries, for example, major families control a conglomerate of companies. Accordingly, an investor looking to buy one of the companies in the family's portfolio may find that legal and accounting professionals, particularly in the larger firms, are engaged in serving that family in numerous roles. The families' influence on the local economy and on the professionals imposes an additional burden on the investor and its due diligence team.

To further complicate matters, leading businesses in many emerging markets are both socially and economically aligned with bankers, suppliers, customers, and other parties. Independent verification of balances of financial data and other economic and business information will require extra time and effort to ensure that the information obtained is complete, accurate, and not misleading. Without such information, risks multiply exponentially.

Accounting Due Diligence Procedures

Experienced practitioners know that accounting is an art and not a science. Thus, accounting due diligence requires experience, training, and knowledge of basic accounting principles, awareness of a country's practices and statutory requirements, and a basic understanding of the tax ramifications of the transaction. Critically, those performing due diligence must know how the proposed transaction will affect the investor after the deal is closed. For example:

Restructurings. From an accounting point of view, a restructuring allows a company to take a one-time charge to operations for expenses directly related to the decision made by management to either abandon or sell a particularly significant area of operations, such as two or three production plants. Although similar to a discontinued operations charge, a restructuring entails continuation of the production and sale of a product in a given line of business.

To illustrate, a shoe manufacturer may have production plants in Poland, Austria, and Germany. The manufacturer decides to close three of the plants in Poland, three in Austria, and four in Germany because the equipment is outdated and because the remaining plants have the necessary capacity to produce the volume eliminated by the closure of the ten plants. The shoe manufacturer did not discontinue any operations, but rather will restructure its operations to make them more efficient. Here, all of the costs associated with the closure of the ten plants must be estimated and charged to operations in the period when the decision is made. Obviously the restructuring process requires many estimates and assumptions. For example, the company generated an estimate of the salvage value of the equipment to be sold at the plants. Once the equipment is advertised for sale, the actual market value may be different from the estimated realizable value, requiring adjustments to the restructuring estimate.

In other cases, employment laws may change during the restructuring process, requiring the company to pay more as a result of the employment terminations. Such changes in labor laws are common and may also cause adjustments to the original restructuring estimate. The generation of assumptions and estimates is critical to any accounting process. However, the due diligence team should be aware of any restructuring charges that may have occurred in prior years, because the effects of the changes in estimates may affect the results of operations for the current year. If the target's management team decides to record adjustments, favorable or unfavorable, to the restructuring charges, the results of operations for the period in question may be either overstated or understated.

The original estimates may have been overly conservative or overly liberal, thus causing effects to be recorded in subsequent periods. The due diligence team should be aware of unusual charges and changes in estimates and investigate their impact thoroughly to establish the reasonableness of the original estimates and the adjustments.

Investments in closely held companies. Determining the value of closely held companies requires making many estimates. Because quoted market values generally do not exist for closely held companies, the carrying value recorded by the target may be influenced by the following:

♦ Cash flows generated by the closely held corporation, in which case an estimate of the value is generated by preparing a discounted cash flow estimate.

♦ Negotiations with potential buyers who have indicated, either orally or in writing, the intent to purchase the company.

♦ Calculation of a value estimate based on other statistical factors, including earnings before interest, taxes, depreciation, and amortization (EBITDA), number of units sold, and other similar factors.

Any time that target management prepares value estimates, the due diligence team should question their reasonableness. In the case of closely held corporations, the target's management may have sought to record excessive valuation provisions (accounting cushions) in earlier years to record higher earnings in later years by selling the understated closely held corporations.

The due diligence team should look for unusual gains recorded on the sale of assets. Time should be devoted to analyze the impact that such dispositions will have on the target's future operations.

The due diligence team should include third-party professionals from the target's country, because, as has been noted, regulatory, legal, and accounting practices are, in many instances, likely to differ from those of the investor's country. For example, the following illustration summarizes the differences in accounting for discontinued operations between different countries, including International Accounting Standards (IAS) and U.S. GAAP (please note that these accounting policies and requirements are subject to change):

DISCONTINUED OPERATIONS

International Accounting Standards. A discontinuing operation is a relatively large component of an enterprise, such as a business or geographical segment, that the enterprise, pursuant to a single plan, either is disposing of substantially in its entirety or is terminating through abandonment or piecemeal sale. Disclosures are required on an initial disclosure event and must be made continually until the operation is disposed of and comparative information is no longer reported.

Australia. Information relating to discontinued operations must be included in financial reports together with continuing operations.

Voluntary disclosure may be made of the results and effect of discontinued operations.

Austria. Discontinued operations are considered to be outside of ordinary business activities. Resulting earnings and expenditures should be included in extraordinary income and expenses.

Canada. The results of discontinued operations should be included in net income. Such results should include and separately disclose the results of operations prior to the measurement date, the net gain or loss from discontinued operations, and any extraordinary gain or loss (each net of applicable income taxes). A net loss should be provided for at the measurement date. A net gain should be recognized only when realized. Income taxes applicable to the results of operations prior to the measurement date and to the net gain or loss from discontinued operations should each be disclosed separately.

Denmark. No specific guidelines exist. If the discontinuance of an operation or sale of a subsidiary has a major impact on the group, the effect on assets and liabilities, financial position, and the profit and loss account is generally disclosed in the note.

France. No specific disclosure is required.

Germany. Provisions should be made for losses and closure costs. Gains and losses due to the disposal usually represent extraordinary income or expenses, if material. Discontinued operations should be disclosed in the notes.

Italy. No specific disclosure is required.

Japan. No specific guidelines exist. Generally, gains or losses incurred by disposal of discontinued operations are presented as extraordinary items in the income statement.

Mexico. Once a formal plan to sell or abandon a segment of a business has been adopted, the related identifiable assets and liabilities should be adjusted to their net realizable value, taking into consideration the cost of separation of related personnel.

The Netherlands. Discontinued operations generally lead to a devaluation of the assets involved. An adjustment to a lower net realizable value should be applied if the asset is no longer to be used in the business and to a lower recoverable amount if the asset continues to be used in other operations of the company. Discontinued operations also can give rise to the formation of a provision. This provision relates to liabilities of uncertain magnitude that will come to bear on the legal entity in connection with winding up activities and reorganization of the company.

Norway. Revenue and expenses from discontinued and discontinuing operations may, under certain circumstances, be presented separately in the income statement in a parallel presentation or as "other items." Reporting entities should prepare pro forma figures for turnover and operating profit from current and prior periods. In accordance with general accounting principles, a provision for expected operating losses and closure costs should be made.

South Africa. Turnover and operating profit arising from discontinued operations must be shown separately on the face of the income statement. Cost of sales, gross profit, and other operating expenses arising from discontinued operations can be disclosed in the notes.

Spain. No specific guidelines exist. Discontinued operations must be disclosed in the notes to financial statements and any impairment of value recognized as an expense of the period.

Sweden. Results from discontinued operations should be included as part of the profit or loss from ordinary activities in the income statement. Provision should be made for losses and closure costs.

Switzerland. In consolidated financial statements only, changes in the scope of consolidation from the prior year, as well as the date of the applicability of the changes, should be disclosed in the notes.

United Kingdom. Turnover and operating profit arising from discontinued operations must be shown separately on the face of the profit and loss account. Cost of sales, gross profit, and other operating expenses arising from discontinued operations can be disclosed in the notes rather than on the face of the profit and loss account. Prior-year comparatives should be restated accordingly.

United States. Discontinued operations must qualify as a business segment (separate major line of business or class of customers), where disposal is expected within one year. This excludes disposals of product lines and restructurings of operations, for which specific loss recognition rules apply. Expected loss on disposal is recorded at measurement date; expected gain is recognized only when realized. Results of operations and gain or loss on disposal should be reported separately in the income statement, net of tax, after continuing operations but before extraordinary items. Previous income statements should be reclassified to conform.

It bears repeating that accounting is an art and not a science. Accordingly, due diligence yields no guarantees. At best, due diligence procedures will identify areas of risk and opportunity in the target, and the investor will weigh these and other factors to arrive at a "go/no go" decision. The accounting due diligence process is influenced and affected by numerous factors, as discussed below.

Integrity and Qualifications of Company Personnel, Their Practices, and Ethical Standards

No due diligence can completely uncover the sophisticated manipulation of financial data by the target company's management. At best, the target's reputation in its community, media coverage of the target, and the target's relationship with local regulatory authorities will create an informational database. These kinds of data together with more obvious evidence of problems, such as existing litigation and lack of compliance with contractual obligations, begin to provide comfort or dismay to the prospective investor.

The backgrounds of all senior and middle managers and of the board of directors should be researched and evaluated by requesting personal background investigations for each of the members of the target's management team, including criminal investigations. Surprisingly, in a number of cases, managers may have criminal backgrounds, have violated securities laws, or have pleaded guilty in criminal cases—suggesting that these individuals may have a propensity to "cook the books." Most international accounting firms will consider resigning from an assignment should such factors surface during the due diligence process.

If it seems that target management is not trustworthy, it is likely that the investment effort will need to be aborted. Accounting information is highly susceptible to manipulation and unethical practices, so the due diligence team should be alert to the possibilities for fraud and deception.

Minimizing employee turnover and disruption should be a major goal of the investing company's due diligence effort. Good employees of the target should be identified and assured that their efforts in facilitating the due diligence process will be recognized and rewarded. The identification of good employees is generally accomplished during the performance of due diligence by evaluating the accuracy and completeness of the information prepared by those employees. Supervisory relationships also should be evaluated to determine whether the data are reliable and accurate. Rewards for the employees to be retained typically take the form of performance bonuses and stock options. Continued employment of the target's key employees will often be a major factor in the success of the proposed transaction, and their departure could be a major contributing factor to its failure.

In a number of European and Latin American countries, the costs of terminating employees may be substantial. Accordingly, the investor may want to take such costs and expenses into consideration in determining the total cost of the proposed investment.

The goal of retaining target employees should not overshadow a thorough evaluation of all of the employees and officers to ensure that the accounting standards applied are reasonable and appropriate. In countries whose governments have historically controlled companies in certain industries, those so-called national champions tend to be bureaucratic and inefficient. Once the privatization of such a company has occurred, the termination of redundant employees often becomes an overwhelming task. For example, before the privatization of Yacimientos Petroliferos Fiscales (YPF) in Argentina in 1991, the company employed 52,000 employees. By 1995, the number of employees had been reduced to 5,800, an 89 percent reduction. Before the privatization, YPF, a petroleum company, owned supermarkets, movie houses, clubs, and even churches. Though painful, the privatization process resulted in a leaner and much more efficient company. YPF's profitability increased dramatically. The restructuring of the operations and reductions in employee levels were critical to the success of the investment.

Relationship with Independent Certified Public Accountants

The relationship the target may have with its independent certified public accountants should be indicative of the quality and reasonableness of its financial statements. Clearly, where the target has used the same accounting firm for years and the relationship is positive, results are likely to be more defensible than if the relationship with the accounting firm is negative or adversarial.

The investor team should evaluate the closeness of the independent certified public accounting firm with the target and the impact of the target's fees on the overall billings of the firm. Although remote, the possibility exists that the target's senior management may be able to influence the decisions of the firm's representatives.

For U.S. public companies with shares or debt securities registered with the Securities and Exchange Commission (SEC), the independent certified public accountants and management must write to the SEC and explain whether there were any disagreements relating to accounting issues. The due diligence team should be able to obtain copies of any such letters from the target's management.

The due diligence team should organize private meetings with the target's independent auditors to discuss issues, including the following:

♦ **Adherence to independence rules.** Ask how material the target client is to the overall practice of the accounting firm.

♦ **Relationship with the management of the target.** Are there any disagreements relating to the application of accounting principles? Were there any limitations on the scope or imposed restrictions on the procedures to be performed during the audit?

♦ **Overall level of fees.** Are there any concerns over the fee negotiation process and the collection of fees?

♦ **Rotation of accounting firm personnel.** How long has the audit partner assigned to the engagement served the target client?

♦ **Access to the audit working papers.** The due diligence team should obtain access to the working papers and read the most significant working papers prepared by the independent accountants. The due diligence team should also ask for access to other important files, particularly those concerning tax matters.

♦ **Principal accounting issues.** Identification of the principal accounting issues should assist the due diligence team in focusing its efforts on the highest risk areas. The principal accounting issues should be analyzed to understand the effect that specific accounting issues may have on the target's financial statements.

♦ **Opinion shopping.** Ask questions relating to the possibility that target senior management may have solicited the opinion of other accounting firms on specific issues.

♦ **Recommendations for internal control improvements.** Read the independent accountant's letters to management. Discuss any concerns over the gathering, preparation, review, and approval of accounting information.

♦ **Accounting adjustments.** The suggestion of accounting adjustments is a sensitive area. Ask the target's independent auditors to provide details concerning any adjustments suggested by target management. Analyze any unexplained adjustments carefully.

Depending on the credentials of the target's independent accounting firm, if the timing of due diligence procedures coincides with the completion of the target's annual audit, consider hiring the target's accountants to execute certain due diligence procedures. The investor's accountants should accompany target management in monitoring and coordinating the work of those auditors.

Considerations in Evaluating Key Accounting Issues

Research and development expenditures. A target's commitment to improving the quality of its products through research and development (R&D) should serve as an indicator of the focus and goals of that company. If R&D expenditures are not material, the due diligence team should determine whether the lack of financial commitment to such an important area should be evaluated.

If the target is involved in significant research and development, the due diligence team should focus on the likely success of the program and the direction in which such efforts are headed. A successful R&D program shows the target's commitment to future growth and expansion. In the United States, GAAP prohibits the deferral of R&D costs; all such costs must be expensed. Accordingly, question any capitalized R&D costs and consider proposing them as one of the adjustments to reduce the target's net book value—and potentially the target's acquisition cost.

Accounting for income taxes. Chapter 6 addresses the due diligence procedures to be performed in connection with income taxes. Suffice to say, however, that income tax provisions and accruals should be evaluated carefully. Timely discussions should be held with the appropriate tax personnel to ensure that no issues are overlooked.

Going concern considerations. Going concern considerations apply to both domestic and cross-border transactions. Financial statements are generally prepared on the assumption that the company will continue as a going concern. But other assumptions may be appropriate, such as the liquidation method, where assets and liabilities are stated at their estimated liquidation value. The going concern concept assumes that the business will continue for at least one year from the date of the auditor's report on the company's financial statements. If target management and its accountants conclude that the business will not be in operation for at least one more year, adjustments must be made to the carrying value of assets and liabilities by adjusting them to their estimated net realizable value, which generally approximates liquidation value.

The due diligence team should determine if the target is experiencing financial difficulties. The following is a partial list of factors the investor team should consider in this context:

♦ Continued losses from operations

♦ Inability to generate positive cash flows

♦ Excessive levels of inventory, combined with decreasing sales and increases in uncollectible accounts receivable

♦ Negative current ratio (current liabilities exceeding current assets)

♦ Inability to meet debt covenant requirements

♦ Delays in the issuance of audited financial statements caused by the uncertainty of the realization of major transactions, such as material sales of assets

♦ Disagreements with the target's independent certified public accountants

♦ Unjustified departure or resignation of key target employees and officers

♦ Overdue accounts payable and instances where major suppliers have refused to deliver goods or where cash-on-delivery terms are required

♦ Termination of employees and curtailment of operations

♦ Inadequate capital (shareholders' equity) levels

♦ Involuntary plant closures or involuntary disposition of assets

The existence of any of these factors sends a strong signal that the target is experiencing financial difficulties, which in turn may require its management to be aggressive in applying accounting principles and reporting the issues faced by the company. The investor team should recognize that the target's owners may be more willing to accept a lower purchase price to salvage whatever may be possible from their own investment—or may try to inflate the price by neglecting maintenance or by cutting back on R&D or on sales promotion.

Employee stock purchase and other employee stock benefit plans. A number of companies issue options to purchase shares and offer grant programs for employees, officers, and directors. These programs generally require that such persons maintain a relationship with the company for a specific period of time.

The issuance of the share options or share grants may not require that any entries be recorded on the issuer's books at the time of the issuance. However, the financial and accounting implications of these awards may be significant to the investor. For example, the share options and grants may include a provision allowing for exercise upon a change in the control of the target. Liberated from the restrictions on their equity participation, target management may be inclined to leave the company with the investor holding the bag. Due diligence should seek to determine the intentions of such recipients. Consideration should be given to including new incentives in the employment agreements as part of the deal to ensure that the employees are contractually obligated to stay with the company postdeal.

Environmental accounting issues. Environmental issues are receiving increasing attention throughout the world. A target may have substantial, and unrecorded, costs associated with environmental cleanup projects. In many instances, companies may not even be aware of the fact that they have violated the law. For example, if an investor acquires a company in a country whose environmental laws require certain monitoring controls and procedures and the target has not complied with such requirements, the investor may be liable for the cleanup costs. In other countries, environmental hazards may exist but with minimal restrictions on them. Due diligence should determine likely cleanup costs if new environmental regulations in such countries appear possible.

The investor team should consider accounting for environmental cleanup costs in completing the due diligence. If necessary, the investor should hire environmental engineers and other professionals to inspect the target's plants and other operation sites.

Provisions for losses. The preparation of provisions for losses requires numerous, significant estimates and assumptions. The target's management must exercise reasonable judgment in preparing the company's financial statements and the relevant disclosures. Aggressive managers will record inadequate provisions for losses, which will generate losses after the investor has committed its funds and controls the target. The investor should review the reasonableness of the allowances for losses to determine whether excessive amounts have been recorded, which may result in additional profits to be recognized by the investor in the future.

Target management also may have been liberal in recognizing provisions for losses for legal and tax contingencies. Accordingly, investor teams should obtain the appropriate professional assistance to determine adequacy of legal and tax accruals. The investor team should recognize that the preparation of estimates is susceptible to target management manipulation. The level of documentation to support the accruals and provisions recorded by the target should serve as a substantial indicator of target management's intention and approach to the preparation of financial statements.

When considering the target's write-off history, investors should be careful in analyzing the adequacy of the allowance for uncollectible account losses. Often, companies will continue to add provisions to the allowance for losses but will not write off uncollectible accounts, thus distorting the write-off ratios, which generally compare write-off amounts to sales and to accounts receivable balances.

Accounting for barter transactions. Barter transactions are generally recorded by determining either the value of the goods or services provided or the value of the goods or services received, whichever is more readily determinable. In cross-border transactions, barter is generally conducted between companies under common control.

In industries such as radio and television, airtime is exchanged for goods and services in lieu of cash payments. Barter transactions, if material, may distort the results of operations and may have an effect on a company's future operations. Accordingly, the investor team should identify the barter transactions by discussing the existence of such transactions with target management, by reviewing the target's financial activity with major customers and suppliers, and by evaluating the financial information on barter transactions provided by the target. Other procedures, including discussions with the target's legal counsel and with other professionals, should be considered.

Effect of off-book transactions and accounts. In the ordinary course of business, companies enter into transactions that are recorded not on their official financial statements but rather in secondary accounting records. For instance, in some industries, companies provide services to customers without taking control over assets or liabilities. Thus, banks provide private banking customers with investment and brokerage services, which are not entered on the bank's official accounting records. That said, legal and financial responsibility for such services and for the customer relationships still rests with the company providing the services.

Financial and accounting due diligence may require inquiry on items not recorded in the target's financial records. Documentation supporting the legitimacy of such transactions is a must. Income resulting from such transactions should be tested to ensure that the income recognition is appropriate. Individual transactions should be tested to ensure that the income was recognized over the appropriate period of time. For example, in cases where the fees charged to a customer are for services to be provided over the course of one year, cash received in payment for such services should be deferred and amortized into income over one year and not recognized at the time of its receipt.

Counsel should be consulted to ensure that any potential contingent liabilities resulting from providing these types of services are recorded properly in the target's accounting records.

Related-party transactions. Related-party transactions are those economic activities effected between parties owned or controlled by the same group of companies. Related-party transactions also include economic activities between companies in which any officer or board member of one company also occupies a decision-making position in the other company. For example, say the president of a company borrowing money from a bank is also a member of that bank's board of directors. The bank and the company are deemed related parties because the president has significant influence over the operations of the company and also influences the actions of the bank's board of directors.

The accounting records of any business are affected by related-party transactions. U.S. GAAP fully applies to related-party transactions. In most countries, generally accepted accounting principles require disclosure of related-party transactions, including the terms of the transactions and the effects of such transactions on the company's financial statements.

Identifying related parties is often difficult and frustrating. Target management may own interests in companies doing business with the target and not disclose the existence of such relationships. For example, in emerging-market countries, several companies under the same family's control often do business with one another and are not identified as being related. The investor team should identify all such entities by requesting a list of all major customers and suppliers and requesting that the owners, officers, and directors of the customers and suppliers of such companies be identified. This inquiry may be critical to determining whether to proceed with the transaction. There is no substitute for interviewing target management, completing background investigations of major customers and vendors, and performing the other tests of the information described earlier. Related-party transactions should be evaluated to determine whether the terms of the transactions were the same as those applicable to arm's-length transactions. Pro forma financials excluding the related-party transactions should be prepared to determine the effect of related-party transactions and the "purified" results of operations.

Statutory, Regulatory, and Legal Requirements

For both inbound and outbound transactions, in certain countries, including the United States, statutory, regulatory, and legal requirements serve to make transparent the presentation, accuracy, and completeness of the financial information companies produce for third parties and shareholders. Similarly, accounting standards are promulgated by government agencies, such as the SEC in the United States and the Central Bank in Spain, to ensure that accounting principles are applied consistently and correctly. Non-compliance with existing laws and accounting regulations may result in criminal prosecution, civil penalties, or other legal claims, which are generally difficult and expensive to defend. Concerns over such penalties will, in most cases, induce company management to be honest and direct.

Tough accounting rules, like the accounting requirements and financial statement disclosure rules enforced by the SEC, will generally improve the reliability of financial information. Professionals and management alike will, as a result of such requirements and under pressure from regulatory agencies, extend additional efforts to comply. The existence of laws, however, provides no assurance of compliance, nor should their existence reduce normal levels of healthy professional skepticism. Conversely, in those countries where transparency does not exist or where regulations do not require much disclosure, the due diligence team should perform additional procedures and tests. Finally, there are countries like the Philippines that have embraced U.S.-style disclosure systems but lack adequate enforcement mechanisms.

Industry Accepted and Generally Accepted Accounting Principles

As non-U.S. companies have adopted U.S. GAAP to register debt or equity securities with the SEC, they've suffered material reductions in earnings and shareholders' equity. As discussed previously, understanding the difference in accounting practices and the effects of such differences is essential to successful cross-border due diligence.

Application of aggressive accounting principles and practices should serve as an indicator of target management's intentions and focus. For example, if the target shareholders are considering selling a portion or all of their share ownership, management may be instructed to accelerate the recording of sales, which may or may not have been completed. In such instances, the goods "sold" may not have been shipped by the cut-off date, may have been sold under terms providing for buyback options, or may have been sold on consignment. On the other hand, expenses that should be recorded currently may be capitalized under the assumption that such expenditures (such as advertising, salaries, software development costs, and organization costs) may have future value. The investor team should exercise caution in evaluating the recognition of sales and the deferral of costs and expenses.

Conversely, when the target's management is well known for applying conservative accounting practices, the investor's due diligence team will recognize that a significant part of the due diligence process has been completed even before any due diligence procedures are applied. When target management is recognized as aggressive, the due diligence should be increased to reduce the risk of not identifying potential accounting issues and differences with the investor's accounting treatment of similar accounts. As noted earlier, if revenues are determined to have been recognized prematurely, the due diligence team should consider performing the following procedures:

♦ Review sales documents to determine whether customers ordered the goods shipped and the dates of the orders as compared to the shipping dates.

♦ Evaluate shipping documents prepared by different company personnel and by third parties to ensure that the information is consistent with the information recorded in the accounting records.

♦ Confirm the existence of receivables directly with the customers receiving the goods and request that any arrangements be described in the confirmation responses. Efforts should be made to make direct contact with the customers to discuss major transactions.

♦ Identify any returned goods subsequent to the cutoff date. Research the target's policies and procedures for issuing credit memos.

♦ Review the aging of the inventory and determine whether any obsolete or excess inventory exists. Pay particular attention to the goods shipped on or just before the cutoff date to determine whether the sold goods were shipped before the cutoff date and whether they were obsolete or excess inventory goods.

Industry Practices

Certain industries are aggressive in the financial reporting of their operations. For example, in the financial services industry, the value of a company may vary significantly as a result of factors external to the company's operations. A decrease in the prime rate, negative information released in labor statistics, and a decline in the economic outlook for a given country may have uncontrollable effects on the company's value and must be monitored to minimize such effects.

To illustrate, assume an investor is planning to buy a bank operating in a stable economic environment. Economic conditions, however, worsen as unemployment and loan default rates rise in the bank's geographic area. Although the target bank's loan portfolio is performing as expected, the due diligence team understands that, considering the economic downturn, the allowance for loan losses may not be sufficient. Application of accounting principles may not require the recording of additional loan loss provisions, and the bank's management may not want to record the additional provisions because they will weaken the bank's capital position and jeopardize its compliance with regulatory requirements. Given these conditions, the investor may wish to terminate or renegotiate the proposed acquisition.

In certain industries, the major companies will influence the manner in which information and accounting disclosures are made. Multinational companies provide benchmarking opportunities for smaller companies in the same industry. The financial statements of smaller companies often mimic those of the majors in the field in order to comply with industry standards. Comparing the target's financial information with that of major companies in the same industry can thus help determine conformity to existing industry practices and ensure that valuable information is not missing.

Income Tax Laws and Regulations

In certain countries, such as Brazil and Mexico, the tax laws are difficult to understand and even more difficult to apply. Not all companies pay their taxes, putting competitive pressure on those seeking to comply with existing rules. In certain countries, management may maintain three or four different sets of books to satisfy different purposes. Thus, the "real books" may contain all of the possibly recognizable and taxable revenues, and the "tax books" will not include all of the revenues required to be reported. Other types of books may include the "regulatory books," in which capital may reflect items not permitted to be recorded under GAAP. But the world is changing. Countries like Italy, where tax avoidance and even evasion traditionally were rampant, are trying to modify the existing tax structure to ensure that taxes are applied equally to all taxpayers and that compliance is strictly enforced.

Investors should identify which set of accounting books is being provided to its due diligence team. The other books may include information relevant to the due diligence team, therefore, all books should be examined. Target company managers should be questioned about the reasons for keeping different sets of books. From time to time, accounting adjustments will be required as a result of comparing and analyzing results from different sets of books.

The investor team should also look for tax avoidance strategies in cross-border transactions. For example, a target may have established royalty arrangements with affiliates to transfer income from a heavily taxed jurisdiction to another with lower tax rates, thereby reducing consolidated company taxes. Other arrangements include manufacturing goods in a high-tax country and recording sales in a lower-rate jurisdiction. All of these strategies, even if legally permissible, should be analyzed to determine their effect on the investor once the transaction is closed, especially if such strategies are not available to the investor. Tax authorities may challenge these and other income tax reduction strategies, thus exposing the investor to potentially serious future tax liabilities. (For further discussion of these tax issues, see Chapter 6.)

Data Processing Systems

In cliches, one may find wisdom. For instance, the cliche "Garbage in—garbage out" is true. Old, inadequate financial information systems will cause due diligence problems for the investor team. For example, in a bank acquisition, the ability to identify all loans to one borrower is critical in measuring the exposure the target bank may have to a single borrower. If the bank's systems do not produce reports summarizing the loans to one borrower, the amount of time and effort required by the investor team may be both excessive and insufficient. As a result, evaluating the adequacy of the provision for loan losses will be an almost impossible task. Manual schedules and analysis will have to be prepared from available reports, summarizing and testing all of the information. The information contained in all data processing systems must be tested and corroborated with credible evidence for the investor team to be able to rely on such information.

Data processing systems are only as good as the personnel inputting the information, the controls over the systems, environmental safeguards, and technical adequacy. If the target's personnel are not adequately trained or lack the necessary skills to input data, the due diligence team must review and test the information produced by the target's systems.

Old or obsolete systems may be not only impractical but also expensive to manage and control. State-of-the-art systems and controls will be

useful in establishing the integrity of the financial and corporate accounting information gathering process.

Depending on the level of sophistication of the target's data processing systems, the investor's team may want to hire experts to assist in the
evaluations of the hardware, software, and control environment.
Employees should be interviewed and observed to determine whether
the systems work as described and in accordance with the target's established policies and procedures.

The sophistication of the target's data processing systems will be
affected by the economic conditions in the target's country. In developed markets, the procurement of reliable and state-of-the-art systems is
much simpler than it is in emerging-market countries. However, the
principal factor in whether a company acquires the necessary software
and hardware for its corporate needs is directly related to the company's
capital resources. Old and inefficient systems will require future cash
outlays from the investor (and should be an element to consider in for-
mulating any offer) and indicate that target management either has not
paid enough attention to data processing systems or lacked the means to
invest in such systems.

Political Environment in the Target's Country

A country's political environment affects potential investors' inclination
or disinclination to complete transactions in that country. For example,
in a country plagued by dictatorships, civil wars, corruption, and other
adversities, investors will not be eager to invest capital. In other countries where fiscal or economic direction is absent, investors will avoid
making capital investments unless the rates of return are much higher
than in other locations.

Changes in the political environment in a country may prompt unexpected requirements to record additional loss provisions. Changes in the
political environment may generate new laws and regulations that must
be reflected in the target's books and records. This is particularly true in
highly regulated industries like banking, petroleum, health care, and
transportation. For example, in dictatorships around the world, auto-
cratic leaders have been known to change the requirements on
allowances for loan losses for banks and other types of financial institutions and for pension and labor costs. New or unanticipated changes in

the law can result in unexpected losses and increased costs. The accounting for such changes should be thought through in advance, calculated, and recorded as required.

In other instances, labor laws have been changed without considering the economic effects of such changes. For example, imposing requirements that employees not be terminated will frustrate the plans of companies trying to streamline operations. In a number of countries, investments are high-risk propositions, and investors must be aware of the implications flowing from the direction a new government may be taking from its proposed new laws. As is the case in any domestic or foreign jurisdiction, effective relationships with government officials will facilitate the due diligence process.

The target's accounting systems may have to be modified to reflect changes in regulatory requirements. The due diligence team should be aware of such modifications and determine whether the required changes have been effected properly, whether the information produced is accurate, and whether the accounting applications are reasonable. If not, and the consequences diminish value, the deal may need either to be renegotiated with contingent payments, like milestone payments or earn-outs, or simply to be abandoned.

In most countries, foreign companies with money to invest will be welcomed guests. Capitalism works because of the incentives created by the investment of capital. Due diligence is one of the tools used to enhance the potential success of an investment. However, the vision, imagination, creativity, and strategic direction required to make a deal profitable depend on the experience and knowledge of the investor's team. Even in the worst economic and political conditions, investors will find opportunities for profitable transactions.

Cross-Border Financial and Accounting Due Diligence

IN AN IDEAL WORLD, target companies would be able to supply all or substantially all of the information set forth below. In the real world, targets may have only a portion of the information sought. Targets in non-U.S. jurisdictions, particularly in emerging-market countries, may not be able to provide all of the requested information. But the investor goes forward at its peril without reasonable compliance regarding the data described in the checklist below.

DOCUMENTS TO BE REQUESTED FROM TARGET COMPANY

General Corporate Matters

1. Certificate or articles of incorporation and bylaws, as amended to date, of the company and its subsidiaries. ❑

2. Minutes of meetings (or written consents) of the company's shareholders and board of directors and any committees of the board of directors. ❑

3. List of all jurisdictions, domestic or foreign, in which the company or any affiliate is qualified to do business or has significant operations or properties, and descriptions of operations in such places. ❑

4. History of the company's formation and development. Detailed organizational chart of the company and all of its affiliates. ❑

5. Minutes of meetings (or written consents) of the shareholders, board of directors, and any committees of the board of directors of each subsidiary of the company. ❑

6. List of officers and directors of the company and each of its subsidiaries or affiliates. ❑

7. List of option holders, warrant holders, and holders of securities convertible into capital stock of the company and its subsidiaries or affiliates. ❑

8. All pre-incorporation, security holder, subscription or registration rights agreements, voting agreements, outstanding proxies, and other agreements regarding the voting, ownership, or other aspects of the company's securities or management to which any shareholder, the company, or any of its subsidiaries or affiliates is a party. ❑

9. List of all corporations, partnerships, associations, joint ventures, and other business organizations in which the company owns, directly or indirectly, an interest or any shares of capitalstock. ❏
10. Shareholder, partnership, or similar organizational equity holder list, with names, number, and type of equity interests held by each equity holder. Pay special attention to voting rights or their absence. ❏
11. History of any transactions in any of company's types of stock securities in the past two years, including documents evidencing transfer of equity interests. ❏
12. Stock book(s) available for examination. ❏

Financial Information

1. Year-to-date financial statements, with comparison to same period of prior year. ❏
2. For the past three years, all annual and quarterly financial reports and financial statements, including accompanying schedules, of the company and its subsidiaries (balance sheets, income statements, statement of cash flows, and reconciliation of retained earnings). If available, include financial reporting (revenues and costs) by line of business and revenues from top ten major accounts. ❏
3. Current trial balance and other significant financial statements and internal financial reports of the company and its affiliates. ❏
4. List of bank accounts, including bank type or account, account number, and authorized signatories. Obtain copies of bank reconciliations for review for all accounts for the last two months and each quarter for the last two calendar years. ❏
5. Bank statements for the last month of the fiscal year-end and of the prior year and all months of the current year. ❏
6. Summary of major accounting policies, noting any that may be controversial or different from the investor country's generally accepted accounting principles (GAAP) or that may not be in accordance with generally accepted industry practices. Listing of accounting methods elections, particularly significant estimates (e.g., accruals, valuation methods, and depreciation). ❏
7. All auditors' and independent certified public accountants' letters and opinions for the company and its affiliates. Obtain auditors' reports to management concerning internal accounting controls and procedures and other matters and any management

responses thereto, and internal memoranda (particularly internal audit or regulatory compliance memoranda) concerning the company or its affiliates.   ❏

8. Financial projections, if any, for the remainder of the current year and next year, including assumptions. Include full-year detailed income statement by month, end-of-year estimated pro forma balance sheet and cash flow forecast, budget for the current year, and comparison of actual versus budget year to date for the current year.   ❏

9. Identification and description of all contingent liabilities not reflected on the company's financial statements, established monetary provisions, allowances and reserves, and disagreements with company's outside auditors concerning the company's financial reporting during the preceding two years.   ❏

10. Copies of letters to management relating to the potential improvement of the company's internal control systems together with any reports, letters, or correspondence prepared by accountants of the company or any subsidiaries or partnership.   ❏

11. Copies of all tax filings and returns (including shareholder, corporate, or partnership) for the last three years, including income taxes, sales, use, property, employment, and franchise taxes (and any other local taxes). Include copies of any correspondence with tax authorities (other than routine transmittals) and copies of tax-sharing agreements between the company and its subsidiaries or affiliates.   ❏

12. Payroll tax reconciliations (two years), reconciling total payroll to the reports submitted to the appropriate payroll tax regulatory agencies.   ❏

13. All income tax audit results and any communication (documented or oral) from the government agencies in all jurisdictions that require tax filings.   ❏

14. Schedule describing ongoing tax disputes, together with copies of tax authority reports, correspondence, and similar matters, with respect to pending tax proceedings regarding open years or items for the company or any affiliate.   ❏

15. Prior year's tax returns for all companies acquired within the past three years.   ❏

16. A schedule of shareholder "due to" and "due from" accounts for the last two years.   ❏

17. A listing of any company expenses that may be regarded as per-

sonal flowing through the business, which may be characterized as "additional pretax profit add-back items." ❏

18. A listing of any significant nonrecurring expenses occurring in the past year or current year. ❏

19. A schedule of accounting firms that have represented the company or any of its affiliates in any material matters in the last five years. ❏

20. A schedule with supporting agreements showing cooperative arrangements with suppliers detailing year-to-date payments and remaining payments to be received for the balance of the year. ❏

21. A schedule with supporting agreements showing commission arrangements with top ten suppliers detailing commissions received year to date and estimated commissions to be received for the balance of the year. ❏

22. A schedule showing current accounts receivable, including quality, aging, and special classes thereof. Include current aged account receivables listing. ❏

23. A schedule showing current accounts payable, accrued expenses, and customer deposits. Include current aged accounts payable listing by supplier. ❏

24. A schedule of property, plant, and equipment; depreciation schedules, and amortization schedules.

25. Detailed listing of capital investments that will be made during the current fiscal year, especially if not completed as of the date of the company's most recent financial statements. ❏

26. Reports on the company from any outside consultants, analysts, or others. ❏

27. Description of contingent liabilities arising from any agreements, severance payments for terminated employees, unresolved legal matters, price redetermination or renegotiation, sales subject to warranty or service agreements, product liability, unfunded pension plan liability, antitrust matters, equal opportunity matters, and environmental or other matters. ❏

Compliance with Laws

1. Documents showing any certification of compliance with or any deficiency with respect to regulatory standards (for example, environmental protection standards) on any of the company's facilities. ❏

2. Principal licenses, permits, certifications, and authorizations to

carry out the business of the company or its subsidiaries from United States federal, state, or local regulatory or licensing authorities or any non-U.S. federal, provincial, or local regulatory or licensing authorities.   ❑

3. Documentation of any investigation of the company by any government agency in any country.   ❑

4. All communication to and other filings with local, state, federal, and non-U.S. government agencies during the last five years in jurisdictions where assets are located or operations are conducted by the company or any of its affiliates. Any reports, notices, or correspondence relating to any purported violation or infringement by the company or any of its subsidiaries or any partnership and any suspended or revoked government permits or licenses and copies of all other material correspondence with government agencies.   ❑

5. Correspondence of the company or its subsidiaries with the following U.S. agencies and their non-U.S. counterparts:
   - ◆ Federal:
     - —Securities and Exchange Commission   ❑
     - —Environmental Protection Agency   ❑
     - —Federal Trade Commission   ❑
     - —Department of Labor   ❑
     - —Department of Health, Education & Welfare   ❑
   - ◆ State:
     - —State Securities Commission   ❑
     - —State Department of Labor   ❑
     - —State Department of Revenue   ❑
     - —State Department of Health   ❑
     - —Secretary of State   ❑
   - ◆ Any other federal, state, local, or foreign government agencies of significance to the company's business or operations.   ❑

6. Press releases or articles concerning the company and its affiliates within the past year in newspapers, magazines, and trade/industry publications.   ❑

Financing Documents

1. Any significant debt agreements to which the company or any affiliate is a party, such as trust indentures, term or revolving loan agreements, bank lines of credit, mortgages, promissory notes, significant property or equipment leases, and other similar agree-

ments and arrangements, and all guarantees by the company or any subsidiary together with any interest rate cap, hurdle, swap, or other hedging mechanism relating to the foregoing. ❏

2. Summaries of all evidences of compliance with the agreements described in preceding Item 1, and any communications regarding defaults, potential defaults, or waivers of defaults. ❏

3. Documents relating to proposed new indebtedness, including but not limited to term sheets, commitment letters, draft agreements, and similar documents. ❏

4. Disclosure documents used in public offerings, sales of control, private placements of securities, industrial development bond financing, or institutional or bank loan applications. ❏

5. Copies of letters of credit, performance guarantees, and bonds. ❏

6. All pledges, security agreements, or other agreements or documents creating or purporting to create liens or other security interest in any assets of the company. ❏

Operational Matters and Other Material or Significant Agreements

1. List of material suppliers. A supplier is considered to be material to the company if payments to such supplier amounted to or exceeded 5 percent of the company's gross revenue in any of the last three years, or if the loss of the supplier would result in a material disruption of the company's business. Provide a list with amount of business with the top ten suppliers for the last three years. ❏

2. Material contracts or agreements concerning business or services performed for, or materials supplied to, the company or its affiliates. ❏

3. List of material customers. A customer is material if it accounted for 5 percent or more of the company's revenues in any of the last three years or if loss of the customer would have a material impact on the company's business or results of operations. Provide the top ten customers for the last three years. ❏

4. Material agreements concerning business or services performed or products supplied by the company or its subsidiaries. Include all contracts, agreements, or other arrangements with airlines, cruise lines, hotels, car rental agencies, ground transportation, or other travel service providers. ❏

5. Marketing information, including advertising, Internet, catalogs, and brochures. Obtain samples. ❏

6. Any material licensing, royalty, trademark, franchising, joint venture, or partnership agreements to which the company or its affiliates are a party. ❑

7. Summary of insurance policies (casualty, property, liability, errors and omissions, officers and directors, general liability insurance, products liability insurance, workers compensation and environmental impairment insurance, and other similar policies and coverage) showing coverage, carrier, and premiums for each coverage. To the extent insurance carriers and coverage have changed during the last five years, identify such changes. Summarize any major claims filed during the last five years. ❑

8. Copies of all insurance policies currently in effect and contact information for insurance agents and brokers. Copies of all policies covering company-owned and personal vehicles used by company personnel. ❑

9. Reports on the company's claims history (loss experience) with respect to general liability and workers' compensation. (It may be necessary to contact the insurance companies to obtain these documents.) ❑

10. All agreements or plans for mergers, consolidations, reorganizations, acquisitions, or the purchase or sale of assets involving the company or any affiliate, or agreements in principle or letters of intent, currently in effect, with respect to mergers, consolidations, reorganizations, acquisitions, or the purchase or sale of assets involving the company or any affiliate. ❑

11. Marketing agreements, including sales agent, representative, dealer, distributor, consignment, and pricing agreements. If there are numerous agreements entered into in the ordinary course of business, simply provide a sample agreement and schedule of parties and terms. ❑

12. Government contracts and subcontracts. ❑

13. Long-term service contracts, including any future contracts. ❑

14. Management and service agreements. ❑

15. Agreements between the company or any of its affiliates and any director, officer, or management executive or consultant of the company or its affiliates. ❑

16. Any contract or arrangement of the company or any of its subsidiaries, that involves payment or receipt in any year of an amount in excess of 5 percent of its earnings or assets. ❑

17. Any waiver or agreement of the company or any of its affiliates canceling claims or rights of substantial value other than in the ordinary course of business, or any document relating to material write-downs or write-offs of notes or accounts receivable other than in the ordinary course of business. ❑

18. Contracts outside the ordinary course of business. ❑

19. Any other material contracts of the company or its subsidiaries/ affiliates. ❑

20. Pricing schedule(s) or commission structures. ❑

21. Policies and procedures for determining contractual adjustments and allowances for bad debts. ❑

Environmental Matters

1. Previous environmental audits or investigations. Phase I or comparable environmental studies, assessments, or similar work done by or on behalf of the company or any affiliate. Reports issued by the EPA and/or state and local authorities and their non-U.S. counterparts. Environmental site assessment reports. Reports filed with, significant correspondence with, and transcripts of any significant proceedings before any state, federal, or foreign regulatory agency during the past five years, including copies of any state or federal surveys, reviews, or inspections. ❑

2. All environmental permits, licenses, or other government approvals. Pending environmental permit applications or applications for other environmental government authorizations. ❑

3. Agreements (other than financing documents) with provisions relating to environmental conditions or liabilities. These would include representations and warranties, indemnities, escrow agreements, and other similar agreements. ❑

4. All enforcement-related documents or agreements, pending or closed, such as consent decrees, administrative or other orders, notices of violation, and agency correspondence alleging noncompliance or relating to cleanup of sites alleged to contain hazardous materials, government requests for environmental or health and safety studies, and the responses thereto by the company or any affiliate. ❑

5. Insurance policies that cover liability for environmental impairment. ❑

6. Documents relating to the existence, monitoring, or insurance of underground storage tanks. ❑

7. Known or suspected environmental problems associated with neighboring or related property.   ❏
8. Policies for handling and disposal of hazardous waste. Policies and procedures governing safety and infection control.   ❏
9. Copy of any safety manual or right-to-know manual.   ❏

Properties and Equipment

1. List of addresses of properties currently owned or leased by the company and related documentation. Obtain a summary of the office floor plan, facility hours (times and hours per weekday), and revenue generated by each facility.   ❏
2. Copies of all deeds or other titles evidencing ownership of the properties owned by the company or a subsidiary/affiliate.   ❏
3. For each property owned by the company or affiliate, a copy of the latest owner or leasehold title insurance policy issued, as applicable, and the most recent survey covering such properties. ❏
4. Copies of all leases for use of the real property owned or leased by the company or any affiliate.
5. Copies of all mortgages encumbering the properties owned or leased by the company or any affiliate.   ❏
6. All equipment and auto leases for a period in excess of two years or that require payments in excess of an immaterial amount annually.   ❏
7. List of all automobiles, including title documentation.   ❏
8. Plans with respect to any facility closings.   ❏
9. Summary of any construction plans for significant new facilities and data on projected construction costs for such facilities and for any facilities currently under construction.   ❏
10. Copies of all principal trademarks, licenses, patents, copyrights, websites, toll-free telephone numbers, or trade names of the company or its affiliates, the expiration dates thereof, and any pending applications therefor.   ❏
11. Details of recent acquisitions, divestitures, spin-offs, or dispositions of assets.   ❏

Management Information Systems

1. Description of core booking and product system (e.g., CRS, front-end, database, developer, year developed, key technologies, key applications, user features or advantages).   ❏
2. Description of website (give name) and key features.   ❏

3. Call-center telecom information. ❏

4. Technology infrastructure inventory, including all technology infrastructure components (i.e., computer and network hardware, operating system software, database management system, and similar items). ❏

5. Telecommunications inventory with details. ❏

6. Information technology (IT) organization

   ◆ Organization chart of current IT organization, including names, titles, and a brief résumé or background information for each employee. ❏

   ◆ IT budget or spending for past three years. ❏

   ◆ Copies of any consulting agreements and/or outsource contracts, including services that may be provided by hardware procurement providers, hardware/software maintenance vendors, or any other MIS service provider. ❏

   ◆ Terms, conditions, and time frames for all existing consultant, contractor, and/or outsourcer product or service arrangements. ❏

7. IT plans and initiatives

   ◆ Copy of most current IT strategy or systems plan. ❏

   ◆ Copies of work plans, design documents, etc., for all current or planned IT projects and/or initiatives. Include name and type of application or project (e.g., "server replacement project"), project objectives/goals, time frames/work plans, estimated project costs, maintenance/operations overview, etc. ❏

8. Schedule of hardware and all maintenance/repair agreements, copies of all contracts, and itemized list of all equipment covered. ❏

9. Application inventory

   ◆ Provide a complete inventory of all current (i.e., operational) and planned (i.e., under development) applications software, including the following:

     —Application name ❏

     —Custom-developed or packaged software? ❏

     —Vendor name and contact information ❏

     —Application age ❏

     —Applications environment (language, database, versions, and similar items) ❏

     —Cost of purchase/development ❏

     —Operating platform/architecture ❏

     —Maintenance specifications ❏

Legal Matters

1. Pleadings, briefs, and other documents pertaining to any material pending or threatened litigation, arbitration, or investigation before regulatory or administrative bodies, in which the company or its officers, directors, employees, or agents, as a result of such status or as a result of action taken in such position, are defendants. Summary of current provisions in the company's financial statements made for estimated liabilities arising out of these matters.   ❏

2. Summary of material prior, pending, and threatened claims or litigation.   ❏

3. Responses of the company's outside counsel(s) to audit inquiry letters in connection with the examination of the company's financial statements for the preceding year, including summaries of litigation, if any. List of law firms used by the company and its subsidiaries for the last five years.   ❏

4. Summary of material prior litigation settlements and all consent decrees, judgments, orders, or other settlement agreements to which the company or an affiliate is a party or is bound, requiring or prohibiting any future activities.   ❏

5. Information about any existing consent decrees or settlement agreements in which the company or an affiliate is not party but which materially affect the conduct of the company's or any of its affiliates' businesses.   ❏

6. Schedule of fines and penalties incurred by the company or any of its affiliates arising out of the provision of its services, the operation of its facilities or equipment, or the sale of its products. ❏

Management and Employees

1. Any employment agreements or contracts, bonus or incentive compensation plans, consulting contracts, or medical reimbursement, death benefit, deferred compensation, or pension plans or arrangements, including "golden parachute" agreements, severance agreements, and agreements not to compete with the company or any affiliate upon termination of employment. Copies of all Internal Revenue Service (IRS) or its non-U.S. equivalent determination letters, if applicable, summary plan descriptions, and Form 5500s relating to the foregoing.   ❏

2. Résumés of key members of management.   ❏

3. All labor agreements, collective bargaining agreements, employment agreements, and non-competition agreements. Provide human resource records, including data on prior strikes, actual or threatened. ❑

4. Employee benefit, pension, health, deferred compensation, and profit-sharing plans or programs, and related trusts, if applicable. ❑

5. Share ownership plans, option and share appreciation rights plans, incentive option plans, bonus plans, or similar arrangements of the company and its affiliates. ❑

6. A schedule of remuneration for the past and present year of all shareholders, the five most highly compensated officers and employees, and all officers and directors as a group, including salaries, directors fees, commissions, bonuses, deferred compensation, insurance benefits, and other fringe benefits. Include a schedule of unpaid bonuses. ❑

7. Summary of ownership of company's shares by each officer and director of the company, including date and price of shares when acquired. ❑

8. Agreements with management or key personnel other than employment or consulting agreements. ❑

9. Indemnification contracts and similar arrangements for officers and directors. ❑

10. Loans and guarantees to or from shareholders, directors, officers, or employees of the company and its affiliates. All agreements documenting transactions between the company and its officers, directors, or stockholders. ❑

11. Any actuarial reports prepared on existing pension plans. ❑

12. List of all options proposed to be granted, if any, including names and addresses of proposed option holders and number of options to be held by each. Obtain similar information regarding all other forms of share subscription, including names, addresses, and agreements. ❑

13. Copies of personnel policies, personnel manuals, employee handbooks, and affirmative action plans. ❑

14. Records showing the number of employees, by division or business segment. ❑

15. A schedule showing family relations among shareholders, officers, and directors of the company and its affiliates. ❑

INCOME ISSUES TO BE EVALUATED AND CONSIDERED IN PERFORMING THE FINANCIAL AND ACCOUNTING DUE DILIGENCE

Income Taxes

1. Review prior two years' sales-and-use tax returns, if applicable. ❏
2. Review any pending income tax disputes. ❏
3. Review employment contracts. ❏
4. Review assignable contracts. Analyze the income expected on sales contracts through the date of their termination, and summarize contract terminations and transferability. ❏
5. Review any stock option agreements. ❏
6. Review contracts with shareholders and/or related parties. ❏
7. Review copies of all prior asset appraisals. ❏
8. Determine whether corporation has nexus outside the United States. ❏
9. Review subchapter S, LLC, or other election or any non-U.S. counterpart thereof, if applicable. ❏
10. Review history of share ownership and classes of share or other equity interests. ❏
11. Review history of cash or share distributions. Determine whether there are disproportionate distributions. ❏
12. Verify any existing affiliates or related businesses. Are there any tax-sharing agreements? ❏
13. Determine whether S corporation, LLC, or their non-U.S. counterparts were previously taxable entities. Assess built-in gains exposure. ❏
14. Document any unnecessary expenses potentially nondeductible pursuant to Internal Revenue Code (IRC) Section 165 or its non-U.S. counterparts. ❏
15. Review documentation of prior spin-off transactions or dispositions of business lines. ❏
16. Analyze appropriateness of an IRC Section 338 or 338(h)(10) election for S corporations or C corporations with net operating losses. Provide similar information for non-U.S. entities. ❏
17. Review for any prior amortizable goodwill, if applicable. ❏
18. Verify whether corporation has any tax attribute carryforwards (net operating loss, general business credits, and similar items). ❏
19. Was there a prior IRC Section 382 limitation? If so, was it properly computed? Provide similar information for non-U.S. entities. ❏

20. Quantify IRC Section 382 limitation, if applicable. Provide similar information for non-U.S. entities. ❏

Additional State and Local Tax Steps

1. Does the company have exposure to any states or their non-U.S. counterparts due to nonfiling of state income tax returns because of aggressive positions toward the nexus issue? ❏

2. Has a review been made of how income taxes are apportioned between the states or their non-U.S. counterparts? Has the apportionment factor been analyzed (i.e., effect of acquisition on property, sales, and payroll factors)? ❏

3. On a going-forward basis, has consideration been given to techniques to push debt down to the target group to increase interest expense at that level and reduce state income taxes? ❏

4. Has the state income tax liability been analyzed (i.e., considering the changes in state income tax liability as a result of acquisition), including an analysis of nexus in particular states or comparable non-U.S. jurisdictions? ❏

5. If the acquisition is structured as a share purchase with an election under IRC Section 338 or Section 338(h)(10), will the election be respected for state and local income tax purposes or comparable non-U.S. jurisdictions? ❏

Capital Franchise Tax

1. Has the capital structure been reviewed for capital taxes? ❏

2. Has the structure been reviewed for net worth taxes? ❏

Excise and Transfer Tax

1. For real estate transfer taxes, review jurisdictions in which real estate is located. ❏

2. Has the company's compliance with the sales and use tax in the applicable states in which it does business been reviewed? ❏

3. Does the company have exposure for sales or use tax on out-of-state purchases of equipment or marketing materials? ❏

4. If the company is claiming an exemption because the buyer of the product is reselling it at retail, is the company obtaining and retaining resale certificates? ❏

5. Has an examination been made of the various states involved to determine whether transfer of assets is subject to state sales or use tax? ❏

6. Do local tax authorities have requirements for bulk transfers? ❑

7. Have allocations of cost of assets between tangible personal property, intangible personal property, and real property been properly made? ❑

Ad Valorem (or Personal Property) Taxes

1. Has the company's position in this area been reviewed? ❑

2. Are there any disputes with local tax authorities over possible major property tax increases? ❑

Escheat

1. Has the company's position in this area been reviewed? ❑

5 | Legal Due Diligence

NORMAN J. RESNICOW, ESQ.
CLIFFORD A. RATHKOPF, ESQ.

LEGAL DUE DILIGENCE is mainly an exercise in proving the negative—or, perhaps, in looking for the proverbial needle in a haystack. Like most detective work, it is largely uneventful and sometimes frustrating. It is not the glamorous part of a deal. The thrill of negotiations with the give-and-take between skilled opponents, and the creative means of financing the deal—these are the stars of the show.

Yet legal due diligence often is the key to a successful closing, and to a deal that works as well post-closing as the parties had envisioned when they shook hands. Legal due diligence requires care, completeness, and sufficient coordination and communication among lawyers and their clients throughout the process. It takes time, patience, focus, and resourcefulness. The people involved in conducting cross-border due diligence must take care not to assume that non-U.S. laws and practices are similar or even analogous to corresponding U.S. laws and practices, no matter how familiar the former may superficially appear. Good due diligence will be reflected in the contracts that document the transaction, including the all-important disclosure schedules. Like the foundation of a building, due diligence is the key structural support, but not much of it is visible when the building is completed.

Legal due diligence is critical in a wide variety of transactions. These include large, multifaceted deals, such as acquisitions of shares or assets of companies, public registrations and issuances of shares, joint ventures and strategic alliances, and secured lendings and other financings, as well as smaller transactions, such as hiring a non-U.S. executive for a non-U.S. subsidiary or establishing a long-term supply contract. The common theme for all such transactions is that one party is purchasing assets or services of the other and expects to be able to receive and preserve the full bargained-for value of the purchase.

In the due diligence process, while the buyer's team is focusing on the target, the target's team may also be engaging in due diligence—a self-examination necessary to produce the required disclosure schedules or to determine the value of the target's or the buyer's shares or assets. Although a target's instinct understandably is to accentuate the positive, M&A lawyers advise that full and broad disclosure is the best protection against post-closing liability. Full disclosure is especially important for smaller privately held companies that may have been "underlawyered" predeal, and for whom post-closing claims can have a major financial impact. Due diligence by the target's counsel is also necessary as the basis of the legal opinion typically required of such counsel as a condition to closing (although the traditionally broad disclaimers in legal opinions are geared toward demonstrating how little its lawyers really know about the target).

"Legalese" across Borders

The greatest risk of legal mishap in the cross-border deal is in failure of communication, especially where a significant part of due diligence takes place in other countries. For example, in a due diligence review of a European company preparing to obtain SEC registration for issuance of American Depositary Receipts (ADRs), the company's U.S. counsel asked the company's local counsel for a review of all "material" contracts between insiders and the company. Just before issuance of the ADRs, the U.S. counsel discovered that only a representative sampling of insider contracts had been disclosed. The registration statement had to be amended, and the issuance was delayed because of this failure to ensure effective communications bridging the U.S. and European legal cultures.

A fundamental consideration in cross-border communications is, of course, the fact that typically at least one additional language will be involved. All contracts in a cross-border deal thus should contain a "languages clause" specifying which language version will be considered official or paramount, and whether translations have any interpretive relevance. Even when the transaction involves a U.S. company and one in the United Kingdom or in another English-speaking country, a real risk exists in assuming there is a common Anglo-Saxon meaning of all technical words and concepts. For example, in British English a "billion" is what Americans refer to as a "trillion," while what Americans call a "billion" is referred to in British English as a "milliard"—an instance where the tedious lawyerly custom of stating written numbers twice, in words followed by numerals, proves its worth.

The risk of misunderstanding is magnified if key participants in the transaction speak and write in English as a second language. In such cases there is real value in involving bilingual lawyers in the due diligence process. After all, words (as much as fees) are the currency in which lawyers deal. But whether or not attorneys understand the foreign language involved, they are charged with transforming the foreign legal elements into the familiar for the client.

The value provided to the client will be significantly enhanced when an investor's lawyers first can focus their foreign counterparts on the key legal questions of concern to the client, and can then act as a critical intermediary between the client and foreign counsel in presenting the results to the client for analysis and decision making. Counsel who fail to act as a critical intermediary, but instead simply pass along foreign counsel's due diligence reports and legal advice to the client, have not earned their fee.

The Purpose of Legal Due Diligence: Insurance against the Unknown

There are two facets to legal due diligence in a cross-border transaction:

1 the discovery of facts having legal, business, or financial implications that could imperil the closing or ultimate success of the transaction, and

2 a review of the legal setting in which the transaction takes place to ensure knowledge of the significance of those facts and the enforceability of the transaction itself.

For the lawyer, the first of these takes place within a collegial setting, coordinating counsel's expertise with that of the business executive, the accountant, and the banker, and perhaps a technology guru or private investigator. The second, however, is primarily the province of the lawyer, although the degree and manner of counsel's involvement may differ from deal to deal and country to country, every jurisdiction having its distinctive legal norms and business customs.

Together, these two facets of legal due diligence provide a form of insurance for the client. If nothing is found to be wrong, the premium for the insurance (the attorneys' fees) will simply be a sunk cost. But if legal due diligence uncovers material problems, the reflected savings may exceed that premium by many multiples.

A Good Deal Is Vastly Better Than a Good Lawsuit

Why should a buyer expend funds for legal due diligence and delay the closing when it will be protected by appropriately worded contractual representations, warranties, covenants, and conditions to closing? Non-U.S. parties in particular may well see precontractual legal due diligence as an expensive and time-consuming duplication of the contractual protections being negotiated. While the question is rarely put that directly, pressure from the buyer on its counsel to rush or simplify due diligence is typically based in part on that thinking.

The blunt answer is that a good deal is vastly better than a good lawsuit, and given a choice between a good lawsuit and an aborted deal, most savvy buyers would choose the latter. The buyer who relies mainly on the target's representations, disclosures, and other promises without a full legal due diligence is a gambler. It is not a matter of trust or comfort levels, for these are of limited value when a target has serious problems of which it, or its top management, is not aware, or has made faulty judgments about known problems.

In cross-border transactions, the value of a good lawsuit may be further discounted. For a purely domestic U.S. deal, the only "foreign" jurisdiction involved may be another state. In a cross-border deal, the process of determining liability, fashioning appropriate remedies, and enforcing a judgment will involve different legal systems. This can increase expense, time, and difficulty many times over. Even if the court or arbitrator rules for the client, the recovery of assets located overseas can be thwarted by roadblocks such as protective local laws, local political pressures, limited currency convertibility, or exchange regulations.

Legal due diligence also addresses the buyer's need to know whether it should even get to the stage of entering into a contract, no matter how ironclad the contractual language is expected to be. One can imagine, for example, potential liabilities such as environmental problems that would bankrupt the target, and possibly the buyer as well, making the transaction a nonstarter. Another concern may be whether there are third parties other than those represented by the target's negotiators who are able to block the transaction.

Information gathered during due diligence also supports and informs the drafting of the agreement and the negotiations surrounding the content and wording of the disclosure exhibits. It is a rare target that does not have some financial or operational problems that require the crafting of legal protective devices. The buyer does not improve its odds of dealing with such problems effectively in the contract by deferring their placement on the drafting and negotiating table.

The foreign buyer should also consider that a contractual indemnity may be insufficient to protect it. The seller may be liquidated immediately after the transaction closes, or may dispose of the purchase price in such a manner that the buyer cannot reach it in an indemnity-based lawsuit. In the worst case, in an asset deal the seller may have been left with liabilities that result in a bankruptcy in which the buyer's damages exceed any available seller financial resources.

Finally, although the buyer's counsel may believe that the deal agreement is the client's ultimate protective device, a court reviewing the pertinent contractual language may disagree. Often, complex issues must be reviewed and the agreement negotiated and drafted under tight time constraints, and what the parties think the contract says may not be what the "trier of fact" (in other words, a court or arbitrator) finally determines (as Tyson Foods found when a court ordered it to consummate its merger with IBP). The risk of unforeseen results in judicial contract interpretation is even higher when foreign law or accounting practices are at issue. The best contract negotiation and drafting are no substitute for effective due diligence.

Defensive Due Diligence in U.S. Public Securities Issuance Transactions: Proving Enough Was Done

In private transactions, due diligence serves as a form of insurance against a broad range of business and other risks. In the area of U.S. public securities offerings, due diligence by the underwriter and other players in the offering process serves two additional functions—as the foundation for preparing the legally required registration statement, and as the key element for establishing these players' (excluding the issuer) statutory defenses against claims of security law violations in connection with the registration statement. Thus, for the underwriters, the buyer's directors and principal executives, and the accountants, engineers, appraisers, and other experts (including attorneys) involved, a central question is whether they exercised, in their respective involvement in preparation of the registration statement, sufficient due diligence to uncover and disclose materially untrue statements or omissions.

In the context of the cross-border public securities transaction, where the due diligence challenges extend well beyond the familiar, there is the additional question of whether, under those unfamiliar circumstances, they employed sufficient due diligence in investigating the issuer's assertions about the nature, materiality, and risks of foreign operations as reflected in the registration statement. Recognition of the heightened need for "defensive due diligence" in cross-border public securities issuances will result in the most effective protection from legal claims under U.S. securities laws.

What will be considered statutorily adequate legal due diligence in the cross-border context will depend upon the circumstances, but three generalizations can be made. First, to the extent foreign operations are material, the legal due diligence should be comparable to that undertaken for the U.S. operations. Second, due care should be taken in choosing foreign counsel, in informing them of what is required, and in properly reflecting the results of their efforts in the registration statement where appropriate. Third, since the statutory defense is based on the adequacy of the due diligence effort, counsel must keep available documents evidencing the effort, including the non-U.S. portions of that effort, and non-U.S. counsel involved should be made aware of that need at the outset.

Forces Working to Limit Due Diligence: Quick Decision Makers versus Slow Scriveners

From the time of the "robber barons," when J. P. Morgan reportedly decided to buy Andrew Carnegie's steel operations simply by saying "I accept this price" in response to Carnegie's scribbling of "$480 million" on a sheet of paper, to the current climate, in which Jack Welch of General Electric reportedly made a fast weekend decision to buy Honeywell, the public has always admired businesspeople able to move quickly. The caveats of the "legal beagles" and the cautions of the "bean counters" go against that grain. Lawyers must accept that those attitudes will not change, and that clients will continue to explain that *this* deal really is a straightforward, friendly deal.

Buyers feeling pressure to rein in or at least foreshorten their lawyers' due diligence should consider some cautionary points. First, legal due diligence can be a moneymaker and not just a cost center. Lawyers often uncover facts that provide a basis for the buyer to renegotiate the deal to its financial advantage. Second, academic studies show that many M&A deals (two-thirds, according to one recent study) just don't work post-closing and result in a loss of value for the buyer. Experience further shows that a significant number of deals do not close because of problems uncovered by legal due diligence in particular. Prudence recommends improving the buyer's odds by taking legal due diligence as seriously as the other parts of the deal. Third, in a cross-border deal, where physical and cultural distances make problems harder to see, the buyer's lack of enthusiasm for legal due diligence may be far more costly than any feared lawyer overexuberance.

In a well-known European beverage manufacturer's long-planned acquisition of the shares of its longtime U.S. distributor, European management decided that, in light of the parties' lengthy and close relationship, no legal due diligence was necessary, and that the deal could be signed and closed in the several weeks before year-end. When the European buyer asked its U.S. attorneys to write a "simple agreement," its managers were astounded to hear that Hart-Scott-Rodino (HSR) antitrust clearance would be necessary, as well as compliance with numerous state and the federal alcoholic beverage regulatory requirements (including fingerprinting of the buyer's president). This significantly threw off the buyer's business and financial planning by delaying the closing into the following year.

Far sadder is the saga of a German machine manufacturer that decided to purchase its U.S. distributor, ending a thirty-year relationship. It closed the deal without the assistance of any U.S. lawyers or significant due diligence. Post-deal, having signed a four-page document largely devoted to the employment terms of one of the distributor's executives for the newly owned U.S. operation, the German buyer asked a U.S. lawyer to review the transaction to see if anything had been forgotten. The lawyer found that the U.S. distributor had kept customer accounts in an unpurchased affiliated company, instead of in the company named in the deal. As a result, all significant accounts receivable remained in the unpurchased affiliate. The distributor's executive who negotiated the deal was fired, and litigation ensued. The German buyer who had sought to minimize use of U.S. lawyers ended up spending a large part of his time with them.

A deal in which the buyer purchases assets and contractually assumes only certain specified liabilities may lure the buyer into a false sense of security, tempting it to limit due diligence (at least on the liability side). Such a deal does not, however, preclude the possibility of successor liability to third parties in certain high-risk areas (environmental and product liability, for example). Also, language limiting the scope of liabilities assumed may not operate as expected when interpreted by courts. For example, in negotiating the memorandum of understanding (MOU) for the sale of the U.S. and Belgian assets of a U.S. manufacturer to an international investment group, the seller's lawyers changed the liability assumption language from "certain specified liabilities" to "all liabilities incurred in the ordinary course of business." Thereafter, in negotiating the final acquisition agreement, when the buyer's counsel tried to exclude various fault-based liabilities from the assumed liabilities, the seller's lawyers prevailed by countering with U.S. case law interpreting "liabilities incurred in the ordinary course of business" to include environmental, product liability, and other fault-based liabilities—which, as the seller's lawyers argued, were assumed liabilities consistent with the MOU.

The business press has warned of the risks of sacrificing due diligence for transactional speed. The Cendant fiasco elicited an article in *Business Week* entitled "M&A Frenzy May Be Scuttling Due Diligence" (August

17, 1998). This unusually candid critique observed that "investors are beginning to wonder whether the frenzied race to do deals has left proper due diligence in its wake." The article noted that unlike in an initial public offering, where nearly everything is to be scrutinized (at least in theory), for M&A "in truth there is no agreed upon definition of proper due diligence." It concludes by prophetically quoting Harvard Business School professor Mark L. Mitchell: "We are going to see more ... deals that turn out to be busts, in part because of a lack of due diligence."

Avoiding Ruffled Feathers and Missed Opportunities

Many midsized and large commercial transactions in today's global business environment involve material cross-border elements. Because the focus of due diligence will vary with the nature of the transaction, the task at the outset is to tailor the due diligence plan to the objectives, demands, and subject matter of the deal at hand, resulting in a focused due diligence process. Counsel should avoid the temptation to take an "off-the-rack" approach instead of custom-tailoring the process, except where the modest size of the deal does not permit tailoring.

A focused investigative approach may not, however, be a welcome one for the company or the individuals being investigated, especially in a cross-border transaction in which the foreign party does not understand the need for and benefits of this approach. The U.S. party's attorney should help the foreign party (whether target or buyer) to understand that the process is integral to U.S.-type deals, and that although it appears adversarial in nature, its true purpose is to uncover problems to ensure that the deal will stand up to scrutiny. This may not be an easy selling job for the attorney.

The acquisition of a private U.S. target by a foreign buyer provides special due diligence challenges. The U.S. target's shareholders and management are, more likely than their non-U.S. counterparts, conditioned to issues of disclosure, even if they have not previously participated in an inbound transaction. Their experience with litigation discovery, government reporting requirements, and the like makes the U.S. target expect the buyer to seek extensive information about its financial and operating condition. If the foreign buyer does not take full advantage of this expectation, two serious and potentially costly mistakes are made.

First, the chance to obtain significant information to mold the negotiations, financially and otherwise, is lost. Second, the target will have a low regard for the buyer's business acumen, which may create difficulties later in the negotiations, and perhaps post-closing as well. Thus, if the foreign party is not transactionally sophisticated, the first and most critical part of legal due diligence may be an educational process.

Providing foreign clients with a full legal due diligence checklist, such as the one at the end of this chapter, is a good starting point, provided that counsel makes sure they understand the reasons why it is seeking those items. This procedure typically results in the identification of a number of issues that require further education of both the client and its non-U.S. legal advisers.

The U.S. client as well may need to go through an education process. Consider, for example, the straightforward scenario of a purchase of an individual's services, where you are the lawyer advising a U.S.-based senior executive recruited by a non-U.S. company for a post abroad in a civil law jurisdiction. You must explain to the client how the familiar two-tier structure of U.S. corporations (board of directors and officers) gives way to a three-tier structure (executive board, management board, and officers). As a result, to assist with negotiating and preparing the employment agreement, you may have to advise the client of the need for some significant legal research (either directly or through foreign co-counsel) regarding how your client would be able to carry out management responsibilities and obligations under the three-tier structure. If you are retained before the compensation package is set in cement, you should advise as to whether it is customary for executives in that country to obtain equity as incentive compensation, and if so, whether equity incentives are available to the executive as a foreigner in that country, and if so, under what circumstances. The education task for counsel in this scenario is no different from that of U.S. counsel advising a foreign buyer of a U.S. business.

Fitting Due Diligence into the Structure and Timing of the Deal: Sooner Is Better

Both the buyer and the target should consider the typical transaction's structure and timing and how the results of due diligence mesh with the contractual protections savvy buyers expect. After initial discussions in which the buyer and target determine there is some mutual interest in a transaction, and after the target discloses some very basic operating and financial information, it is common for the parties to enter into the MOU, typically a nonbinding letter of intent and confidentiality agreement. Characterizations of MOUs as nonbinding are only partly correct, because various provisions of the agreement are meant to be legally binding (such as confidentiality clauses, "no shop" covenants during exclusive negotiation periods, "no raid" clauses to protect the target's employees, and "breakup fees," among others), while the remaining parts are meant solely to describe the parties' current intentions regarding the transaction.

After the MOU is signed, the buyer may present the target with a document disclosure list that forms the initial subject matter of the due diligence inquiry. Thereafter, the parties usually move into a process of due diligence and contract preparation that can last anywhere from a few weeks to several months or longer.

Despite some differences between the structures of an acquisition of shares versus assets and the acquisition of private versus public targets, the main parts of the acquisition contract are much the same. The target is expected to agree to a long list of representations and warranties concerning, among other things, ownership, authority, legal capacity, line items on its financial statements, and various nonfinancial statement liabilities, and to disclose exceptions to the representations and warranties on disclosure statements attached as schedules to the contract. The target is also expected to agree to specified covenants governing the conduct of the target's business and finances between contract signing and closing. After providing for these so-called reps and warranties and covenants, the contract typically contains a detailed list of remedies for any breach of the target's reps and warranties or covenants—specifying, among other things, how much the target or selling shareholders must pay back to the buyer as indemnities, as well as whether, when, and under what circumstances the buyer may withhold part of the purchase price against payment of any indemnities.

This common structure for a U.S. acquisition is similar to those used outside the United States, although U.S. contracts tend to be longer and more detailed. This difference occurs largely because foreign parties and counsel in civil law countries are accustomed to legal code-based contracts, while U.S. and other common law parties and counsel operate on the basis of caveat emptor (buyer beware), where "the law is the contract." The U.S.-style contract typically evolves as the due diligence process develops and areas of concern are identified. This fluid process may be disconcerting to foreign parties, and it is up to U.S. counsel to walk them comfortably through the process.

Some buyers may be tempted to delay investing significantly in legal due diligence until the definitive acquisition contract has been negotiated and signed, with serious legal due diligence efforts to be conducted between contract signing and closing. While understandable, this approach risks giving legal due diligence short shrift. It also makes negotiating changes in the contract as due diligence unearths new information more difficult—changing a signed contract is much more difficult than changing a draft. Finally, in a cross-border context, legal due diligence requires additional time, which may increase the length of the due diligence process and, in consequence, delay the closing. Thus, it is strongly preferable to conduct full legal due diligence after signing the MOU and while still negotiating the final contract.

Organizing and Executing Legal Due Diligence: The Buck Stops at the Top

Four key elements of effective legal due diligence are:

1 assigning qualified personnel;
2 organizing and delegating duties;
3 ensuring a searching investigation; and
4 communicating results effectively.

Assigning Qualified Personnel

Especially in cross-border transactions, counsel must initially determine what the key issues will most likely be and who can most appropriately handle each. This means that very early in the deal, usually when the MOU is being prepared, the buyer and its counsel must start lining up the troops. Will foreign counsel be needed? Likewise for foreign accountants, or does the buyer's current CPA firm have offices in the countries involved? Does counsel or the client know the foreign counsel personally, or is the person merely a referral? What is the depth of practice and experience of the foreign counsel? In a transaction involving a company in an emerging market country, can competent counsel be found who doesn't have a prior association with the target—and therefore a conflict of interest?

One may have to choose between the best technical lawyer and the best-connected lawyer; or one may be able to choose both if cost permits, and if coordination issues are manageable. Is there a need for specialized consultants (often a euphemism for a local lobbyist who knows where and how legitimate pressures may be brought to bear in critical areas)? Although the legal team may change over time, it is often difficult to replace a key foreign team member in a timely manner; the first choice must be a good one.

In addition to the lawyers, the legal team should include representatives of the buyer's management. Which executives should help identify and field legal issues? Obvious examples would be the CFO, general counsel, and any internal legal staff, as well as the managers of human resources and information technology. The target's legal due diligence team, which prepares the critically important disclosure schedules, should include managers who have responsibility for sensitive areas such as environmental risk, tax compliance, product liability, intellectual property, antitrust, labor relations, and litigation and other third party claims.

In the twenty-first-century business environment, where job changes are increasingly frequent, companies may lack the breadth of human historical memory that once existed when people spent a working lifetime at a single company. This employee mobility presents a particular challenge to the target's counsel, who may have to chase down former employees and dig for buried files in order to prepare disclosure schedules. Also, the target's management and other employees who are aware of the deal may be skittish about their futures and thus less than fully focused on assisting with due diligence disclosure. Some of them may suddenly depart for new employment in the middle of the deal. Keeping their knowledge of the deal confidential may be critical, so it is important to determine what information key personnel, whether currently or previously employed, have received. For that to be done, they must first be identified and located. Therefore, the target's counsel should begin this task earlier rather than later in the due diligence process.

The legal due diligence team may also need to import specialized domestic or foreign legal expertise in technical areas that the buyer's law

firm does not cover. These areas may include certain environmental liability and compliance, intellectual property, pension and benefits, and
labor union issues. One of the first decisions to be made is which of these
issues will be sufficiently important in the deal to require an outside legal
specialist on call from the beginning.

In addition to investment bankers, there are outside nonlawyer
experts who may be needed in various ancillary areas that may surface
within the legal due diligence context. If the target's operations, for
example, involve significant real estate, an environmental audit firm, a
surveyor, and an architect or civil engineer may be required. If the target engages in import/export transactions, consider involving a good
customs broker. Although asset valuation matters are traditionally han-
dled by the client and its accounting firm and investment bankers, the
parties might also require the services of an experienced insurance agent
to see if the policies in place are sufficient in coverage and protect the full
value of the acquired assets.

The next issue, touched on briefly already in this chapter, is one of
language: Are translators needed? This question is not as simple as it
seems, because the terms being translated may not have local meaning.
Counsel's foreign counterparts may appear to be fluent in English, but
if the context is missing, fluency does not help much. In one transaction
in which a U.S. buyer was acquiring a German company, the buyer's
U.S. attorneys had no significant German experience. The target's executives spent several days trying to figure out what the buyer's attorneys
meant when they asked for "certificates of good standing or the local
equivalent" and were even more baffled when these attorneys tried to
explain that such documents would be necessary to ensure that all "franchise taxes" were paid. As a result, the target's executives hired a U.S.
attorney familiar with German practice to assist them and their German
attorneys with the transaction. The matter was quickly resolved when the
target's U.S. attorney was able to explain to the buyer's attorneys that
Germany has no franchise tax, and that unlike in the United States, failure to pay franchise taxes cannot lead to a corporate dissolution by the
state, so no official document resembling a certificate of good standing
exists. The buyer's attorneys were finally satisfied that they could address
their concerns adequately by reviewing the target company's entries in
the local *Handelsbuch* (the official commercial registry). This problem

might have been resolved much sooner if the buyer's attorneys had hired German attorneys who could "translate" the request.

Because translations (whether or not by certified translators) are costly and time-consuming and are rarely sufficient for legal analysis, it is best, if feasible, to bring to the team an attorney with the relevant foreign language and foreign and domestic legal skills. This attorney should review non-English language due diligence material in its original language, understand the legal issues resulting from the review, and prepare English-language summaries of those documents, without the need for any intermediate formal translations.

Finally, counsel should not overlook the critical assistance that a private investigator can provide. More often than not, one of the most valuable acquired assets is target's management team. It is surprising how few due diligence investigations ever bother to do even cursory background checks on key management members. This can be a delicate issue if management learns that it is being investigated, so counsel needs to discuss the use of a private investigator first with the client. Practical reasons (beyond issues of attorney-client privilege) will incline the client to have the "private eye" be engaged by the outside law firm, instead of engaging it directly. For more on the role of private investigators, see Chapter 8.

The personnel assignment process may also involve establishing a secure and sufficient document "war room," which is a data room where copies of all the documentary disclosures will be organized and stored (traditionally at the offices of the target's outside counsel), and assigning the professional and clerical personnel to operate and control it. Although a controlled data room is more frequently used when multiple buyers view the same data, the procedure is recommended for all larger transactions. It assists in the organization of the data and serves a further purpose: Employees will not be disturbed by troops of "outsiders" poring over company records at the target's sites.

In more complex due diligence situations involving transactions whose budgets allow for more up-front costs, consider setting up a restricted intranet site on the target counsel's network server (preferable to the target's server, as there may be issues of business confidentiality or attorney-client privilege involved). All documents are scanned, indexed, and electronically stored, usually in a format permitting electronic comments on the scanned document itself or in a corresponding file. This is an invaluable way to share information among team members who can log on to the site. It also avoids the traditional issue of whether all appropriate pages or copies of critical documents have been distributed to all team members. Another option is to have one document intranet site serve as a "virtual war room" available (on a strictly controlled basis) to both parties' due diligence teams, and have a separate site for comments and analysis restricted to the buyer's team. Especially in cross-border transactions, where time differences often complicate communications, these electronic data rooms have proven increasingly useful, because they accelerate the process and reduce the need for air travel and face-to-face meetings.

Organizing and Delegating Duties

Each deal typically has one individual lead counsel (in-house or outside). The lead counsel is the logical person to designate the head of the due diligence team, who will be directly responsible for leading, coordinating, and communicating the results of the legal due diligence effort. Because the attention of lead counsel will necessarily be divided, another partner should focus primarily on due diligence. As noted above, it is helpful to have lawyers who speak and read the language of the other party's country as team members, but this is not the principal qualification for the team leader—deal experience, common sense, efficiency, and organization and communication skills all rank higher.

Once the team members have been identified, the due diligence team leader must clearly delegate to each team member his responsibilities, the time frames in which particular responsibilities must be completed, and the manner of reporting findings. The leader's first administrative task is to ensure that each person involved, including the lead counsel for the buyer and the target, is provided with a contact list containing the names, addresses, telephone and fax numbers (including mobile, home, and weekend numbers), and e-mail addresses of all other team members and a brief description of each team member's responsibilities.

The team leader's final organizational task is to have the key team members assemble and distribute to all team members a confidential initial briefing book about the target, based on documents and information that were disclosed at the MOU stage or that are publicly available. This briefing book should be periodically updated (using discretion as to sensitive matters) with important findings as they develop.

Ensuring a Searching Investigation

Due diligence should proceed on two fronts: a review of documents and other data from selling shareholders and the target, and an independent investigation of public information concerning the target together with expert evaluations of the target.

The investigation typically takes place off-premises and secretly unless the target has already made public, as legally required or by choice, the news that it is for sale. Targets are understandably concerned about the deleterious effects an inspection tour may have on employee morale. Once news of a possible sale of a company (or division or plant) becomes known to employees, the rate of employee injury, sickness, and defection increases significantly. Also, the minute the news of a possible transaction goes out, salespeople of the target's competitors will be knocking on the doors of the target's customers, trying to win them away with tales of the target's financial woes and impending doom.

The legal due diligence team must review documents to see if there are any major impediments to the transaction or to the buyer's continuation of the target's business post-closing. Thus, the team must examine all major contracts to ensure that there is no bar to continuity. In the case of an asset transaction, this analysis is of greatest importance, because if there is a limitation on the target's right to assign, the customer, landlord, or other third party whose consent is required may then refuse to do so or, more likely, seek to squeeze concessions on pricing or other terms as a condition to its consent. This is less likely to occur in a share transaction, but a number of contracts may have change-of-control provisions that act in the same manner as a nonassignment clause, even in share transactions.

In obtaining third party consents to assignment, counsel should look for the consent documents to include "estoppel certificates" stating that no defaults have been formally called and, to the consenting third party's best knowledge, no basis to call a default exists.

Counsel should request such a certificate even if the underlying contract between the target and the third party does not require it to be given; the resulting protection afforded to the buyer can be significant.

In borderline cases where it is unclear whether a third party consent is required, consents should not automatically be requested, especially for nonmaterial contracts, because the very request may set in motion a chain of "stickup" events that would not otherwise have occurred. In other words, the third parties may refuse to consent unless prices or other terms are renegotiated in their favor. Instead, a negotiated sharing of identified risks between the buyer and seller may be the preferred solution (with a carefully worded provision in light of the possibility of forced disclosure of such provision in any subsequent litigation with the third party).

Counsel should examine permits and licenses to see whether they will survive the closing; if not, the team must work with the buyer to see whether there is a way to be ready to do business following the closing by putting in place new permits and licenses. Permits and licenses pass immediately and automatically by law in share purchase transactions, so (absent a change of control restriction in the permit or license) this problem tends to be limited to asset deals, unless a condition of granting the permit or license has been a guarantee or other undertaking of the target's shareholders.

The legal due diligence team may also be involved in the buyer's interviews of the target's executives and key employees, as well as of any regular legal counsel the target uses. Understandably, the executive interviews are often less a matter of due diligence and more in the nature of negotiation and planning sessions.

The Internet is a useful source of information about a target and its assets, liabilities, business, and personnel. A good search engine and a properly thought-out search pattern can often generate an amazing wealth of information about a target. Except for official government websites, the information obtained may not be wholly reliable, but it provides a good starting point.

In the United States, subscription-based searches can be performed in the Public Records search area of Lexis-Nexis, where one can find current and historical information on any existing or previously satisfied judgment debtors. However, because this information is recorded by state, and by county within a state, tracking the history of a peripatetic executive can become expensive. Likewise, obtaining a credit report from one of the national credit agencies can be an invaluable source of information on individuals. If the target has had any significant borrowing history, usually there will also be a Dun & Bradstreet, Moody's, or Standard & Poor's (or equivalent) rating history. Although such reports are not particularly geared toward legal due diligence, if available they should be used, as they may point to specific problems or general credit trends that will provide guidance to the contract drafters.

Broad information-gathering due diligence is more difficult in outbound transactions, and obtaining access to the local old-boy network may become fairly important. Such networks may be found in informal groups within the legal community. For example, in Australia, lawyers capable of dealing with labor union matters exist as a sort of informal club; either you are in it or you are not.

That said, the key objective in ensuring a truly searching and successful due diligence process is to be certain that red flags are not missed or misconstrued. A proper, and promptly updated, briefing book is the start. But because the team's junior members typically perform the bulk of the hands-on due diligence, the key to success is regular and meaningful partner supervision and intervention as needed. This should be supplemented by the use of specialized personnel when feasible (which is where the expert evaluations come in; see the list in item #1 of the checklist at the end of this chapter) and a constant flow of clear communications within the team to encourage informed skepticism for the detective work being undertaken.

Communicating Results Effectively

In most transactions involving larger law firms, the due diligence team leader will not be the person negotiating and drafting the contract or reviewing the disclosure schedules. Thus, the team leader needs to see to it that what the investigators in the field have discovered is properly and promptly put into writing and distributed to the negotiators and drafters. She should receive copies of all field memoranda and ensure that sufficient time is set aside to review and analyze them. It is also critical that the team leader take the time to discuss promptly with the buyer (either directly or through the negotiators/drafters) the nature and scope of problems that may have arisen and to explore potential solutions.

Details matter, and due diligence is heavily focused on them. A single detail of communication became an issue in the above-noted 2001 litigation between Tyson Foods and IBP. An outside lawyer for IBP received by e-mail a letter from the SEC relating to proxy and financial statements. His quick look at the document led him to conclude it concerned a prior, irrelevant matter, so he did not forward it to Tyson Foods or his client. The mailed version of the SEC letter arrived more than a week later, and this communication time gap became a major issue in the lawsuit.

Once the deal has closed, all the due diligence documents (as well as drafts of acquisition agreements reflecting the ongoing negotiations prior to signing) should be gathered together and stored rather than discarded. All too often, post-closing disputes arise concerning whether or when a particular liability was disclosed, or what the buyer did or did not know before entering into the acquisition agreement. These work papers can be excellent evidence regarding such questions.

When the buyer's counsel discovers a material matter during due diligence that the target did not previously identify, the matter should very quickly be brought to the attention of the target's counsel, particularly if further clarification is desired or if the matter may affect price or other contractual negotiations. If, however, the buyer perceives that no such clarification or adjustment is necessary or obtainable, the due diligence team may be tempted to keep the matter from the target's attention, in order to hold the matter in reserve for possible use if the buyer later seeks to abort the closing or to assert or defend post-closing claims.

With that possibility in mind, the target's counsel will want to include provisions in the contract to preclude such "sandbagging" by the buyer, thereby preventing the due diligence process from becoming a game of "gotcha." Such an antisandbagging provision would state, in effect, that the buyer cannot abort the closing, or assert claims against the target post-closing, based on matters discovered by certain dates in the buyer's due diligence but not brought to the target's attention by other certain dates. These provisions can be complex, because they necessarily require determining who knew what, and when.

It is bad practice for either party to sit silently regarding matters found in due diligence. The far wiser practice is to bring them promptly to the other side's attention and request an explanation and further information, because it is always better to know more, not less, about the other party. This is especially true for buyers, because targets are typically in a far better position to know their business than are the buyers. In cross-border transactions, in which the process of obtaining and analyzing information is significantly more difficult and complex, full disclosure is even more important. Thus, even putting aside the ethical issues and legal risks arising in a sandbagging strategy, the buyer's disclosure to the target of discovered matters is greatly preferable to nondisclosure. Similarly, as noted above, disclosure is the selling shareholder's best friend, for that which is fully and fairly disclosed, especially as clearly set forth in the contract, cannot be the subject of future liability. For both sides, candid disclosure will prevent good deals from blowing up due to lack of trust arising from efforts to conceal or mislead, and will abort deals that have fatal flaws—in both cases saving time, effort, and expense in the process.

The final communication concern is to ensure that the all-important disclosure schedules are not presented or modified at the last minute without informed input from those junior attorneys who were in the trenches conducting the due diligence investigation. Inevitably, the drafting, analysis, and negotiation of those schedules lag far behind the wording of the body of the agreement, even though the schedules are of equal importance. In the end, the schedules and the agreement must be integrated to form the complete document. (Interpreting the contract text together with the wording of the disclosure schedules became an issue in the previously mentioned lawsuit between Tyson Foods and IBP.) To treat the schedules as less than a key part of the contract is to run the race only to slow down before the finish line.

Certain Key Risk Exposure Areas in Legal Due Diligence

Not all due diligence concerns are equal. The key areas described here (by no means an exhaustive list) are often of dramatic concern simply because the financial and business consequences of nondiscovery or faulty analysis are potentially cataclysmic.

Environmental

In any U.S. transaction involving significant real estate or production facilities, a large part of due diligence should focus on the target's compliance with federal and state environmental laws and regulations and its exposure to potential joint and separate environmental liability. In places outside the United States that have meaningful environmental legislation, such as Western Europe, the buyer should have many of the same concerns. Larger problems attend environmental due diligence in countries emerging from an era of planned economies, and in developing-market countries where environmental regulation is still in its infancy or nonexistent.

The most common property contamination and toxic tort concerns in a U.S. transaction include:

1   unregistered or abandoned underground storage tanks;

2   abandoned landfills and other disposal sites, septic systems, and wells;

3   failure to store, transport, or dispose properly of hazardous wastes (possible exposure to CERCLA or "Superfund" liability); and

4   smokestack emissions and water and other liquid emissions.

Due diligence also should determine the historical uses of the target's sites by the target and its predecessors on the properties, and whether there has been any historical use of asbestos in existing buildings and what steps must still be taken for remediation. ASTM (formerly the American Society for Testing and Materials) has established a number of standards relevant to environmental due diligence, including the Transaction Screen Process, Phase I and Phase II studies, restoration of brownfield properties, and evaluation of USTs (underground storage tanks).

Steps in the review process. The first step in environmental due diligence is to examine all permits to verify that they are still in force; that they are in accordance with current regulations (or if not, are properly grandfathered); in a stock deal, whether there are change of control restrictions affecting continuation of the permits; and, in an asset transaction, whether the permits are transferable. Part of due diligence should be to prepare for the timely continuation or transfer of permits (or if not continuing or transferable, to obtain new permits in the buyer's name) so that, post-closing, the target can continue to do business seamlessly. A problem that arises in acquisitions where new permits must be issued is that the buyer must meet current conditions for obtaining the permit—often more stringent than the conditions of the target's original permit grant. If there are significant problems with permits vital to the continued operation of the target's assets, the buyer may want to weigh the additional costs and risks of undertaking a share transaction instead, where such permits pass to the buyer automatically by law.

The buyer's counsel should be aware that land use permit issues can arise even when the buyer plans an operational change that may not appear to affect the land. For example, the Japanese purchaser of a U.S. golf course complex planned to market memberships as tradeable interests (which had become the investment craze in Japan). The buyer signed a purchase contract with the assistance of U.S. counsel, and then brought in new U.S. counsel to conduct due diligence and close the deal. The new counsel advised the buyer that the membership scheme could not be implemented without permits from the California Coastal Commission. Unfortunately for the buyer, the contract did not make such permitting a condition to closing, and the buyer was unable, post-closing, to implement its membership plan.

The second environmental step is to review all existing violations of record to determine whether they have been corrected, whether there are any outstanding remedial or financial obligations regarding the violations, and whether the violations might have any material effect on the continued viability of permits needed to conduct business post-closing. In addition, counsel should discuss with the appropriate target personnel whether there are any actual or suspected violations not yet officially reported or investigated.

The third customary step in the United States is for the buyer to determine whether it wants to obtain a current so-called Phase I study of the property. This study is typically undertaken by an expert environmental consultant and consists primarily of the expert's on-site review of operations and their potential environmental risks, including a review of permit and violation problems. Quite often, sophisticated targets have a set of records already prepared for the transaction, including its own Phase I studies. Although these records may be helpful, the buyer should still determine whether to rely on the target's studies or to obtain an independent study. A Phase I study is relatively quick and inexpensive, so it is the rare case where having such an independent study done is not recommended. In addition, lenders for the transaction typically require a recent one.

Significant problems appearing in a Phase I study are likely to trigger a demand for a Phase II study, which consists of test borings at the site; laboratory examination of and reports on soil, water, and air samples; and remediation suggestions. The process may be costly and take weeks to complete. Depending on the nature of the historical use of the property and the extent of the potential exposure, this may be a serious issue to the buyer.

The target also may have some concerns with respect to the Phase I and Phase II studies, especially if they involve a situation as yet unreported to environmental regulators. Even if the deal fails to close, the target probably will be under a legal obligation to report and remedy violations uncovered in due diligence. On occasion, this leads to sometimes difficult negotiations between the parties on how to handle the situation and which party is to bear particular risks. For these reasons, the environmental consultants (and other consultants) are typically retained by the buyer's counsel, in an effort to bring the results under the protection of the attorney-client privilege.

Special considerations. In cross-border deals, the process of environmental due diligence depends largely on the level of applicable administrative regulation. In Europe, for example, three levels of law and regulation shape the examination process: European Union, national, and regional or state regulations. Consider Belgium: In addition to the uniformly applied EU and Belgian environmental rules, there are three distinct local regulatory authorities: the Flemish Region (strictest), the Brussels Metropolitan Region, and the developing Walloon Region.

Nonetheless, sticky problems for environmental due diligence arise much less often within the EU—where a considerable body of expertise has developed on which U.S. buyers can rely— than in the old Soviet-bloc countries of Eastern Europe, where the pressures for production in the centrally planned economies did not permit any extensive concern for the environment. There, environmental problems are endemic. Shortly after the latter countries adopted Western economic models, the first generation of privatizations commenced. Western investors typically negotiated very tough site rules regarding remediation by the states involved. This was not the case where nationals were able to purchase production facilities by voucher or other systems. Now, when second or third generations of transactions are involved, due diligence requires an especially careful review of all remediation procedures, of any state guarantees or waivers of enforcement, and of the degree to which the latter would be applicable to a current buyer. The careful buyer should also be prepared to import Western environmental experts to work with the business and legal teams in order to prepare a useful pre-closing environmental audit.

Not all of the former Eastern Bloc countries continue to suffer from this problem. The Czech Republic, for example, gave massive guarantees to Western private investors early on. After a major legislative overhaul of environmental regulation in 1993, the Czech Republic now has overall strategic planning based on a brownfields solution to risk assessment and risk taking, and a respectable body of environmental expertise and information is available to the potential buyer. Nonetheless, the risks remain that legislative or administrative concessions in such countries could be modified by successor governments or as integration with the European Community or other groupings moves forward.

Antitrust

The concerns of antitrust counsel in due diligence are both factual and transactional. Not only does the predeal process have to seek to uncover the target's possible violations of various antitrust regimes, but the process itself must be carried out in a manner calculated to avoid antitrust violations. The latter encompasses two issues: (1) If the transaction involves a horizontal relationship between the buyer and the target, care must be taken with pricing disclosures and preclosing control mechanisms; and (2) Assuming the transaction is large enough to qualify, the parties must obtain clearance for it to proceed, such as compliance with HSR filing procedures in the United States. The need for such compliance can affect the timing and manner of the due diligence process.

Key issues in inbound versus outbound transactions. Antitrust issues are generally most important to lawyers who represent inbound buyers, because the potential for antitrust liability is strongest in the United States (although the EU antitrust blocking of General Electric's worldwide acquisition of Honeywell and EU scrutiny of other deals has arguably raised the profile of foreign antitrust risks to a comparable, if not greater, level). In outbound transactions, the most active government antitrust agencies are found in Canada, Japan, Australia, the EU and its affiliated countries in the EEA (European Economic Area), and other neighbors that have adopted EU law as a precursor to EU membership. The major difference in these regimes is that unlike in the

United States, counsel for potentially injured parties cannot bring private antitrust lawsuits featuring treble damages and attorney fees. The U.S. statutory provisions governing such litigation were meant to promote and supplement government efforts in antitrust enforcement.

Due diligence for inbound transactions should focus primarily on the issues of price-fixing, territorial restraints, intellectual property restraints (discussed below), and exclusive dealing—all areas in which the so-called per se rules can find application. These court-developed rules provide that once a per se violation is proved, there is no need to go further to prove the effect of the violation on commerce (contrary to the so-called rule of reason violations). Thus, for a per se violation the deleterious effect on interstate or international commerce is presumed, and the only remaining issue for the plaintiff is establishing the nature and extent of the remedy.

With those priorities in mind, legal due diligence should not overlook other federal antitrust issues, such as interlocking directorships, violations of resale price maintenance rules, price discrimination, and the various state antitrust rules. Recall that the antitrust actions against Microsoft involved not only the U.S. government as a plaintiff but also many state governments as prosecutors regarding violations of state antitrust rules.

The mechanics of antitrust due diligence vary with the type of transaction. It may be that the transaction will be subject to such antitrust provisions as Section 7 of the Clayton Act, governing what types of mergers and acquisitions are illegal or potentially so. If this is the case, the investigation should focus on the prospect of antitrust liability, and counsel should engage economists and other professionals to dig deeply into the details of the structure of the target's market and its business practices to try to come to grips with the buyer's legal exposure.

In transactions that meet the size-of-parties and size-of-transaction tests of the HSR preclearance mechanism, the due diligence team often must also assist the buyer in preparing, submitting, and monitoring the required HSR filing. In this regard, particular attention should be paid to identifying all affiliates of the buyer and target around the world, and collecting and analyzing their sales and market share data. (Note that all market studies and other competition-related analytics prepared for the buyer's directors or officers must be furnished with the HSR filing.) In outbound transactions, similar procedures are required for preclearance of acquisitions in certain countries.

In conducting antitrust due diligence, basic questions should include the following:

1 Whether the target maintains a written set of antitrust policy guidelines for its personnel (which, if properly prepared, updated, and enforced, give some comfort that inadvertent antitrust violations have not occurred, and in certain cases can also significantly reduce liability if a violation has occurred)

2 Whether the target regularly uses outside antitrust counsel (in which case many of the due diligence questions can be dealt with more quickly through such counsel)

3 Whether the target or selling shareholder is or has been the subject of any enforcement proceeding or consent decree anywhere in the world (in which case the target will already have antitrust counsel, and the issues of possible liability or violation should be discussed with that counsel in depth)

The following key areas of inquiry apply in both inbound and outbound transactions. The inquiry should take into account the structure of the relevant markets and the parties' relative market shares when considering potential antitrust exposure. Due diligence questions include: Does the target maintain membership in any trade associations or groups that set some qualitative or quantitative standards for industry members? If so, do any of the target's officers, directors, or shareholders act as officers or committee chairpersons for such groups? Are there written minutes of meetings that can be reviewed? Are meetings attended by antitrust counsel watchdogs to ensure that price-fixing, territorial divisions, or similar discussions do not occur?

Do any of the target's officers, directors, or shareholders act as directors of or in other key positions in any supplier, customer, or competitor? Do they or key sales personnel of the target regularly attend industry conferences? Are there periodic reports filed concerning meetings and other activities that the target's antitrust counsel has not reviewed? This area of competitor cooperation has been the focus of antitrust enforcement agencies for the past decade and has given rise to some record-setting fines for international price-fixing. A well-publicized example is Archer-Daniels-Midland's involvement in the lysine cartel, which led to worldwide fines and settlements for the corporation and others well in excess of $100 million.

The buyer should determine whether the target terminated any dealers or distributors within the relevant statute of limitations period for contract actions (which are typically longer than those for antitrust actions). If so, there may be antitrust issues, especially if the termination was at the request of a competitor of the terminated dealer or distributor, or was caused by the dealer or distributor failing to follow suggested retail prices, reselling at deep discount or otherwise being disruptive in the marketplace. There are draconian antitrust-based rules applicable in certain industries to terminations of distributorships (franchises, car dealerships, and beer distributorships, for example) in the United States that should be considered if the target is in an affected industry.

Typically, the buyer's counsel reviews any significant form contracts that the target uses with its customers, as well as the actual contracts entered into with its top customers and suppliers. When requesting these contracts, counsel should consider stipulating that the prices charged to the target's customers (or by the target's suppliers) be redacted if the buyer is a competitor of the target or of any significant customer or supplier of the target. This consideration is important because the due diligence process itself can raise antitrust problems, especially when the buyer and target operate in the same market.

Confidentiality concerns and other risks. If the buyer and the target are competitors, the target will naturally be concerned about revealing its pricing and discount structure to the buyer, as well as the identity and sales volume of its top customers. If, for any reason, the deal does not go through, the target is left with critical sales and marketing information protected at best by the rather cold comfort of a confidentiality agreement. Aggressive buyers may, however, insist on disclosure of these pricing and customer details in the period between contract and closing and seek to impose controls over the target's marketplace activities. Antitrust issues will be a factor in negotiating such items.

Sometimes creative lawyering can solve these confidentiality concerns. In the long negotiation of the agreement for the U.S. subsidiary of a foreign manufacturer to acquire the subsidiary's main U.S. competitor, the target objected to a presigning inspection of its facilities and machinery by the buyer's executives. The target was concerned about what would happen if the deal didn't close. The target's response to the buyer's insistence on this score was an offer to acquire the buyer. The buyer's counsel broke the logjam by suggesting that

1 the parties first complete negotiations to arrive at a contract they would both be comfortable signing subject to a satisfactory inspection by the buyer of the target's facilities and machinery, and

2 in the days before a scheduled signing, each would conduct an inspection of the other's U.S. facilities and machinery. This strategy was successful in providing the needed trust, motivation, and deal momentum for the target to proceed to a signing and closing.

Antitrust concerns arising from steps taken preclosing caused the U.S. Department of Justice to file a lawsuit against Computer Associates International Inc. (CA) over CA's two-year-old purchase of Platinum Technology International Inc. (PTI). Although this transaction eventually closed, CA had contractually required a significant set of controls to be placed on PTI that were effective during the thirty-day waiting period under the HSR law. These controls included requiring PTI to obtain CA's approval before entering into certain contracts with customers, and installing a CA employee at PTI headquarters to review customer contracts and other management decisions. By reason of this preclosing jumping of the gun, the Department of Justice was, at this writing, seeking $1.27 million in civil penalties from CA and PTI, as well as an injunction barring CA from engaging in similar future conduct. With such risks in mind, counsel for the buyer and target should, before closing, review how and what materials to disclose and what actions to control between signing and closing.

Intellectual Property

In an age in which intellectual property (IP) is often more important than hard assets, IP due diligence may be critical to a buyer's "go/no go" decision. International treaties covering patents, trademarks, and copyrights have made due diligence in the IP world somewhat uniform, especially in determining whether IP assets exist and are registered in the target's name. However, checking the relevant national registries for registrations, renewals, and assignments is only the beginning of IP due diligence. There are five larger issues:

1   ownership of employee inventions or creations;

2   trade secrets and other nonregistered confidential information;

3   the terms and conditions of licenses;

4   potential liability for infringements of third party IP rights; and

5   special problems associated with databases.

Each of these areas may have similarities from country to country, but the differences can be crucial to the continued post-deal conduct of the target's business.

Ownership of employee inventions or creations, copyright issues, and trade secrets. Issues relating to the ownership of employee inventions or creations tend to fall into the patent and copyright areas. For employee inventions, some countries require that the employee receive reasonable compensation for assigning a patent or patentable invention to the employer; in others, the terms of an existing employment contract will govern. If due diligence uncovers any registered or unregistered employee inventions, the team should ask the target to produce a waiver and confirmation of assignment letter from the employee, including a confirmation that no other parties have any rights in or claims to the invention. If such a letter is not obtainable, the buyer should at least confirm that the employee made an effective assignment to the target and is not instead licensing the invention to it.

The danger of not looking carefully into this kind of issue is illustrated by a German buyer's acquisition of a U.S. target that had certain key technology protected by an employee patent previously assigned to the target. The buyer possessed complementary technology that it wanted to exploit worldwide jointly with the target's technology. The buyer was given a copy of the waiver and confirmation of assignment signed by the employee. Soon after closing the target's new management terminated the employee. The former (and now aggrieved) employee then contacted an earlier employer and signed an affidavit stating that he had invented the technology while employed there. Thus, according to his employment contract with the earlier employer, the technology belonged to that employer and could not properly be assigned by the target. The fact of when the technology was created was the crux of the matter, so the waiver and confirmation letter was invaluable evidence for the German buyer to rebut the credibility of the former employee's affidavit given to his earlier employer.

The typical copyright issue, especially in the United States, is whether the party creating the material (often important computer programs created by a person hired specifically for the task) was an employee acting within the scope of employment or, alternatively, an independent contractor. If the former, in the United States and in most other countries, the employer owns the registerable rights in the material (subject in certain foreign countries to the issue of compensation). If the person was an independent contractor, the question becomes whether the material is a "work made for hire" (with unique U.S. legal ramifications if the parties have not signed a written document designating the work as a "work made for hire") or whether the independent contractor has retained some or all of the rights in the work. (The computer program example applies to all copyright issues; this could just as well relate to advertising copy, or photographs shot by a freelance photographer.) Especially where key technology for the operation of the business is involved, due diligence should focus on such issues as whether there is any source code available (in escrow or otherwise), as well as the terms of the agreement with the person in question.

The independent contractor's written agreement should specify that the material or program is a work made for hire, and that any aspects of the material or program not covered by such protection are assigned to the company, together with any rights of registration. Special attention must also be paid to "carve-outs," in which the contractor retains rights to use certain elements of the material or program for her own purposes. The problem becomes infinitely more complicated if due diligence must pin down all rights, especially in situations where the independent contractor may have a development team linked by e-mail but located, for example, in Ireland, India, and Indonesia.

Trade secrets and other confidential information are proprietary IP and not protected by any registration. Therefore, in most areas of the world, these properties are transferred and protected only by contract. The task in due diligence is to determine whether the contracts are valid. The first contractual relationships to consider are those involving the target and its employees and independent agents. Quite often, no employment or consulting agreements are in place, and the issue is whether a general policy statement of the employer provides binding legal protection. Determining this may require investigating the target's entire system for maintenance of confidential information and documents, such as log-in or log-on procedures, safekeeping, encryption, and employee or consultant hiring and termination processes. The second contractual relationships to consider are those with third parties such as licensees or licensors, where the contract terms are key to successful trade secret due diligence. In a cross-border context, the due diligence team must pay careful attention to local laws that may require disclosure of critical confidential information for safety, health, or other public policy reasons, notwithstanding contractual agreements requiring confidentiality.

An IP license, or conditional waiver by an IP owner of its right to sue for infringement, may be of great importance to the target acting as licensor or licensee. Due diligence regarding licenses (what is licensed, to whom, for how long, for what compensation, and to whom the license may be assigned or sublicensed) is often inadequate in cross-border deals because U.S. targets, or those within the EU that are subject to possible antitrust regulation, are often skittish about disclosing information to potential buyers.

Global differences in IP focus and regulatory approaches. In the United States, the IP issues to examine are fairly predictable and often overlap with antitrust issues, and arise in a traditional legal context. Examples include:

1   Horizontal cross-licenses, tying and full-line forcing (in other words, compelling purchasers to buy additional goods, services, or rights as a condition to the requested purchase or license)

2   Collection of royalties beyond the scope or term of the IP

3   A determination of whether any misuse of the IP is sufficiently material to suspend or extinguish the IP rights

4   Analysis of exclusive licenses under the terms of Section 3 of the Clayton Antitrust Act, with the required relevant market and competitive injury determinations

U.S. counsel doing a transaction in the EU will meet with a different IP focus and regulatory approach. The EU has certain per se rules on IP licensing (so-called black list clauses), but the EU also grants advance clearance to a number of restrictive clauses ("white list clauses") that are permitted so long as the licensor does not have more than a 40 percent market share.

Potential liability for violating third party rights is one of the core concerns of due diligence in cross-border as well as domestic deals, but one of the most difficult to ascertain. The only real tools available to the due diligence team are official registry searches and reviews of all threatening correspondence. In the first category, all trademarks and patents important to the target's operations should be reviewed to determine whether there are third-party-owned trademarks or patents that might present infringement issues—infringement either by or against the target. Counsel should consider retaining a commercial search company to conduct the search and at least a partial evaluation of potential infringements on a relatively expedited basis; the benefit of using an outside search firm—freeing up the due diligence team for other matters—often is far greater than the cost. Of course, all correspondence addressed to the target over an extended period (six years would be comfortable) that describes possible violations of IP rights must be investigated to see what responses were made. In addition, the drafting team must deal with these issues carefully in the "reps"—and not just by listing the possible violations on a disclosure exhibit.

A cautionary note: In some countries there are new legislated forms of IP, such as the British database right, that have no U.S. equivalent. In doing any cross-border IP due diligence, the practitioner should first review the general scope of IP laws in the countries in which the target operates to see whether any of these new forms of IP exist.

Finally, if the target is located within the EU, due diligence must focus on the current use of customer information accumulated in any databases and the potential use for such database information post-transaction. European database regulations are quite strict in protecting consumer information that would customarily be extensively mined and used in the United States. If the transaction involves any contemplated use of the European target's databases, the due diligence must determine whether the buyer is properly organized to take advantage of the U.S. safe harbor rules that the EU has accepted. These rules enable a U.S. company, upon voluntary compliance with other rules that the United States and the EU have agreed upon regarding the use of personal information, to achieve substantial compliance with the EU database regulations. Absent such safe harbor, the mining of the target's data, not to mention the use of the results, could result in significant fines in Europe.

Taking a broad view of IP due diligence. Successful IP due diligence takes a broad view of what constitutes IP, whether high tech or low tech, because IP issues tend to surface where least expected. In the worldwide merger of two of the largest international accounting firms (carried out in each country by merger of the respective two local firms there), due diligence turned up the fact that the "international practice" name (in addition to the local practice name) of some of these national firms had been registered by them—and in some instances by their founding partners—as service marks (trademarks). These registrations became a major issue in several countries where the national firms refused to merge. When, upon such refusal, one of the two national firms was chosen as the merged worldwide organization's member in that country, the other firm refused to relinquish its "international" name, now part of the worldwide organization's name. This led to litigation in which the non-chosen firm claimed the right both to continue to use the "international" name and to block use in its country of the "international" name by the other firm or any other representative of the merged organization.

M&A due diligence of a dot-com or similar company, in which IP is far and away the most important asset, requires a different (or expanded) due diligence effort. Certainly the due diligence on such companies should be heavily focused on IP. As these tend to be newer businesses, counsel can rely less on their management, who may lack business experience. Particular scrutiny should be given to noncompete agreements. Still, dot-coms and other new-tech companies are businesses, and as more businesses integrate fully into an information technology world, the distinctions for due diligence purposes will fade. Nonetheless, in a dot-com or similar type of acquisition, the composition of the due diligence team should be heavily tilted toward those with IP fluency and experience.

National Security Implications

The national security preclearance procedures for M&A transactions under the Exon-Florio Amendment are sometimes lumped conceptually with the HSR antitrust preclearance procedures, but are really more a matter of technology, and thus of IP. In a nutshell, if a deal may result in foreign control over defense or other national security-related operations or assets, the parties would be well advised to avail themselves of the voluntary Exon-Florio preclearance procedures. The obtaining of such clearance minimizes the risks of a later forced divestiture action by the government. In the post-9/11 environment, the government may take a broader view of what deals have national security implications.

Litigation

The focus of due diligence is at least as much the avoidance of unanticipated liabilities as it is verification of the assets, so investigation of potential or actual litigation or administrative claims is central to the process. The buyer wants to know what the opening balance sheet will look like after the closing, and it certainly does not want to find any unexpected red ink. There is, however, a conceptual gap confronting counsel seeking to evaluate litigation or administrative claims when one of the parties comes from a common law jurisdiction and the other from a civil law jurisdiction.

Process and timing issues. At common law, the parties largely control the process and timing of litigation. The parties use pretrial disclosure devices as widely as possible to obtain whatever information they can about their adversary's actual or potential position. As a result, discussions with the target's litigation counsel can take place on a rather informed basis, and counsel undertaking a due diligence investigation of the target can often independently review claims and evidence in the dispute in order to form opinions on liability and damages.

These procedures are truly anomalous to many European attorneys. They view litigation as something largely conducted by the judge or magistrate, who develops the evidence, conducts the witness interviews, determines the relevance and weight of the evidence, and controls the timing of the lawsuit. Pretrial discovery is not generally available. Further, the civil law attorney may not comprehend U.S. counsel's view of litigation: whether the facts of the case fit into (or can be distinguished from) a prior decided case that can serve as legal precedent. The civil law attorney is trained to view litigation issues in terms of general legal code provisions, as refined by the writings of "eminent jurists" and "noted authorities" (in other words, legal scholars). Also, consideration of industry norms and standards is more important than prior case law (unless from, for example, a country's constitutional court or equivalent).

As a result, the request for an opinion on litigation must be carefully explained, and the common and civil law attorneys must focus on the likely ultimate outcome of the litigation rather than the particulars of the ongoing litigation process. Whether the deal is inbound or outbound, the goal is the same: to determine the potential liability and damage risks to any of the target's material assets. If the target is a U.S. public company or provides audited financial statements, the process may be easier to start, because all material claims and litigation *should have* been provided to the auditors and, thus, disclosed in public securities filings. In that event, due diligence will include a review of all of the target's attorneys' responses to the auditor's requests for information regarding any of the claims or lawsuits they are handling. This information should cover the same historical time period for which the buyer has requested the financial statements themselves—usually the prior full three fiscal years before the date of the acquisition agreement, and sometimes up to five years. Of course, as the Enron meltdown has reminded us, relying solely on publicly filed information without further due diligence review and analysis is risky, as things may be brewing below the public radar screen that can have devastating effects on a buyer.

The target should be prepared to document for the buyer all claims or proceedings that exceed a specified amount related to the size of the transaction, or where the continued existence or use of a right or privilege, such as a permit or license, of at least some importance could be suspended or lost. In any case where there is a financial exposure, a critical issue is whether the event is insured and whether the insurer has been notified, has conceded defense and indemnity for the claim, or has disclaimed coverage. This issue applies even in the case of an asset transaction where the specific liability is contractually stated to be left with the selling side—in which case the cautious buyer may want the target to add the buyer as an additional insured or loss payee under the applicable insurance policies, in light of successor or liability concerns. If a key permit or license is involved, due diligence should also determine whether the buyer can obtain the permit or license in its own name, and whether this can be done in a sufficiently timely manner so as not to interrupt the target's post-closing operations.

Exposure issues. While due diligence concerns regarding litigation are fundamentally the same in inbound and outbound transactions, some important differences in the details can affect the amount of the exposure. For example, in the United States in cases of blatant civil wrongdoing, victims commonly request punitive damages. Such damages are unconstitutional in Germany. U.S. counsel in an outbound transaction may not have been exposed to the "English rule," in which the losing side pays the legal fees of the winning side, or the "German rule," which adds the element of legislatively fixed legal fees at each stage of the proceedings based on the amount in controversy. Conversely, English and German counsel are likely to find the U.S. system of contingent fees to be equally strange and probably unethical. Class actions present a U.S. litigation risk not always well appreciated outside the United States. The presence of local counsel to sort out these and other differences can be quite useful to avoid misunderstanding.

If the target makes consumer products, a foreign buyer's litigation concern should focus on exposure for product liability. Foreign businesspersons and professionals generally view the United States as a product liability claimant's paradise, and this is often the one area where U.S. counsel gets little argument from its foreign client about the extent of the due diligence. Counsel may have to calm the foreign buyer's concerns instead of rousing the buyer to appreciate the potential risk exposure. For example, in the acquisition of shares of a U.K. manufacturer, the U.S. buyer had been subject to product liability litigation. The target required the U.S. buyer's counsel—before any further due diligence could proceed—to travel to London to review with the target's barrister all of the buyer's actual and threatened product liability litigation and the insurance coverage for it. This demand required hiring an international insurance adviser on issues of coverage and policy limitations.

A foreign buyer's inquiry into a target's product liability exposure must go beyond a review of existing one-off cases and claims. Counsel should look for any developing claims patterns that could ripen into a class action or a product recall. In reporting to the foreign client on the amounts claimed in the complaints filed in pending product liability, securities violation, employment discrimination, and personal injury cases, among others, U.S. counsel must explain that the amounts claimed are routinely inflated by multiples in the filed complaints, and she must make a realistic assessment of the financial exposure for the material litigation claims. Foreign clients may be unaccustomed to such claim inflation.

Security Interests of Creditors

U.S. lawyers acting as a buyer's due diligence counsel are accustomed to relying on several external sources of information regarding a target's creditors and the security interests they hold in a target's assets. Primary among these is the Uniform Commercial Code (UCC) search, seeking evidence of secured creditors and the particulars of the security interests. This search is often one of the very first things that U.S. attorneys will do, if the buyer's CFO has not done it already. In the United States, in order to "perfect" (assure the priority of) a security interest in goods and intangibles of a corporation where the security interest is otherwise not recorded or perfected by possession, a creditor would typically file a UCC-1 financing statement in a central state registry maintained by the secretary of state (or like officeholder) of the state where the debtor is incorporated. This security *filing* is in addition to the security *agreement* with the target that creates the security interest (but not its priority) and that is often embodied in a document separate from the loan agreement or debt instrument. That two-step process—security agreement and UCC filing—provides the means of determining (by filing date priority unless otherwise agreed by the creditors) the relative seniority of the lien.

U.S. counsel for a buyer in an outbound transaction will find that experience with the UCC recording system offers help only in countries that follow the Anglo-American common law system. For example, the Canadian Registration of Personal Property Obligations Act provides a similar system, as do a series of Australian statutes. While there is legislation establishing the framework for a system of recording liens in Russia, the actual practice of recording is rather chaotic. Thus, placing any reliance on whether a security interest is or is not properly recorded in Russia, or actually exists, requires a large degree of faith.

Very few foreign countries using a legal system based on the Roman law civil code system have any formal system of lien recording for personal property generally, and their laws regarding security interests are usually much different from the U.S. model. If the target is located in France or Germany, for example, the French lien (a *privilege*) or the German security interest (a *Sicherungsrecht*) is good only to the extent that a third party purchaser of the assets actually knows about it and can be said to be purchasing in bad faith.

Absent such evidence, what can the lien holder do, and how can the buyer conduct due diligence on liens? A common practice in the United States and elsewhere for larger tangible items is to place a plaque asserting ownership on the asset itself; a part of outbound due diligence would then be a physical inspection of the major assets. In a deal involving the financing of oil barges in Venezuela, the creditor had foot-square steel plaques made announcing its security interest. These plaques were securely bolted to the barges' pilothouse doors, and the captains (who, importantly, were not government employees or agents) were paid a small gratuity to ensure that the plaques did not disappear.

In the case of intangibles like accounts receivable, there is little the creditor can do to perfect a security interest, other than to force the account debtor to arrange to have payments on its accounts to be made directly into some sort of escrow fund or to the creditor, from which it is redistributed to the debtor so long as the debt is kept current. Enforceable commitments obtained from account debtors, and lockbox arrangements, represent the best possible buyer protection.

In some outbound deals the ability to identify recorded liens may be limited. If so, the appropriate course of action is to add belt-and-suspenders security in the acquisition agreement itself, such as lengthy and sizeable escrowed purchase price holdbacks.

In the case of real estate assets, foreign registry systems for ownership are much the same as in the United States. What is different from the U.S. system is the answer to the questions of the nature and location of the property, and how you can be sure that there are no liens, encumbrances, or rights of usage attaching to it. In a U.S. transaction involving any significant real property, the U.S. lawyer should ask the target for a copy of its most recent title search report and current title insurance policy. Counsel should then arrange to obtain a current title search report and to purchase title insurance effective as of the closing. The title report points out almost all known impediments to the buyer's receiving the bargained-for ownership interest in the real property. This report makes the transfer and the securing of mortgages and other liens on real property relatively easy. If unusual problems emerge (such as the federally supported Native American land claims against New York State uncovered in the sale of upstate New York manufacturing facilities to an international investor), the target, the buyer, and the title insurance company can negotiate a special coverage provision in the title policy plus a contractual representation stating that there is insurable (not just marketable) title to the real estate in question.

In most outbound transactions, a title report is not available. Thus, in Australia the buyer should have the solicitor or title agent, rather than a title insurance company, review title. Personal property liens on chattels and intangibles can be searched at the same time, because the registry office serves for both personal and real property.

In cross-border transactions involving European real estate (assuming foreigners are permitted to own real property, which they are generally not in Switzerland), the purchaser of real property must have title transferred before a notary public, who in Europe is a professional with significant powers. It is the duty of the notary to make sure the parties are aware of any mortgages, liens, encumbrances, and tax bills affecting the real property, and that they have taken appropriate steps to discharge them, before he officially reads the deed and has the parties sign it. The notary system does not, however, give the buyer the same financial assurances that American title insurance does.

Terminating Employment and Marketing Relationships without Liability

A buyer typically expects to streamline costs and reorganize the target's personnel after the acquisition. However, the traditional "at will" termination that, although eroding at the edges, remains the cornerstone of U.S. nonunion employment law is repugnant to both law and practice in most developed countries. Accordingly, in cross-border deals involving employees outside the United States, the matter cannot be resolved by reviewing a few employment contracts and the company handbook. Rather, it involves understanding the target's historical employment practices, the detailed administrative regulations that may protect employees, and the costs incurred upon making changes and upon failing to honor such practices and regulations.

Plant closings also can create legal and political problems. If closings are part of the acquisition plan, they must be organized in advance with the precision of a military campaign. Among the local advisers engaged should be skilled public relations professionals. U.S. law has its counter-part with the procedures required under the so-called WARN statute.

In a number of jurisdictions, legal protection regarding termination extends beyond employees to certain third parties, such as distributors and independent sales agents. In Germany, for example, legislative provisions govern in some detail the circumstances under which a terminated sales agent must receive post-termination compensation ("indemnity"), whether or not the issue has been reflected in the contract. As a result, the review of a German target's commercial contracts and business arrangements must focus on, among other things, whether the third party individual or entity may be deemed to be a sales agent and, if so, whether any part of the contemplated transaction might constitute an actual or de facto termination.

A Belgian statute similarly protects terminated distributors. This protection is considered a "mandatory" provision of Belgian law, and thus cannot be circumvented by contrary provisions or waivers in the distributorship contract, by contractual designation of non-Belgian law or courts, or by arbitration provisions. Likewise, if the contract has been extended, either formally or informally, several times beyond its contractually stated term, it is likely to be considered subject to the statute as a "contract of indefinite duration."

Such statutes are not unknown in the United States. For example, Puerto Rico has a statute protecting distributors generally from termination without compensation, and Wisconsin has a strong dealer protection statute not limited to specific industries or to franchises. Ironically, a Belgian-owned company, which decided to do its own contract due diligence review in its acquisition of a U.S. competitor, missed a reference to a "joint venture" product supply relationship in the target's contract with a Wisconsin customer. Because of the Wisconsin dealership statute, the Belgians were stuck with an ongoing product supply contract that it had intended to terminate post-closing. The lesson is that terminating employment and marketing relationships and closing facilities are often unforeseen triggers to liability outside the United States, and sometimes within it as well.

The Preferred Result of Legal Due Diligence: No News Is Good News

The best evidence of a legal due diligence job well done is that post-closing, nothing happens: No skeletons in the closet are discovered, no surprises come out of the woodwork, and none of the parties' expectations are unfulfilled because of something that could or should have been unearthed in legal due diligence. The invisibility of these non-events (except perhaps when contractual or statute of limitation claims periods quietly expire) provides no occasion for cork-popping expressions of satisfaction. There is, however, a quiet but profound sense of accomplishment in a job well done.

The quest for such accomplishment should prevent those performing legal due diligence from turning it into an unimaginative, rote, one-size-fits-all process that fails to accomplish the job and may sow the seeds of future problems. Thus, every due diligence assignment on a sizable transaction should be customized, mustering the best counsel can provide, so that the buyer can receive what it bargained for: nothing less on the asset side, nothing more on the liability side, a seamless transition, and an enhancement of value.

Cross-Border Legal Due Diligence

IN A WORLD where risks of legal consequences touch on almost every aspect of business, any legal due diligence checklist for major transactions is inherently incomplete. The following checklist is intended to serve as a template to be adapted to the transaction at hand. While this checklist is geared principally toward buyers, targets may engage in similar due diligence in transactions in which the buyer's shares are a material part of the consideration. There is inevitably some overlap with the checklists used by other professionals on the deal team, but proper coordination should minimize duplication of effort. Moreover, professionals may examine the same document for different purposes (i.e., on environmental issues lawyers seek to analyze legal exposure, accountants review balance sheet reserves, and operations people evaluate the effect of such matters on day-to-day operations). Thus, much of the perceived duplication is more apparent than real and is necessary to the conduct of proper due diligence.

1. Division of Responsibility
- ❏ Counsel (is local—including foreign—or special counsel needed?)
- ❏ Target's personnel (including in-house counsel)
- ❏ Accountants
- ❏ Investment banker
- ❏ Private investigator/information specialist
- ❏ Title company
- ❏ Consultants (such as pension, environmental, OSHA, insurance, customs)
- ❏ Translators
- ❏ Information technology personnel (to create due diligence sites)
- ❏ IP commercial search company

2. Memorandum of Understanding (MOU)
- ❏ Determine whether the parties have entered into any understanding in the form of a MOU or other form of letter of intent, whether oral or written, concerning the proposed transaction.
- ❏ If so, determine whether all legally operative conditions to the transaction in the MOU were fulfilled or waived.
- ❏ If not, determine whether a MOU is necessary and which provisions, if any, should be stated to be legally binding. Note risks under foreign laws of inadvertently entering into binding MOU obligations.

3. Publicity and Confidentiality

❑ Determine whether the target, on the buyer's request, should agree not to disclose information about the buyer obtained in negotiations, not to negotiate with others for a period of time, and/or not to disclose existence of negotiations.

❑ Determine whether the buyer, on the target's request, should agree not to disclose information obtained in negotiations and/or existence of negotiations.

❑ If joint public communications are to be made, establish which individuals must approve before dissemination.

4. Access to Books and Facilities

❑ Arrange for access to the target's books and records, including off-site storage locations.

❑ Arrange for access to the target's facilities and to third party facilities where the target's property is located.

❑ Obtain the target's document retention and disposal policies and procedures. Consider requesting suspension of document disposal.

5. Capitalization and Shareholders

❑ For a non-publicly-traded target, obtain list of voting and nonvoting shareholders specifying their holdings and cross-check against the stock transfer ledger.

❑ Obtain particulars of bonds, debentures, and any other debt or hybrid securities of the target, including indentures and other pertinent documents. Examine covenants in trust indentures and similar documents for effects on transaction.

❑ Confirm the status of preemptive rights or any other similar rights and privileges.

❑ Inquire about the existence of, or agreements to issue, options, warrants, or other rights or commitments relating to the purchase, sale, or issuance of securities. Investigate for convertibility features of any debentures or preferred stock and obtain vesting schedules, pricing, and other conditions for options.

❑ Determine status of shareholders (such as minors, trustees, deceased or legally incompetent individuals, joint owners, partnerships, bankruptcy estates).

❑ As necessary, obtain trust and partnership agreements or other pertinent documents to determine if any shares are held in fiduciary or partnership capacity or by an entity.

❏ Inquire about the existence of any stock option plans, employee stock option plans (ESOPS), stock bonus plans, profit sharing, or other plans that are holding the target's shares.

❏ Determine if shares are fully paid for legally adequate consideration and nonassessable.

❏ Inquire about compliance with federal securities and state blue-sky laws for original and subsequent issues of the target's shares (to avoid rescission actions).

❏ Check that shares issued do not exceed amount of authorized shares and that shares are validly issued under state corporate law.

❏ Determine whether there are any voting agreements or trusts, outstanding proxies, or other shareholder agreements relating to voting of shares.

❏ Verify that no restrictions or trigger events exist regarding the transfer or pledge of the target's shares contained in stock purchase, buy/sell, or repurchase ("put") agreements. Check for first-refusal rights; leases, licenses, service contracts, or other agreements making sale of assets or shares an event requiring third party consent; loan agreements collateralizing the shares; tax liens on shares; and other shareholder or employment agreements relating to securities, assets, or change of management of the target.

6. Seller's Authorization of Transaction

❏ Review specific authorization resolutions, and make sure authorization is not contrary to articles of incorporation or bylaws of the target.

❏ Determine whether shareholder approval is necessary (e.g., sale of substantially all of the seller's assets).

❏ Check whether any third party approvals are necessary (private or governmental, including foreign governments).

❏ If possible, review reports to the seller's shareholders or other owners requesting consent or otherwise describing transaction.

❏ Inquire whether there are any pending litigations or disputes with or among the seller's shareholders or other owners.

7. Target's Organization, Good Standing, Structure, Subsidiaries, and Affiliations

❏ Obtain a certified copy of articles of incorporation, with all amendments, and any other filings with the secretary of state. If the target is required to file with other state government agencies relating to its corporate purposes (e.g., banking department), also verify those filings.

For foreign entities, obtain a certified copy from corporate registry, which may also show names of individuals authorized to sign for the company and additional information. (Note whether more than one signature is required.)

❏ Obtain a copy of the corporate minute books, including bylaws with all amendments, certified by the corporate secretary. Consider comparing the copy to the original minute books.

❏ Obtain good standing certificates in states where the target is incorporated and states where the target is qualified; also obtain any pending applications to qualify.

❏ Ascertain jurisdictions where the target has substantial contacts or files tax returns, and determine whether the target should be qualified in any other states.

❏ Review all (for past five years) minutes of meetings (or written consents in lieu of meetings) of shareholders, board of directors, and board committees (e.g., executive, nominating, compensation, and audit committees and any nonboard committees); for major matters, consider requesting materials, if available, distributed to the board in connection with deliberations.

❏ Obtain charts of corporate organization: corporate structure, including names, locations, and functions of all subsidiaries and divisions, and key personnel (directors, officers, and other key management and technical personnel). Determine which directors and officers will have to be replaced at closing. Identify any familial relationships between shareholders/directors and employees.

❏ Obtain annual reports for the past five years. Verify history of the organization (i.e., how did the target come into existence?), and investigate predecessor entities or businesses and terms of any prior acquisitions, mergers, or consolidations.

❏ Inquire about the existence of any partnership, joint venture, strategic alliance, joint research and development, or joint marketing arrangement, or any trust, agency, or nominee relationship, or any investment to which the target is a party. Check for "no assignment" and other restrictions in these agreements, and for potential capital or loan calls on the target or requirements to provide loan guarantees, security, or indemnities.

❏ As applicable, obtain all of the records mentioned above in this section for relevant U.S. noncorporate entities (limited liability companies, general and limited partnerships, etc.) and for foreign corporate and noncorporate entities. For entities in foreign jurisdictions, check the local ownership regulations and restrictions, and determine any citizenship or residency requirements where directors or officers will have to be replaced at closing.

8. Securities Filings

❑ For publicly traded targets or sellers, obtain all filings made with the Securities and Exchange Commission (SEC) and relevant state securities agencies, including relevant 10Ks, 10Qs, 8Ks, proxy statements, and registration statements (S-1s, S-7s, or S-8s).

❑ Determine whether there are any enforcement proceedings or investigations by the SEC or state securities commissions.

❑ Determine federal and state securities implications of the acquisition, including registrations, exemptions from registration, and restrictions on resale.

9. Financial Statements

❑ Obtain the target's financial statements for the five preceding years (and those of significant subsidiaries and divisions).

❑ If financial statements are not audited, determine if a limited audit by the buyer is necessary.

❑ Obtain the target's approval to have access to the target's auditors' work papers, and consider meeting with the target's auditors.

❑ Obtain interim financial statements, and ensure that statements are prepared on a comparable basis with prior periods.

❑ If in existence, obtain the target's financial projections.

❑ Obtain auditors' letters to management, and management's responses, for prior five years.

❑ If there has been a change of auditors within the preceding five years, investigate the circumstances, including review of relevant target files and inquiry of prior accountants.

❑ Identify and analyze off-balance-sheet financing and other off-balance-sheet structures, including securities law disclosure and insider trading compliance. Confirm true ownership of entities involved, and compliance with conflict of interest policies, and whether terms are arm's-length. Check for trading, swap, and other arrangements that may amount to financings.

10. Bank Accounts and Securities Holdings

❑ Obtain a list of all bank accounts, safe-deposit boxes, money market accounts, escrow accounts, brokerage accounts, and other account holdings. Determine who has signature power or access, and what changes will need to be made at closing.

❏ Obtain a list and particulars of all third party (nonsubsidiary) securities owned or held by the target (including corporate name, number and class of shares, certificate numbers, location of certificates, or restrictions on transfer). Determine whether such securities are pledged or otherwise noted as security for obligations and, if so, which obligations. Determine whether the number and type of securities held by the target subject it to regulation under the Investment Company Act of 1940. If such securities appear on the balance sheet, determine whether they have been marked to market or are booked at lower of cost or market.

11. Loans, Contracts, and Commitments

❏ Obtain loan and similar documents relating to third party and internal (affiliated entity or individual) loan and financing agreements and instruments, whether the target is debtor or creditor (e.g., bank loans, notes, letters of credit, factoring and other receivables financing agreements, or compensating balance arrangements). Consider the effects of any covenants in those agreements on the acquisition.

❏ Obtain security agreements, financing statements, pledges, conditional sales agreements, and other evidence of security for indebtedness.

❏ Obtain correspondence with lenders for past three years, including all compliance reports submitted by the target or its accountants, and computations demonstrating compliance with covenants.

❏ Obtain presentations given to lenders in the past three years in connection with obtaining credit.

❏ Determine whether debt can be refinanced or prepaid without penalty.

❏ Obtain contracts with significant customers. Determine accounts receivable (by customer), and identify any disputed items and reserves for bad debts. Determine any formal or informal arrangements permitting any customer later payments, discounts, rebates, or other special financial treatment.

❏ Obtain standard forms of all purchase and sale orders, quotations, contracts, invoices, and lease, license, service, and support agreements, and other documents used in connection with the purchase, sale, or other ordinary course disposition of the target's goods, other property (e.g., technology, real estate, etc.), and services.

❏ Obtain purchase and supply contracts, including for raw materials, outsourcing, contract manufacturing, processing, toll milling, warehousing, utilities (energy, water, etc.), waste removal, and transport, and agreements for technology support and maintenance. (For equipment and other capital expenditures on order, check if cancelable, with or without penalties.) Determine any formal or informal arrangements permitting the target later payments, discounts, rebates, or other special financial treatment.

❏ Obtain contracts and identify other arrangements with insiders or affiliates.

❏ Obtain installment sale, installment purchase, and sale/leaseback agreements.

❏ Obtain membership agreements and identify other relations with trade associations.

❏ Obtain guarantees, indemnities, and similar agreements.

❏ Obtain franchise, distributorship, sale representation, sales agency, commission, and other marketing agreements.

❏ Identify arrangements with foreign agents, representatives, and intermediaries, to ensure compliance with the Foreign Corrupt Practices Act.

❏ Obtain brokerage, consignment, sale, and return arrangements.

❏ Obtain agreements with or commitments to attorneys, accountants, investment bankers, business brokers, finders, consultants, advertising and public relations firms, executive search firms, architects, interior designers, engineers, lobbyists, charities, etc., and other nonprofit organizations (universities, public institutes), and government or quasi-governmental agencies. Identify political contributions (U.S. and foreign) by or identifiable with the target for legality and publicity risks, especially if the target's business involves government contracts.

❏ Obtain product and service warranties given and received by the target.

❏ Identify and analyze agreements with respect to obligations or liabilities for the return of goods in the possession of customers or other third parties, including arrangements obligating or permitting the target to buy back its products.

❏ Identify and analyze agreements expected to result in loss to the target upon completion or performance.

❏ Identify and analyze agreements restricting the target from carrying on its business (or a portion thereof) in any geographic, product, or service areas.

❏ Identify and analyze long-term agreements permitting pricing or other financial adjustments.

❏ Obtain any other agreements involving more than *(specify appropriate dollar threshold)* or relating to obligations or liabilities outside the target's ordinary course of business.

❏ In reviewing terms of all existing contracts, consider whether they can be assumed or terminated; whether they can, by their terms, be renegotiated to the buyer's advantage or disadvantage; and whether they have been modified in practice without any (or legally adequate) written amendments.

❏ Determine whether any powers of attorney have been given by the target, and to whom (e.g., taxes).

❏ Determine the existence of any prior (past ten years) or pending acquisition, merger, stock or asset sale, or similar agreements, or agreements for sales of material assets of the target or for acquisitions of the shares or assets of any other business. Note whether rights and remedies accrue to successors in interest, the contractual time limits for claiming remedies, and whether any claims already have been asserted, threatened, or expected.

❏ If applicable, obtain agreements and offering documents relating to sale of the target's equity or debt securities for the past five years.

❏ Determine existence of any commitments to brokers or finders, written or oral (if binding in the applicable state), for this transaction.

12. Inventory

❏ Determine whether any inventory is in the hands of vendors, at customer locations, field warehoused, or otherwise not on hand to the target, and whether it is owned by someone other than the target (e.g., work in process, demos, etc.).

❏ Determine obsolescence or salability; consider inspections on sampling basis.

❏ For contracts with U.S. government, confirm adherence to its cost accounting requirements.

13. Real Estate, Machinery, and Equipment

❏ Obtain list and particulars (location, type, acreage, building square footage, date of construction, date of purchase, etc.) of all real property owned or leased (as lessor or lessee) by the target, and all other real estate interests (e.g., easements, subsoil rights, concessions, and construction air rights).

❑ Note any recorded building or other violations, and identify easements and other burdens on the target's real property.

❑ Where the target is a lessor, determine creditworthiness of tenant or subtenant.

❑ Order new title reports and obtain past title reports (five years) and all existing title insurance policies.

❑ Obtain surveys and maps, building plans, and engineering studies.

❑ Obtain all mortgages and mortgage notes and related financing statements, rent assignments, and guarantees. (Note any due on sale and change-of-control provisions.)

❑ Obtain Uniform Commercial Code, tax, judgment, and other lien searches in all applicable jurisdictions, and check for items affecting real property interests and improvements (including machinery and equipment affixed to land or buildings).

❑ Obtain all pending real property purchase or option agreements, and all agreements for construction, alteration, or furnishing of real property.

❑ Review deeds, bills of sale, and leases. Check leases for assignability (obtain consents if needed) and for use limitations and rights of affiliates to use property. Obtain estoppel certificates from landlords, tenants, and mortgage lenders.

❑ Determine location and condition of all plants and other facilities and all machinery and equipment, and arrange inspections (for buildings, especially asbestos, and "sick building" complaints).

❑ Determine presence of any machinery, equipment, or other fixed (to real property) assets held by the target but owned by persons other than the target (e.g., leased).

❑ Obtain existing or new appraisals of properties and compare with balance sheet values.

❑ Confirm zoning and other land use restrictions. Determine if these would affect any planned post-closing changes or additions by the buyer.

❑ For leased property, obtain list of all leasehold improvements, showing total cost by major items, amortization reserve, rates used, and present unamortized cost.

❑ Obtain any building or facilities management agreements and other agreements for servicing real property (e.g., trash removal, cleaning, landscaping, and exterminating).

❑ Note and review any trust or other arrangements to comply with foreign restrictions on nonlocals owning real estate.

14. Environmental and OSHA

❏ List all states in which the target previously owned, operated, or leased property, conducted operations, or disposed of wastes.

❏ For each site, identify the nature of operations or activities, and chemicals or other toxic, caustic, or hazardous substances or wastes or by-products that were used, generated, or otherwise present. Describe handling procedures for such substances.

❏ Determine whether the target has received a hazardous waste treatment, storage, and disposal permit and, if so, whether there have been any notices of violations or warnings with respect to the site.

❏ Determine whether the target has generated "hazardous wastes" and, if so, the location of storage or disposal of wastes, the maximum period of on-site storage of such wastes, and the volume of wastes generated per month.

❏ Determine whether the target disposes of its wastes off-site and, if so, whether the target is or could be a potentially responsible party in connection with any past or present off-site landfills on which it has disposed of wastes.

❏ Determine whether the target discharges wastewater or storm water into something other than a publicly owned treatment works and, if so, obtain the discharge permit and analyze any notices of violations and any treatment facility changes required (noting costs involved).

❏ Describe effluent streams (gaseous, liquid, solid, and particulate) at each plant, present means of control (e.g., scrubbers), and any steps being taken to bring nonconforming operations into compliance; determine whether the target holds any permits under federal water or air regulatory statutes or any other air emissions or water discharge permits, and, if so, analyze any notices of violations or warnings. Also, determine whether the target is aware of any air emissions or water discharges for which it is not currently required to hold a permit.

❏ Determine methods and viability of current means of handling solid waste and effluent problems, and identify probable longevity of present arrangements, potential liabilities that may result from the use of current methods, and expenditures and timetable to correct existing problems.

❏ Determine whether the target ever had releases, spills, or fires and, if so, whether the target reported them properly and ascertained the level of cleanup necessary. Describe details of each such release, spill, or fire (including type of substance involved, extent of spread of the

released substance into or onto the air, soil, and/or water, and remedial measures taken to prevent a recurrence). State whether the target has filed any official notifications relating to release of any hazardous substances on any property owned or leased by the target.

❑ Determine whether any tank for storage of a petroleum product or
other material is located at the target (typical if the target operates
its own fleet of vehicles, forklifts, etc.), and for any such tank, list
contents; capacity; whether located above or below ground;
whether any permit, license, or other approval for tank has been
applied for or obtained or any notification has been submitted; the
nearest waterway or body of water and its distance from tank;
whether tank is covered by spill prevention control and countermea-
sure plan; and last date tank was leak tested and whether it was
determined not to be leaking.

❑ Determine whether the target has received notice relating to involvement in a superfund site and, if so, whether notice relates to on-site
contamination at the target's property or to off-site disposal of hazardous substances by the target or one of its contractors.

❑ Determine OSHA compliance and complaint experience of the target, review all files relating to OSHA matters, and consider having a
private OSHA consultant inspect major facilities and review paperwork for compliance.

❑ Determine whether any hazardous substance (including asbestos)
has been detected in any monitoring, testing, or other similar internal or private study conducted by the target on buildings, air, soil, or
water (including groundwater and nearby surface water bodies) at or
near any of the target's facilities and, if so, review copies of all relevant documents.

❑ Determine whether the target has ever acquired any enterprise or
line of business, or held an interest in one (e.g., in a joint venture),
having environmental problems and, if so, determine the target's
potential exposure.

❑ Determine whether the target has created reserves for potential environmental or OSHA liabilities and, if so, analyze adequacy of reserves.

❑ Review existing Phase I and II environmental assessments on the target's sites, commission Phase I assessments, and, as necessary, commission Phase II assessments.

❑ Examine any foreign environmental and worker safety problems,
upon obtaining pertinent documents.

15. Intellectual Property and Information Technology

❏ Obtain a worldwide list of registered and pending applications to register patents, trademarks, service marks, and copyrights owned or used by the target. Also obtain list of domain name registrations and applications.

❏ Determine any oppositions to pending applications to register, or current or threatened claims challenging existing registrations of, target's owned or used intellectual property.

❏ Identify key trade secrets, including past and current procedures to maintain confidentiality, and known or suspected breaches of confidentiality; verify internal compliance with confidentiality procedures; and examine any claims of industrial espionage by or against the target.

❏ Obtain and review all nondisclosure and similar agreements and commitments involving target as discloser or disclosee.

❏ Obtain and review copies of all license agreements from or to the target, and review records of royalty payments and receipts; note any pending or threatened disputes over royalties.

❏ Review the target's compliance with license restrictions, in particular copying of software or journals.

❏ Review records retention, oversight of employee communications, privacy, and other policies concerning employee use of the target's information technology and equipment.

16. Employees, Benefit Plans, and Compensation

❏ Obtain chart setting forth the name, title, function, and years of service of management and key technical employees.

❏ Obtain list of all individuals (or entities acting for individuals) who are consultants to the target, and determine whether they should be classified as employees under tax rules.

❏ Obtain and review existing employment contracts and résumés or summary biographies of key personnel, noting golden parachute/ change of control/change of title or responsibilities provisions in contracts. Also obtain and review all other agreements for compensation to key employees.

❏ Obtain and review all severance agreements, compensation plans, or other agreements or arrangements with key personnel that involve payments or other compensation to them or any other person in connection with resignation, retirement, or other termination.

❏ Obtain schedule of all compensation paid during the last three fiscal years to key personnel, showing separately salary, bonuses, and noncash compensation and perquisites (e.g., use of cars, club memberships). Look for patterns of charging personal expenses to the target or expense account abuse.

❏ Obtain and review documents establishing or defining any stock option, bonus, profit sharing, pension, retirement, deferred compensation, or similar plan currently in effect or proposed; the most recent summary plan description and annual report filed with any government agency concerning any such plan; any qualification letter from the Internal Revenue Service concerning such plan; and any actuarial reports or other documents from actuaries regarding such plan.

❏ Obtain and review documents establishing, or summary descriptions of, employee benefit or similar plans, including employee booklets for each employee benefit plan (i.e., life, long-term disability, short-term disability, dental, medical, vision, and flexible spending accounts).

❏ Obtain and review personnel policies, personnel and code-of-conduct manuals, and employee handbooks.

❏ Obtain and review confidentiality, noncompetition, and invention agreements between the target and employees, including standard forms of such agreements as currently used by the target.

❏ Obtain list of former key executive employees who have left the target in the past two years and a brief description of circumstances of their leaving. Consider obtaining statement whether the target has any reason to believe such former employee has violated any nondisclosure, noncompetition, nonsolicitation, or similar agreements or is contemplating legal action against the target.

❏ For business where certain employees must be licensed (e.g., registered representatives), obtain chart showing registrations by employee, type, and jurisdiction.

❏ Review employee recruitment and hiring procedures, forms, and files, noting compliance with procedures to avoid unlawful discrimination and hiring of nonqualifying aliens.

❏ Verify compliance with requirements to pay overtime, including proper classifications of employees for overtime.

❏ For foreign operations, check adherence to and compliance with applicable codes of conduct toward foreign employees and evidence of protests in U.S. or abroad regarding the same.

17. Labor Relations

❏ Determine scope of collective bargaining contract over specific employees, job categories, and work functions, noting geographic reach of contract and union's jurisdiction.

❏ Determine collective bargaining contract restrictions on plant movement, subcontracting, and internal modification of work methods.
❏ Determine rates of compensation and size of workforce in each category.
❏ Identify specific collective bargaining contract references to obligations for the target and buyer, especially obligations calling on the target or buyer to notify or bargain with union regarding sale and (as often seen in outbound transactions) the buyer's obligation to adopt collective bargaining agreements containing obligations to employ target's employees, including seniority, vacation and holiday benefits, severance pay, etc..
❏ Identify collective bargaining contract obligations (including trust agreements) to establish, maintain, or contribute to fringe benefit funds for medical, pension, apprenticeship, or other welfare purposes, noting contribution levels, eligibility formulae, and possible contractual commitments to increase these at future dates.
❏ Identify unions, their principal leadership, history of strikes and organizational drives, and ambitions to organize nonunionized employees or invade jurisdiction of other unions.
❏ Check outstanding recent litigation before the National Labor Relations Board (NLRB) and other relevant federal and state labor agencies, and identify labor-related judgments, settlements, consent decrees, conciliation agreements, compliance agreements, etc., with outstanding obligations or that affect future operations.
❏ If closing a facility with 100 or more employees, prepare for compliance with WARN (Worker Adjustment and Retraining Notification Act) requirements for sixty days' advance notice.
❏ Check relations with other government agencies affecting employment, e.g., compliance with minimum wage laws, Title VII of Civil Rights Act, and minimum standards imposed by statute on parties contracting with U.S. government (Walsh-Healey and Davis-Bacon Acts).
❏ For foreign operations, review history of strikes and other labor unrest, as well as union representation.

18. Taxes
See Chapter 6 for a more extensive tax checklist.
❏ Identify all tax litigation pending, determine status, and analyze prospects.
❏ Obtain all tax litigation settlement documents and tax dispute-related correspondence for prior three years, and determine compliance with settlements.

❏ Obtain and review law firm tax opinions (including backup opinions and certificates) for material transactions within past five years, and determine whether conclusions are in question, or whether regulations or case law underpinning opinion has changed.

19. Litigation, Claims, Investigations, and Contingent Liabilities

❏ Obtain complete pending litigation, mediation, arbitration, and other legal proceedings list, and, for material claims, review files of the target and the target's counsel.

❏ Obtain documents and information on all threatened litigation, arbitrations, contested claims and complaints, notices of default, investigations, legal inquiries, internal compliance or incident reviews, disciplinary proceedings, grievances, labor controversies, condemnations, and other such prelitigation events, current or concluded in the past five years.

❏ Obtain target's auditor's attorney inquiry letters and replies for the prior five years, and have the most recent updated by letter from counsel.

❏ Obtain any current litigation reports to the target's board of directors by the target's attorneys.

❏ Inquire about existence of judgments, consent decrees, injunctions, other judicial or administrative decrees or orders, stipulations, settlement agreements, and other agreements or requirements arising from contentious matters, noting those still requiring or prohibiting future activities.

❏ List products/services that historically exposed the target to product liability or recall claims, and check for any newly emerging patterns of claims or customer or user complaints or inquiries.

❏ Obtain documents and correspondence relating to contingent liabilities, including performance specifications guaranteed by the target, penalty provisions in contracts, and investigations or violations that may lead to civil or criminal penalties or forfeitures.

20. Insurance

❏ Obtain all insurance policies and fidelity bonds, including general liability, product liability, key executive life, director's' and officers' indemnification, business interruption, employee claims, workers' compensation, product recall, kidnapping, or acts of terrorism.

❏ Determine involvement in any group or company captive insurance arrangements, and, if any, confirm tax deductibility of premiums paid by the target to captive.

❑ Analyze pending claims and claim notices, whether claims have been promptly reported, past claims experience, refusals to provide coverage, and cancellations of coverage.

❑ Review most recent applications for coverage, and determine if any applications or coverages were denied in the past five years.

❑ Evaluate adequacy of insurance coverage, both as to types and amounts of coverage, including extent to which the target is self-insured. Note the geographical extent of coverage, and whether foreign subsidiaries are covered.

❑ Contact the buyer's and the target's insurance carriers regarding possible continuation of coverage.

❑ Investigate "tail insurance" for products liability coverage for unreported, unknown preclosing occurrences, and determine whether this coverage should be carried by the seller or the buyer.

21. Antitrust

❑ Consider antitrust aspects of acquisition under Section 7 of Clayton Act, Hart-Scott-Rodino (HSR) filing requirement, and other federal antitrust and state unfair competition statutes. Also consider foreign antitrust compliance, especially under the European Community regulatory regime.

❑ Determine, for antitrust purposes, business objectives of the buyer and the target, including whether prices are to be increased or decreased, products and services are to be bundled, operations are to be vertically integrated, etc.. Also, obtain and review any analyses by buyer stating reasons for acquisition or plans for post-closing operations.

❑ Identify business lines of the buyer and the target.

❑ Determine relevant markets (products and geographical areas) involved in acquisition.

❑ Evaluate competitive effects of acquisition on business of the buyer, the target, and their competitors.

❑ Inquire about the target's past antitrust problems (e.g., allegations or investigations of price-fixing, price discrimination, or monopolization, and injunctions and consent decrees).

22. General Regulatory Requirements for Operations and Transaction

❏ Obtain a list of all of the target's other permits and licenses, and determine requirements of all federal, state, local, and foreign regulatory authorities as to transfer, assignment, or sale of such other permits and licenses (Food and Drug Administration, Interstate Commerce Commission, Army Corps of Engineers, etc.).

❏ Review such existing permits and licenses to ascertain their terms and conditions for continuing compliance by the target postacquisition, and whether acquisition triggers additional obligations (e.g., additional bonding) or the need for additional related permits or licenses. Note if any grandfathered exemptions under such permits or licenses will be lost upon acquisition.

❏ Review the target's compliance, policies, manuals, and records for matters subject to government regulations.

❏ Focus on regulation of the target's particular lines of business, and survey applicable federal, state, local, and foreign laws and regulations for legal requirements of completing the transaction and for how they affect post-closing operations of the combined company.

❏ For inbound acquisitions involving the defense, technology, or other national security sectors, consider whether to apply for U.S. government pre-clearance under the Exon-Florio Amendment. Upon approval, later forced divestment action by the governed is barred, absent false information in the application.

23. Successor Liability

❏ If an asset purchase, determine the target's liabilities not intended to be assumed by the buyer but that may, as a matter of law, become the buyer's responsibility as successor, including bulk sales liability; sales/use, unemployment, and employee withholding tax liability; product liability (injury, product recall); environmental liability; pension benefits; labor union contracts; employment discrimination; liabilities under regulatory permits or licenses; etc..

6 | Tax Due Diligence

ROBERT T. BOSSART, ESQ.

C ROSS-BORDER TAX DUE DILIGENCE for any investor involves a balance between tax compliance review and future tax planning. The weight the investor gives to each can be a function of the type of investment. An investor planning a purchase of a target's assets may spend more time planning future tax operations than worrying about the target's past tax compliance. This is true because in asset deals, the target's tax attributes and tax liabilities usually do not pass to the investor (though some customs duties, sales and use, personal, or real property tax liabilities may). Conversely, an investor acquiring the target's shares will be inheriting all of the target's prior tax liabilities, structures, and planning. Thus, tax compliance due diligence will likely present a heavier burden in a share purchase than in an asset purchase.

Compliance versus Planning

Too many investors believe that tax due diligence focuses solely on the target's past compliance activities. The truth is that tax due diligence needs to begin at the moment the investor decides to actively consider the target. This allows the investor to carefully consider the structural and financing form of the potential investment at the start. Too often, tax advisers are brought in to look at a deal after the parties have already structured it. In due diligence, tax experts may discover major tax problems arising from the planned form of the transaction or major tax opportunities that can be seized only if the parties employ a deal structure other than the one contemplated. Typically, investors are unwilling to retrace any part of the deal because it could open the entire transaction to renegotiation. The result is often poor strategic tax choices that fail to capture major tax benefits.

Due Diligence Coordination

It is important for those performing tax due diligence to coordinate effectively with other members of the due diligence team. Many investors wrongly assume that tax, financial accounting, strategic, intellectual property, environmental, and other due diligence activities are performed in watertight compartments. Nothing could be further from the truth. In one deal involving a Swedish investor, the intellectual property attorneys discovered many potentially valuable unregistered intangible assets, such as patents, trademarks, or copyrights, that were not visible on the target's tax returns. The investor was going to establish a U.S. incorporated subsidiary to purchase the target's assets for cash. By coordinating tax and intellectual property due diligence, it was possible to create large and permanent tax savings to the investor.

Even in a share acquisition, tax planning performed during due diligence can significantly improve postacquisition tax efficiency. For example, a U.S. company was going to acquire the shares of a target in Italy, a high tax rate jurisdiction. The target's principal asset was a manufacturing intangible for products sold around the world. The non-Italian individual selling the target would not sell the Italian company's assets, only its shares. Here, tax due diligence practitioners from a number of jurisdictions coordinated with other experts on the due diligence team. Immediately after the acquisition, the investor subdivided the intangible asset rights between the United States and the rest of the world. The investor then transferred those rights from Italy at virtually no incremental tax cost to the global acquiring group. The subsequent taxation of the earnings of the transferred intangibles at a rate of approximately one-quarter of the Italian tax rate paid for the total due diligence effort and permanently reduced the investor's global effective tax rate.

Local, National, and International Perspective

Another important area in international tax due diligence that affects both compliance and planning is nonfederal taxes. Too many investors focus solely on taxes at the national level and then only on income taxes. Although national-level income taxes are exceptionally important, the existence of nonfederal taxes should never be underemphasized. Provincial, territorial, or state income or franchise taxes; local income taxes; value-added or sales and use taxes; excise taxes; property taxes; transfer taxes; and mortgage-recording taxes, among others, must be considered in due diligence.

In a world of deals that cross many borders, the need for multifaceted tax due diligence is of increasing importance. Traditional deals had an investor looking at a target whose operations were primarily confined to a single nation. Thus, traditional transactional tax due diligence focused on whether the proposed deal was an asset or a share purchase and was taxable or tax-deferred. Today, even a taxable asset acquisition of a target in one country is likely to involve the target's ownership of shares of subsidiaries in many different countries. Likewise, the growth of multinationals and their related party transactions has increased the likelihood that tax authorities in different countries can review the same international group's transfer of goods, intangibles, services, or capital, and come to contrary conclusions about how much profit is taxable in their jurisdiction. Intergroup transactions across national borders have grown, causing taxpayers to more aggressively pursue an optimal global effective tax rate. As a result, tax disputes with tax authorities and exposure to tax disputes at all levels are rising. These events have only increased the importance of involving internal and external tax personnel as early in the deal process as possible.

A Word about Joint Ventures

Joint ventures are increasingly common and complex. Nevertheless, both parties normally view themselves as investors rather than targets, and each transfers assets or shares or both into the joint venture. Thus, to a very great extent, applying the due diligence techniques described below for asset acquisitions or share acquisitions will normally suffice.

However, one additional step of due diligence should be considered. Since most joint ventures do not endure, each investor's exit strategy must be taken into account. Particularly important are the disposition of intangibles—those each investor contributed to the joint venture and those developed inside it. Likewise, the possibility of inheriting unwanted liabilities at termination should receive very close attention before the parties enter into the joint venture.

Taxable Purchase of Assets

A taxable purchase of assets provides the investor with the greatest opportunity to generate future tax benefits from the investment. Hence, the focus of initial due diligence is on those aspects of the target's compliance providing the investor the best information to use in planning the transactional structure and the target's postdeal operations. Before examining specific compliance documents, however, the tax due diligence team should have a very good idea of the target's global legal, operational, and tax structure and business functions. It is important in reviewing the target's legal structure to understand whether the purchase will involve all or only some of the target's assets.

Let's assume the target will be selling *assets* in its country of incorporation but may be selling the *shares* of specific (primarily foreign) corporate subsidiaries or selling operating divisional assets in various global subsidiaries. Each scenario presents problems and opportunities for tax due diligence to uncover for compliance and planning purposes.

Understanding the Target's Operations and Structure

Operational considerations. One key to a successful asset acquisition is to understand the target's production, distribution, and/or service functions. It is particularly helpful to obtain functional flowcharts. They allow tax advisers to coordinate with other due diligence team members in reviewing the target's operational structure, thinking about exposure areas, and planning. For example, the investor may wish to know the tax consequences of continuing all existing operations versus discontinuing some. The tax due diligence team should clearly understand any proposed changes in the target's operations and whether such changes involve the acquisition of designated assets or whole businesses outside the target's country of incorporation. (For a complete discussion of operational due diligence, see Chapter 3.)

In one situation, Corp X was selling all of the assets in its country of incorporation. These assets included the shares of subsidiaries in twelve other countries. Corp X had production facilities in nine countries. The investor determined that, postdeal, it would cease production in five of those countries. Therefore, it was important to focus the planning efforts on the surviving production facilities, while simultaneously considering future tax costs or opportunities generated by the discontinued operations. In this case, the discontinued facilities were all in high tax rate jurisdictions and were participants in a cost-sharing agreement that funded new manufacturing intangibles. Appropriately revising the cost-sharing agreement provided income to entities that otherwise would have had unused tax losses and gave the investor the opportunity to centralize many of the manufacturing intangibles in a very low tax rate jurisdiction.

Similar care should attend due diligence on distribution operations. If the target has distribution subsidiaries outside its country of incorporation, it is important to understand whether the investor plans to continue those facilities in those countries, to integrate their operations with its own in those countries, or to eliminate the workforce of those subsidiaries while maintaining the function. Each scenario can have significant tax consequences that will affect the investor's future global effective tax rate. Likewise, international tax due diligence should review service functions to create tax opportunities for the investor.

Service functions can be offered to external customers or internally. In one case, UK Target, Ltd., performed customer assistance/support and warranty service locally, usually at a loss. The investor created a centralized call center, an Internet tech support site, and an Internet distribution function that reduced costs and increased income that was taxed at low rates. In another case, acquiring only one of a French company's four operating divisions meant that the investor would not acquire support functions that the French company performed as a centralized service. As a result, the investor was able to create a shared service center in a low tax rate jurisdiction outside of France to perform the vast majority of support services for the acquired division. By charging these internally shared services at a markup to each of its operating divisions in high tax rate jurisdictions, the company lowered its overall taxes and reduced global support costs.

Fully understanding the target's structure and operations requires understanding the target's tax operations. For example, if a type of entity in any country is not designated in the U.S. income tax regulations to be treated "per se" as a corporation for U.S. tax purposes, it is possible for the shareholder to make a "check-the-box" election. This election treats the entity as a branch (one shareholder) or partnership (more than one shareholder) solely for U.S. tax purposes even though it retains corporate limited liability in its local jurisdiction. In reviewing a target's tax status, it is important to understand whether, for U.S. tax purposes, there are differences between the target's global legal structure and its tax structure. A U.S. target may have an Irish subsidiary, which itself has subsidiaries in the United Kingdom, Germany, and Japan. For U.S. tax purposes, whether these three entities are treated as corporate subsidiaries or branches of Ireland will affect both U.S. tax deferral and foreign tax credit planning. Many non-U.S. companies also make use of the "check-the-box" rules either to help structure their U.S. operations or, before putting some of their non-U.S. operations up for sale, to maximize their value to U.S. buyers.

The 80/20 rule. Understanding the target's legal, tax, and operational structures helps determine where to expend the tax due diligence compliance review and the acquisition and postacquisition tax planning effort. Here, as elsewhere, the 80/20 rule applies. In most situations, 80 percent of the critical operations of a group are contained within 20 percent of its entities, and 80 percent of the critical operations of an entity are contained in 20 percent of its functions. Without time to review every entity for every transaction, it is important to focus on the 20 percent of those operations that provide 80 percent of the target's revenue. The due diligence team can review other aspects as time permits or by exception.

Considerations relating to legal structure. Most target corporations prefer a share sale to an asset sale, because a selling shareholder's returns from an asset sale are diminished by taxes at the corporate and shareholder levels. However, in today's global economy there are many opportunities for asset sales. A major multinational with many operating divisions may sell the assets of one division because it can shelter the gain inside the company with other tax attributes or other expenses. Sometimes, it simply has no other choice from a business operations perspective. Alternatively, it may have no intention of distributing the after-tax proceeds of the asset sale.

Owner/operators of pass-through (nontaxable) entities for federal tax purposes are more receptive to asset sales because of the possibility of one level of tax. Subject to certain limitations, these entities can include partnerships or U.S. S corporations. Perhaps the most important format used by most new U.S. high-tech and other companies is the limited liability company, or LLC. A U.S. LLC has all of the corporate limited liability attributes of a regular corporation, but it is a pass-through entity for federal income tax purposes. Thus, a start-up or growing company in an LLC format is more likely to be willing to sell its assets than would a regular "C" corporation, because the LLC is exempt from the double taxation of the C corporation format.

An LLC format may therefore make a company a more inviting target because that format enhances value to prospective buyers. For example, assume that Softco, Inc. (a regular U.S. C corporation), establishes an Irish operating subsidiary ("Ireland"). Softco and Ireland also enter into a cost-sharing agreement to develop all future software wherein Softco retains all of the American intangible rights and Ireland retains all the non-U.S. intangible rights. A U.S. buyer wishes to acquire Softco. Because Softco is a taxable corporation, its shareholders would greatly prefer to sell shares and have only one level of U.S. taxes at U.S. capital gains tax rates.

Under such circumstances, the U.S. investor would obtain a new member of its U.S. consolidated tax return group, and Ireland would remain a subsidiary of that entity. None of the intangible property rights of Softco or Ireland would change hands in the share acquisition, thereby forcing all intellectual property planning into the postacquisition period. Meanwhile a non-U.S. investor seeking to acquire Softco would be forced to acquire Softco's shares. This creates a major tax problem, because a non-U.S. investor would be forced to remit all of Ireland's low-taxed earnings through the U.S. tax system en route to the investor's home country. This is exceptionally costly and inefficient and would probably result in a lower purchase price for Softco's shares.

But there is a better way. Assume Softco LLC is a U.S. tax pass-through entity that owns Ireland. As before, both companies own or have beneficial rights to their respective intangible assets through the cost-sharing agreement. Under these circumstances, any investor—U.S.- or non-U.S.-based—could make a more tax-efficient acquisition of Softco LLC's business than of Softco, Inc.'s business. Such improved tax efficiency should raise the purchase price. In both of these situations, the LLC's shareholders should consider their structural advantage in determining their asking price. All other factors being equal, investors should also seek entities outside the United States with the flexible characteristics of an LLC.

International Federal Tax Compliance Due Diligence

Reviewing prior federal tax returns from all relevant national tax jurisdictions only sometimes offers significant help to the investor. Assume the target has three divisions globally and is selling the assets of one. If all three divisions are in one entity in each country, reviewing the target's federal tax returns may not provide the investor with any insight into tax aspects relevant to the assets to be conveyed. In these circumstances, the target's divisional financial statements (or for purposes of the sale, the target's pro forma financials) may provide greater insight into the nature of the assets in question.

On the other hand, assume the investor is acquiring all the assets of a U.S. target. Here, a review of the target's federal tax return may provide valuable insights into tax planning opportunities. The target's federal tax return will show most of the types of assets the company owns, excluding self-developed and previously expensed intangible assets. It will also provide a history of prior tax capital cost allowances or depreciation for real and personal property and disclose acquired or capitalized self-developed intangible assets currently being amortized for federal tax purposes. The federal tax return will provide insight into issues like amortizable bond premium, organization expenses, start-up expenses, and the tax amortization of R&D or purchased goodwill.

Federal tax compliance review also considers inventory cost accounting and employee benefit matters. It also may include special industry-related issues or requirements, tax credits, or negotiated agreements with the federal tax authorities as well.

Research and development expenses. If the target currently expenses R&D, such expenses may, at best, be found as a supporting line item in some countries' tax returns. Otherwise, they might be found as a separate line item (although global in amount) in the target's financial statements. Knowing R&D expenses can be important in determining the level of expenditures that meet the tax definition of deductible research and experimental expenditures. In some countries, this definition is narrower than the one used for financial statement purposes and can be important for two reasons. First, many countries permit companies to claim a credit for research and experimental expenditures as defined under tax law rather than as defined under financial statement principles. Second, if the investor acquires a U.S. business where either the target or the investor owns non-U.S. subsidiaries of a U.S. entity, one of the expenditures that must be taken into account in allocating and apportioning expenses to foreign source income for U.S. Foreign Tax Credit Limitation purposes is research and experimental expenditures. Specific U.S. tax regulations determine how such defined expenditures are allocated and apportioned and can affect repatriation costs.

Inventory accounting methods. The target's tax return will disclose the types and levels of its inventory. The target may be using first-in first-out (FIFO) or last-in first-out (LIFO) or some other method for its inventory accounting. Many countries outside the United States do not allow the use of LIFO. In addition, some companies in the securities industry are required to use the "mark-to-market" method to account for their securities inventories. Observing the types of costs used in determining inventories, their levels, and the accounting methods in use can help provide information that may be valuable to the investor for future tax planning purposes.

Employee benefits. Many issues arise on employee benefit matters, even in an asset acquisition. Top management may have bonus payments triggered upon a sale of the company's assets. In the United States, these golden-parachute issues can create a large additional cost to an investor who acquires assets. Tax due diligence professionals should review material employment-related documents for the existence and impact of such executive benefits.

An asset transaction also may cause employee share options to vest and be immediately cashed in, with the resulting additional compensation being a liability to the target. It is therefore important to determine whether the acquisition agreement makes such option payments the target's responsibility. Material obligations of this sort may cause the investor to rethink the price.

Assuming that the target's workforce will transfer to the investor's company at the date of the asset acquisition, several issues arise regarding employee benefit plans. Even in an asset acquisition, group health and welfare plans may transfer from the target to the investor. The investor may want such plans to transfer only to the target's employees. The investor may want all the members of the target's management team to become members of the investor's existing health and welfare benefit plans. It is therefore important to understand the investor's expectations on such issues.

Even in an asset acquisition, no area can create more uncertainty than the target's pension and profit-sharing plans. Due diligence should first focus on the plans and tests under the national tax and/or labor rules on what makes and keeps a plan qualified. For example, in the United States the Employee Retirement Income Security Act (ERISA) of 1974 provides a series of rules that require annual testing. These tests include whether highly compensated individuals are receiving greater than a defined "fair share" of benefits. They also contain limits and requirements concerning the funding of liabilities. A disqualified plan represents a disaster to both the employees and the company. It is therefore important in due diligence to review the plan's compliance with all of the federal tests. However, such concerns may not apply in countries where pension funds are managed and controlled by the national government.

If the plans meet all of the tests, the investor still may need help deciding whether to retain the plans or to liquidate them at the acquisition. Thus, where all the assets of a business are acquired, in some countries it is possible for a liquidating plan to acquire annuities for each beneficiary to be set aside until that employee retires. Under such circumstances, the target's employees become members of the investor company's plans but do not put their prior vested benefits at risk in their new company. Alternatively, the entire plan might be assumed by the investing company and kept separate so long as a separate trade or business exists inside that entity. Here, coordination among tax counsel, HR personnel, and investor management becomes critical. In countries where the national government maintains the plans, fewer alternatives may be available.

Withholding taxes. Employment taxes are another key area. Most countries view such taxes as a fiduciary obligation of the company. Therefore, tax and financial accounting members of the due diligence team should coordinate to make sure that the target properly withheld and paid prior employee payroll taxes, including social insurance contributions, and properly filed the appropriate tax returns. This prevents the possibility of a contingent liability (such as a lien) reducing the value of the acquired assets.

Special circumstances. Reviewing the target's federal tax return also may offer the investor greater insight into industry-specific issues. For example, many countries have specific rules regarding the taxation of industries like banking, securities, energy, forest products, insurance, and real estate. Under such circumstances, a review of the target's federal tax return will demonstrate how its assets have been deployed under the rules for that industry and reported in the company's tax return. Likewise, many countries provide tax credits for specific activities even in situations where they may not have special tax accounting rules for an entire industry, such as, for example, research and experimentation, energy, or investment tax credits.

The United States and other countries provide special tax credits for activities outside their boundaries. Likewise, some countries provide special tax credits or exemptions for activities in particular locations. The United States has the Possessions Tax Credit, and countries like France, Italy, and Israel have designated specific regions to receive special tax breaks. Often, the income subject to the special tax regime is disclosed either on the target's federal tax return or on a separate tax return for that tax regime. Reviewing such documents helps confirm that the target appropriately filed prior tax returns and paid the required taxes. It also provides valuable information for future planning.

In some countries, the target may have reached a negotiated deal with that country's tax authorities covering how or on what income it is going to be taxed. Typically, the target will have approached the tax authority before starting operations in that place and negotiated a deal. In such an instance, tax due diligence should confirm that the tax holiday, tax exemption, or tax base that was negotiated will continue postdeal. In some jurisdictions, the tax authorities do not automatically approve the continuation of such tax arrangements when a change in the assets or

ownership of the business takes place. Therefore, reviewing every negotiated tax deal will help you comply with its terms or conditions postacquisition or determine whether the arrangement should be renegotiated.

Foreign Subsidiary Shares as Part of the Target's Assets

One of the most important due diligence issues in an asset acquisition
arises when shares of a target's foreign subsidiaries are among the assets
conveyed to the investor. The challenge is to provide appropriate due
diligence—while recognizing that these entities are scattered and of different sizes and importance—with scarce time and due diligence
resources. Here is another opportunity to employ the 80/20 rule, where
80 percent of the target's foreign operations reside in 20 percent of its
foreign subsidiaries. Absent special circumstances, the investor's review
of only those key entities usually provides sufficient comfort.

For each foreign entity chosen for review, examine the tax returns it
filed in its jurisdiction. For example, say the investor will succeed to the
target's foreign subsidiary shares and inherit the entire tax history of
each subsidiary. This puts a premium on compliance due diligence. In
addition, due diligence will focus on how the target parent's home
country taxes the receipt of dividend, interest, royalty, and other income
from sources outside its own jurisdiction. Usually the regulatory focus
is on dividends, because interest and royalties from foreign sources are
typically taxable. Nevertheless, some countries provide a total exclusion
for foreign source income, while others provide it only if certain tests
are met.

A Hong Kong entity's Hong Kong source sales, for example, are subject to Hong Kong tax, but its sales sourced outside of Hong Kong are
exempt from Hong Kong tax. Likewise, if a Dutch company owns at
least 25 percent of a non-Dutch subsidiary, a dividend paid to the Dutch
parent is exempt from Dutch tax under the Participation Exemption.
Switzerland has a 20 percent ownership threshold for its Participation
Exemption. That same dividend paid to some other parent might be
fully taxable. Moreover, countries that tax receipt of the dividends may
provide either a partial or full foreign tax credit for income or withholding taxes paid by the foreign subsidiary. That said, every country with a
foreign tax credit system has its own foreign tax credit rules. Thus, the
tax due diligence team requires members who understand the rules of

each country where an entity receives significant dividends to apply the relevant foreign tax credit rules appropriately.

Note, for example, that for many years Japan allowed foreign tax credits only on dividends from first-tier non-Japanese subsidiaries. It now allows them from the second tier. The United Kingdom allowed foreign tax credits on dividends in a way that favored putting all of the non-U.K. operating subsidiaries underneath a Dutch subsidiary to blend their effective tax rates. Unfortunately, the United Kingdom in recent years proposed revising its foreign tax credit system. If the United Kingdom adopted a per-country system, the amount of foreign tax credit the U.K. dividend recipient could claim would be limited to the U.K. tax rate, applied on a dividend-by-dividend basis, thereby increasing repatriation costs from countries with rates lower than those of the United Kingdom.

The United States has the most complex foreign tax credit system, one that currently allows deemed-paid foreign tax credits from as low as a third-tier foreign subsidiary and is scheduled to allow U.S. taxpayers to claim deemed-paid foreign tax credits from subsidiaries as low as the sixth tier. In addition, the U.S. foreign tax credit limitation calculation has a series of income groupings referred to as "baskets." Foreign tax credits are related to each type of basket. So, for example, the United States has the overall foreign source income basket, the financial services income basket, the passive income basket, and a variety of other baskets. Different types of income from different countries can blend effective foreign tax rates relating to that income within a specific basket. However, foreign tax credits in excess of the U.S. statutory rate in one basket cannot be used to offset the U.S. tax liability on income sourced to a different basket that does not bring sufficient foreign tax credits to eliminate the U.S. tax.

Likewise, exceptionally complex rules exist for the sourcing of income received by a U.S. taxpayer. Depending on the type of transaction involved, such as the sale of product, performance of a service, receipt of a royalty, or other types of income, the sourcing rule is potentially different. Thus, tax due diligence for the acquisition of non-U.S. subsidiaries that would ultimately pay dividends to a U.S. taxpayer would have as one of its highest priorities understanding the non-U.S. operations and their foreign tax credit history. The investor can then do whatever planning is possible regarding the acquisition structure and the postacquisition period to improve the tax efficiency of those operations from both a non-U.S. and U.S. tax viewpoint.

Finally, understanding the tax structure of the foreign subsidiaries can lead to other tax planning opportunities. Some of the opportunities will be covered later when we describe taxable share purchase transactions.

Transfer Pricing

If the target has assets in one country and subsidiaries in others, thorough tax due diligence will necessarily include a review of transfer pricing issues. Transfer pricing is the exchange for a measurable value of goods, services, capital, or intangibles between two related parties in different tax jurisdictions. Assume a Japanese parent licenses a patent to its Singapore manufacturing subsidiary in exchange for a sales-based royalty. Disputes arise from the tension between companies' desire to pay the lowest possible tax and governments' desire to raise revenue from companies rather than voters.

A multinational group that makes products it sells globally would typically account for as much of the total profit as is legally possible in low-tax rather than in high-tax jurisdictions. Governments are aware of such corporate behavior and routinely complain that multinationals in their country do not pay their "fair share" of tax by "artificially" shifting profits out of the country through overly aggressive transfer pricing schemes. In the example cited above, Japan would be concerned that an unusually low royalty from the Singapore manufacturing subsidiary would shift significant profits from Japan (36 percent national tax rate) to Singapore (10 percent tax rate) to generate a large (26 percent) tax rate savings. Concerns about the potential shifting of taxable profits from high- to low-tax jurisdictions has prompted many industrialized countries with tax rates above 25 percent to examine closely the tax affairs of multinationals in their countries for transfer pricing "abuses." Such tax examinations have led to transfer pricing disputes between multinationals and governments around the world. It is small wonder, then, that transfer pricing is the number-one tax examination issue worldwide.

Tax due diligence requires obtaining copies of all tax examination reports from any country in which the target has tax operations. This is especially important in obtaining an understanding of any risks posed by existing transfer pricing policies among group members. In most multi-

national transactions, there are one or more transfer pricing disputes at
the parent or subsidiary level. All of this information is important in
advising the investor on the risks involved in making the investment.
With effective due diligence, the investor's acquisition of the target's
assets can allow it to redefine the group's transfer pricing practices.

Consider the following example: U.S.-based HardwareCo, Inc., had
significant intellectual property in a product line, produced that product
in subsidiaries around the world, and decided to sell the entire product
line as an asset sale. More than 70 percent of the product line's revenues
were from non-U.S. sources. The investor's primary goal in the global
asset purchase was to acquire all, or almost all, of the target's intangible
asset rights in an international intellectual property holding company
(IPHC) in a low tax jurisdiction. The investor established a global corporate tax structure to facilitate the licensing of the intangibles to all
manufacturing operations in exchange for royalties that resulted in low
or no withholding tax. The IPHC also acquired the marketing intangibles and licensed them to its sales and distribution subsidiaries in
exchange for royalties. Overall preacquisition planning minimized
income subject to tax in high tax rate jurisdictions and maximized the
income in low tax rate jurisdictions—a tax home run.

Consider another example: In addition to the assets of FrozFood,
Inc., an investor also acquired FrozFood's foreign corporate subsidiaries
holding such operations. Here, it was not possible for the investor to
acquire all of the marketing intangibles on the acquisition date, because
the foreign subsidiaries owned them. FrozFood had also previously
owned all of the manufacturing intangibles and licensed them to foreign
subsidiaries in exchange for royalties. Unfortunately, all of those royalties were being returned to a high tax rate jurisdiction (the United
States). Once those royalties exceeded the ability of FrozFood, Inc., to
offset the excess foreign tax credits that came with its high-tax-rate
foreign subsidiary dividends, they were subject to a full U.S. tax instead
of being deferred offshore—an inefficient tax structure. During the
acquisition, a team including corporate, intellectual property, and tax law
practitioners arranged for the investor to establish a cost-sharing agreement immediately upon closing the acquisition. Although the establishment of a cost-sharing agreement would typically have the temporary
impact of increasing the effective tax rate of the overall group, this detri-

ment was offset by implementing other tax planning. The result was a gradual decline of the investor's overall global effective tax rate.

Nonfederal Tax Due Diligence in an Asset Acquisition

As we have described, almost every country imposes significant provincial, territorial, state, or local taxes. Depending on the form of the transaction, some of these taxes—such as income or franchise taxes, capital taxes, sales and use taxes, value-added taxes, property taxes, property transfer taxes, and mortgage-recording taxes—will, to a greater or lesser degree, adversely affect the investor. In an asset deal, the investor must cope with the nonfederal tax aspects of the target whose assets it is acquiring. Typically, those assets also include shares of subsidiaries outside the target's country of incorporation. As a result, it is necessary for the investor to undertake due diligence at the nonfederal level for each country in which the target has an incorporated subsidiary whose shares the investor is also acquiring.

Nonfederal income taxes. Starting at the outbound target level, some countries have relatively simple nonfederal tax systems. Consider a country with eight provinces. In this country federal taxable income is allocated to each of the separate provinces based on a formula (somewhat like Canada's) that takes into account the receipts, payroll, and property in each province. Each province then applies a tax rate to the allocated federal income for provincial income tax purposes. As long as the provincial tax rates are roughly equivalent and due diligence can determine that 100 percent of federal taxable income has been allocated to the eight provinces, due diligence at the provincial level is straightforward. However, like Canada, each province may have special incentives, credits, or tax rates that increase the provincial due diligence effort. In Japan, for example, the enterprise tax allocates federal taxable income among those prefectures in which the entity has business offices or factories. Each prefecture applies national standard tax rates that it can increase within limits. In Switzerland the federal tax rate is fairly low, and cantonal taxes are the primary taxes to take into account. Effective cantonal tax rates can be very low or as much as triple the national tax rate. In most countries the tax base for jurisdictions one step below the federal level is generally similar even if different tax rates apply.

In the United States, no single national model exists to allocate income across all states. Virtually every state that taxes income has a different method for doing so. Wyoming and Nevada have no corporate income taxes. Some states have special tax vehicles that can receive passive income without incurring significant income tax. For example, a Delaware intangible property holding company can receive dividends, interest, and royalties at no Delaware income tax cost with only a small return filing fee.

Many states use a method of apportionment to determine how much of adjusted federal taxable income to tax. Some states start with that entity's federal taxable income and make specific state adjustments, such as depreciation method adjustments or add-backs of the federal tax deduction for state income taxes. Others use a three-factor apportionment formula that compares the amount of payroll, property, and receipts in that state to the total payroll, property, and receipts everywhere else in that company. After each factor is added, the total is divided by three to determine the apportionment factor against which to multiply the adjusted federal taxable income to compute the amount of income the state may tax.

Some states, like New York, have used a double weighting to the receipts factor. Michigan and others have a single-factor formula. Each state has absolute discretion on whether to impose an income tax, whether to allow or require adjustments of federal taxable income, to determine its allocation or apportionment factors, and to impose its own tax rate. Inbound investors are justifiably flummoxed.

The nexus concept. Many inbound investors believe that the state in which they locate their U.S. headquarters or, alternatively, where they incorporate will be the state that taxes them. Both beliefs are partly correct and wholly inadequate. States tax corporations based on a concept called "nexus." Nexus requires that, for state taxation purposes, the corporation have "sufficient contact" with the state for that state to tax it.

What "sufficient contact" means varies from state to state, because each state defines its nexus differently. However, an office in a state is clearly sufficient. If a company headquartered in one state employs salespeople who live and work in another state where the company has no formal office but who have a contract to sell the company's goods in that state, the company may have sufficient nexus in both states. In some states, having a warehouse from which goods are shipped by common carrier is sufficient nexus even if the warehouse is operated by a third party. A South Carolina court held a Delaware corporation subject to tax in South Carolina because it received royalty payments from an entity in South Carolina despite having no other contacts there.

Many non-U.S. investors are surprised when they first establish U.S. operations without incorporating a U.S. subsidiary. Often, inbound investors comfortably rely on an income tax treaty between their country and the United States to shield them from U.S. federal income tax, only to find that states in which they have nexus tax their operations. This occurs because states are not parties to the U.S. government's income tax treaty network. Hence, a non-U.S. company may decide to begin U.S. operations by merely having a warehouse from which it displays and ships goods in the United States. Virtually every U.S. income tax treaty provides that such activity alone is not sufficient contact to give rise to a tax liability for the non-U.S. party. Nevertheless, if that warehouse, marketing office, subsidiary, agent, or intangible asset is located in some states, those states may attempt to tax the U.S. sales proceeds of the non-U.S. company.

Likewise, a non-U.S. party may have an office in the United States that gathers market research but does not take orders for products. Again, this may create sufficient nexus for the state to attempt to tax the entity. As a result, whether or not the non-U.S. investor establishes a U.S. subsidiary to make the investment, issues concerning state nexus will continue to arise. These uncertainties will expand with new developments. For example, typical nexus issues concerning subsidiaries, agents, or intangibles expanded with the advent of new types of entities such as limited liability partnerships (LLPs) and limited liability companies (LLCs). Likewise, technology advances involving satellites, software, and the Internet have generated new nexus issues.

From a tax due diligence viewpoint, the key issue is whether the target has filed the appropriate nonfederal income or franchise tax returns in the appropriate province, territory, state, or locality. Where all federal income is allocated to various provinces, the issue is easy to resolve. In the United States, however, with its multiple forms of state and local tax jurisdiction and different nexus rules, the issue can be very nettlesome. It is important to remember that should the target be subject to taxation, the statute of limitations begins to run only when a tax return is filed. In an asset acquisition, the non-federal due diligence should focus on making certain that the tax advisers know exactly where liability on the target's filed returns exists and identifying tax liabilities on unfiled returns.

For example, assume that a single U.S. target entity has assets in approximately twenty states, manufacturing operations in a single state, and distribution operations in forty states. Assume further that the investor has identified those states where liability or potential liability exists. As a result, the investor may decide to acquire the target's assets using a variety of investor entities to reduce state taxes. For example, it may be possible to hold all manufacturing and marketing intangibles in a Delaware IPHC, isolate the manufacturing operations in a single entity, and place other distribution operations in one or more entities. In addition, the investor may give consideration to using some LLCs as part of the acquisition structure. Thus, the planning technique is to isolate income in a low-tax state even if other operations are in states with high tax rates. Splitting up the target company's assets among two or more investor companies sometimes provides a measure of state tax planning. But in California, for example, and elsewhere, unitary tax means that all of the members of the group must be taken into account, perhaps even globally, unless the entity files a "water's-edge" election with the state of California.

Transactional taxes. Transactional taxes are another area of nonfederal due diligence. Many countries have value-added tax (VAT) systems in which each party handling a product or performing a service is required to charge a value-added tax for that portion of the product or service attributable to that party. Many non-U.S. VAT exceptions exist for exports and certain effects. The European Union is in the process of harmonizing its VAT system but has not yet reached the total agreement that it achieved on customs duties. Due diligence on VAT will provide the asset-transaction investor with the opportunity to see whether VAT is being paid and under what circumstances. This will help the investor determine its VAT responsibilities and provide it with certain postdeal planning opportunities.

In the United States, state sales and use taxes apply to transfers of goods and, in some cases, services. Every state has its own rules concerning these taxes. Some states do not tax food and clothing; others do. Some states have bulk sales rules that exempt a sale of all the assets of a business from their sales taxes. However, an asset sold in one state may move to another and become subject to the second state's use-tax provisions, typically with a credit for the sales taxes paid to the first state. It is important for the inbound investor to understand these issues on a state-by-state basis, particularly for portable assets like trucks, fleets, or rolling stock.

Although states have nexus rules for sales and use taxes, the definition of nexus for income tax purposes versus the definition of nexus for sales and use tax purposes in the same state can be different. Generally, nexus for sales and use tax requires some level of physical presence. The expansion of the Internet and federal legislation prohibiting new sales and use tax applications to Internet sales has caused states to scramble to find ways to apply nexus concepts for sales and use taxes to such transactions. In a recent state court case, a bookseller owned stores in one state and an Internet bookselling business in a separate entity. The latter had no physical presence in the state, but its bricks-and-mortar affiliate accepted returns and allowances for books purchased over the Internet. Under such circumstances, the court ruled that the Internet company had to pay sales and use taxes in that state. Similar Internet entities may trigger VAT levies, particularly since the European Union has recently attempted to apply VAT where non-EU Internet sellers ship merchandise to EU recipients or allow EU customers to download items from non-EU-based websites.

Other areas to which local due diligence may properly apply include property taxes, mortgage-recording taxes, and similar local tax issues. Here the investor should ask the due diligence team to determine the appropriate taxes. Likewise, a review of such taxes in due diligence may provide planning opportunities. In a famous case, the deal design of a $400 million real estate transaction avoided paying a real property transfer tax by putting the real estate into a separate corporation and selling the shares of the corporation rather than the real estate itself.

If members of the target's group import goods, tax due diligence should include a customs review of each relevant entity, subject to the ubiquitous 80/20 rule.

Asset Acquisition Planning Opportunities: Overview

Investors can convert their tax due diligence efforts on compliance issues into tax-saving ideas consistent with their plans for the target. These ideas can affect such items as asset valuation, structure, acquisition indebtedness, and accounting methods.

Purchase price allocation. Allocation of the purchase price among the target's assets provides the investor with both challenge and opportunity. Part of the challenge comes from the investor's desire to achieve the speediest recovery of its investment by allocating as much of the price as possible to short-lived assets. For example, this can generate revenue without taxation of the cash through tax basis in a short-term contract. However, the investor's proposed allocation of purchase price between short- and long-term assets to achieve fast cost recovery may conflict with the seller's desire to create capital gains income either exempt from tax or subject to preferential capital gains rates.

In some places, the clash between the investor's and seller's goals results in inconsistent tax positions, particularly if the acquisition document is silent or vague. In some countries, such inconsistent tax return positions are not resolved until government examination, thereby putting the taxing authority at risk. Other jurisdictions, like the United States, require that the parties either consistently report the allocation of the purchase price in their tax returns or identify the areas in which they differ. U.S. tax law further prescribes the rules by which the investor and target are to allocate the purchase price among seven classes of assets defined in the income tax regulations. These seven classes of assets range from cash as the most liquid to goodwill and going concern value as the most broad based. However, even within broad classes of assets, it is important for the investor to be as specific as possible to accelerate the time at which a tax deduction or an exclusion from income takes place.

In one case, an investor was acquiring Biotech LLC in an asset acquisition. Biotech LLC had one product on the market and five in various stages of R&D. To the extent that the investor assigned a lump sum payment price to the five projects in the R&D pipeline, no amortization or write-off of that amount could occur until the last of the projects either resulted in a marketable product or was discontinued because no product was likely to result. However, by assigning a specific value to each of the five R&D projects, it could amortize or write off the related amount as each of the separate R&D projects came to fruition or was abandoned. The same type of analysis applies when the investor acquires the assets of a target that has contracts expected to generate income over time. To achieve the optimum result, the investor should separately allocate the purchase price to each of the contracts as part of a combined due diligence effort involving the tax advisers in concert with the appraisal and valuation group.

Because many cross-border asset acquisitions involve the acquisition of shares of the target's foreign subsidiaries, it is important to understand the consequences of allocating purchase price to such shares. Different outcomes result when all foreign subsidiaries are held through a single foreign holding company versus when all foreign entities are owned directly by the target whose assets are being acquired. It is also important to determine whether the country in which the subsidiary is located allows a step-up for the basis in the assets inside the company despite the fact that its shares were acquired. (This topic is discussed in greater detail later in this chapter in the section on share acquisitions.)

Asset acquisition structuring. Due diligence will usually provide the tax due diligence team with a good idea of which tangible and intangible assets should generate the greatest value. Take particular care to review intangibles not specifically set forth on the target's balance sheet. Such a review can help determine the appropriate structure for making the acquisition. Often the simplest structure is best, such as incorporating a single entity in the target's jurisdiction to make the asset acquisition. However, asset acquisitions almost always provide opportunities to achieve a more tax-efficient result. For example, consider the possibility of having a new or existing investor subsidiary in a low-tax jurisdiction acquire the target's intangibles (a typically tax-efficient strategy whether or not the target is a high- or low-tech company).

Also consider whether hybrid entities should be used. A hybrid entity is an entity treated as a corporation by one tax jurisdiction and a partnership or branch by another. Because of this hybrid concept, the U.S. "check-the-box" rules noted earlier have become important to many investors. Assume a U.S. entity seeks to acquire the assets of one of several business lines of a French company. Suppose that the French tax rules prohibit the deduction of direct acquisition indebtedness. To reduce taxes, the U.S. investor might set up a holding company entity ("SARL") that could be treated as a corporation for local national tax purposes but as a branch for U.S. tax purposes, and designate SARL as the borrower. SARL would then form a wholly owned French subsidiary ("SA") capitalized with the funds required to make the acquisition. Assuming France allows for consolidation, the interest might be deductible. Because the holding company would be treated as a branch of the U.S. parent, so long as the interest is paid to anyone other than a member of the U.S. shareholder's consolidated tax return group, the interest paid by the SARL also would create a tax deduction on the U.S. tax return. If the debt runs directly from SARL to the U.S. shareholder, the interest would be viewed as a payment from a branch to a home office and disregarded for U.S. tax purposes.

Structure can be important where the target has a series of foreign subsidiaries that it owns directly. The investor may prefer to use a single foreign holding company with each of these entities beneath it. The holding company becomes a deferral technique or central funds facilitator without the need to repatriate funds from subsidiaries back to the parent to reuse them outside the target's country. Alternatively, in an asset acquisition with all subsidiaries held as brothers/sisters by the target, a multinational investor with a variety of business segments or subsidiaries around the world may wish to have one particular group own a target subsidiary in one such segment and a different group own a target subsidiary in another business segment. This strategy is much easier to facilitate in an asset acquisition than in a share acquisition.

Asset acquisition debt considerations. Using a combination of debt and equity to fund the acquisition can substantially increase its short- and long-term tax efficiency. Two questions arise on acquisition debt. One is whether the investor's country subjects interest deductions to limitations on the ratio of debt to equity. Many countries have a formal rule that disallows interest expense where that ratio exceeds 3:1. Germany previously allowed a 9:1 debt-to-equity ratio at a holding company level but a 3:1 debt-to-equity ratio at an operating company level. Germany has since revised the former down to 3:1. This is a typical rule of thumb outside the United States, which has no formal rule.

Whether or not a country has a formal debt-to-equity ratio for purposes of deducting interest, the country may have limits on the ability to deduct share acquisition debt or interest in general. Thus, France has denied any deduction for interest on share acquisition debt. Other countries, like Canada, have disallowed interest paid to third parties when the funds are invested outside the borrower's country of incorporation in assets that generate only passive income. Here, it might be important to have two entities make the acquisition so that the entity with the debt can acquire operating assets inside the target's country. This allows the interest deduction because the second entity would acquire the foreign subsidiaries using all equity funds. In the United States, the "earnings stripping" rules can limit the ability of a taxpayer to deduct interest when such interest is paid to a non-U.S. related party with U.S. withholding tax at less than a 30 percent rate or to a third party that is the subject of a guarantee by the non-U.S. related party.

Post-asset acquisition considerations. How can you most effectively tax plan for the surviving entity? Prior due diligence will have already disclosed all of the key tax accounting methods the target used under the laws of its jurisdiction. However, because the investor usually forms new entities to make the acquisition, it gets to choose new accounting methods, which may employ the same tax accounting method as the target did or another one. Investors should take advantage of tax-minimizing possibilities by considering deductions for R&D, LIFO versus FIFO, inflation accounting in some countries, revaluations, redefinitions of fixed assets, and a change of tax fiscal year-end.

Taxable Share Purchases

From a tax perspective, when the investor acquires the target's shares, it steps into the shoes of the target's shareholders, inheriting the target's entire tax history. This inheritance includes the current-year tax structure and contingent tax liabilities based on open tax years of all entities currently under tax examination or to be examined by the tax authorities because the statute of limitations is still open. The investor also inherits all of the target's existing accounting methods, capital cost recovery methods, and asset tax basis. Thus, the fundamental difference between an asset purchase and a share purchase is that the investor's purchase price in a share purchase typically winds up in tax basis of the target's shares rather than in its assets. The inability to write up the target's assets reduces the transaction's tax effectiveness. Acquiring shares also increases the investor's exposure to the target's prior tax return positions. The investor may or may not inherit carryover loss and credit attributes of the target, which may be subject to limitations even if inherited.

Tax Compliance

Because of the inherited character of a share acquisition, due diligence is critical for compliance determination, a process that includes confirming that all tax returns, in all jurisdictions, were accurately filed on time for all prior periods and that all required payments were made. If any taxing jurisdiction has issued within the past four years a report for the target or any member of the target's group, the tax due diligence team should review it for the issues raised, the amounts paid, or those in dispute. If the target is the subject of any ongoing tax examinations at any level for any type of tax, the due diligence team should obtain access to ongoing examination materials and get an assessment from the target or its outside advisers of the likely outcome in that examination. It is also important to obtain copies of extensions of the statute of limitations for any tax under examination. The investor should view years in which the statute of limitations has not expired as "open" years. A master list or matrix of open years by entity and by type of tax will help focus due diligence efforts. Although, as a practical matter, not every year or type of tax dispute can be thoroughly reviewed, it is a point from which the due diligence team can put the 80/20 rule to effective use.

The investor's tax due diligence team should closely scrutinize all tax cases currently at administrative appeals or in court. The very fact that the case is at administrative appeals or in court means that it could not be resolved at the agent level and that the tone of the negotiation on the disputed items already has been set. Because the likelihood of an additional payment is probably beyond the investor's ability to control, the tax due diligence team should write a strong tax indemnification clause to add to the final acquisition agreement.

Transactions and Tax Reserves

A key area for tax due diligence in a share acquisition is the target's prior history of major transactions arising from deals—major acquisitions or dispositions of assets or companies inside its group anywhere in the world. In a prior major acquisition, the target may have deducted expenses that should have been capitalized, thus creating a tax exposure for open years. Likewise, gain recognized on the prior sale of divisional assets may have been overly weighted toward items that would generate low or no tax treatment.

Reviewing the target's tax reserves is critical. There will be tax accruals for liabilities that have been incurred but not paid and reserves for matters existing in returns already filed at parent and subsidiary levels. Tax accruals will be a matter for the financial accounting due diligence team to confirm, but in some cases, that team will be able to confirm only the total amount of reserves for contingent tax issues. It is therefore the tax due diligence team's responsibility to review all reserves on contingent tax items. Given the prospect of a big tax bill down the road as a result of these items, it is unacceptable for the target to resist producing tax reserve schedules.

In all cases, have a lengthy discussion with the target's in-house and adviser tax personnel on the nature of the matters that are the subject of the reserves and the degree of exposure. Many non-U.S. jurisdictions require that the tax return conform to the statutory books. Thus, tax reserves relating to such countries typically exist outside that country either at the parent level or in consolidation. If a tax dispute results in an additional tax, the amount of prior reserve at the parent or the consolidated level equal to the additional payment is reversed and booked by the entity responsible for the tax payment during the accounting period in which the additional taxes are required to be paid. The offsetting entries should have no financial statement impact.

As in the case of asset transactions, if the target has a parent company and several foreign subsidiaries, the single most important tax examination for the investor will involve a hard look at internal transfer pricing of goods, services, capital, and intangibles among members of the related party group. This is especially important in the case of a share acquisition because, by acquiring the target's shares, the investor inherits the target's history of transfer pricing. It is thus up to the tax due diligence team to thoroughly understand the target's transfer pricing policies as well as its production, distribution, and service functions in order to appropriately evaluate such practices and the tax exposure resulting from such practices.

Consolidated Returns, Attributes, and Accounting Methods

If two or more members of the target group file a national consolidated tax return in their home jurisdiction, the cross-border investor should know how the consolidated tax rules work in that country. There may be deferred tax items between members of the consolidated tax return group, basis adjustment accounts that need to be resolved on a change of group members, intercompany transactions within a given tax jurisdiction that can affect subsequent tax liabilities, and tax attributes calculated on a consolidated rather than a separate entity basis. These include net operating losses, tax credits, and charitable contributions. This review is especially important if any target member of a consolidated tax return group worldwide is not going to be part of the overall transaction and is being transferred by the target from its existing consolidated return group. The transfer has special impact when there are existing tax-sharing or tax indemnification agreements.

Given the successor liability character of a share transaction, the team must review in great detail items like tax accounting methods for inventory, capital recovery, research and experimental expenditures, and amortization of intangible assets. Like any other aspect of due diligence, problems that emerge from this sort of review may affect the price and structure of the deal; the target's representations, warranties, indemnifications, and covenants; or the investor's conditions to closing expressed in the merger documents.

Withholding Taxes

Within a target's multinational group, withholding tax issues are doubly important. From a national tax perspective, withholding includes all payroll and social insurance obligations. Moreover, payments of income from one tax jurisdiction to another may be subject to a 25 percent to 30 percent withholding tax unless otherwise reduced by an existing tax treaty. It is important to review intragroup payments that might be subject to withholding tax for appropriate calculations, reporting, and payment to the national tax authority. Assume a U.S. subsidiary paid dividends or interest to a Dutch shareholder, but the Dutch shareholder was ineligible for the benefits of the U.S.-Netherlands Income Tax Treaty. Here, the U.S. subsidiary should have withheld a 30 percent tax under the U.S. withholding tax rules. If the target used the treaty rate of 5 percent for dividends and 0 percent on interest, it is liable to the IRS for the payment of those taxes. Exposing this problem in due diligence prepares the investor to ask for a tax indemnification or an escrow of some of the purchase price.

Employee Benefits

In share transfers, target employees are "assets" that transfer directly over to the investor, thus requiring a review of all of the target's benefit plans and compensation, welfare, and benefit practices. Due diligence should focus on the target's compliance with national rules, including highly compensated individual tests, discrimination tests, coverage tests, and other tests imposed by national tax authorities in order for such plan contributions to be deductible by the corporation and not constitute income to the individual. One proposed share acquisition was dropped within minutes of the tax due diligence team's informing investor management that the target had improperly changed actuarial assumptions for its pension plans at the end of the prior year. This change made one plan appear to be overfunded by $500,000, but it really was underfunded by $2 million.

In countries where the government runs all pension plans, payment to the government is sufficient. However, there are a variety of non-U.S. jurisdictions where employee benefit plans, particularly pension and profit-sharing plans, do not have the same strict funding and testing requirements as they do in the United States. In some countries it is sufficient that the pension plan is established by the company and is carried as a liability on the company's balance sheet. Sometimes under those circumstances, no separate arrangement with an independent trustee need be set up, nor does the plan have to be funded on a current basis. The tax due diligence team should review and report on every type of compensation, welfare, or benefit plan in each tax jurisdiction so that the investor understands the ramifications of completing the transaction given any tax exposures in the plans.

Two other areas for review include golden parachutes and share compensation plans. Golden parachutes typically benefit a few very senior members of top management and can create a significant nondeductible cost to the company. Share compensation plans may take the form of qualified stock options, nonqualified share options, thrift plans, warrants, or other forms of share compensation based on the tax rules of a given jurisdiction. Often, such plans have clauses that provide for vesting immediately before a change of the control of the target. Likewise, some target plans call for immediate vesting and cashing out of the target's shares should there be a change of control. This poses a potential contingent liability to the investor that the team should investigate early on in due diligence.

Foreign Tax Credits and Exemptions

The target may include a variety of foreign subsidiaries that may be in almost any structural format. Use the 80/20 strategy once again when considering which of the affiliates to examine. There may be exposure items appearing at, above, or below the organizational level of a subsidiary. It is important to understand how the target's country treats the receipt of income from foreign subsidiaries. As previously noted, many countries have a foreign tax credit system allowing the recipient of foreign-source income to take a credit in its country for all or part of the taxes paid by the dividend-paying foreign subsidiary. But take care, because virtually every country's foreign tax credit system is different. While the United Kingdom, France, the United States, and Japan all have foreign tax credit systems, each has its own distinct rules. In all cross-border deals it is important to understand the foreign tax credit rules in the country of each constituent party.

In the case of a U.S. investor, it will be important to develop a significant amount of data on each foreign subsidiary for future foreign tax credit planning purposes. These data should include the subsidiary's history of earnings and profits, the tax equivalent of financial statement retained earnings. It will also include the history of non-U.S. taxes previously paid, by entity and by year. Because the United States has many antideferral rules, a flowchart of intercompany transactions can help identify existing and prospective issues for U.S. and non-U.S. targets alike. With a U.S. target, it is also important to determine whether the target had income earned by a foreign subsidiary previously taxed in the United States because of the U.S. antideferral rules that has not yet been distributed. The absence of relevant information on this score can create a significant risk to the investor and endless hours postdeal to straighten things out.

If the target is a non-U.S. company with foreign subsidiaries, it is unlikely that the target will have this kind of information on hand. If the investor is also a non-U.S. party, there is no need for such information unless the target has a U.S. subsidiary that owns non-U.S. subsidiaries. But if the investor is a U.S. party and the target a non-U.S. party, it will be up to the non-U.S. tax due diligence team to try to estimate such information as best as it can given the available time.

Tax Attributes

Typically, in share acquisitions the target's tax attributes and those of its subsidiaries carry over to the investor. These include net operating losses and the carryforward of tax credits, including investment tax credits, research and development tax credits, and foreign tax credits. These carryover tax attributes may survive a change of control of the target in a share transaction. However, the United States and some other countries impose limitations on the ability to carry over such tax attributes. Some tax experts believe that an investor should pay only for the ongoing business and attach no value to carryover attributes, because of the difficulty of using them.

Structuring the Share Acquisition

During due diligence, the tax team should consider the form that the share acquisition structure should take in order to provide the investor with the best possible subsequent tax results. This is an often daunting task, because the typical share acquisition investor inherits the target's tax history and those of its subsidiaries without basis step-up. But even share acquisitions can sometimes be structured to effect tax savings. For example, the investor may wish to consider establishing an entity inside the target's country to make the acquisition, or making the acquisition from an entity outside that country. The tax decision is often a matter of choosing either the best jurisdiction from which to deduct acquisition interest or the jurisdiction that permits the filing of consolidated returns.

There may be special circumstances under the laws of either party's jurisdiction that allow for attractive results. For example, the United States has a special "Section 338" election. When a U.S. investor acquires the shares of a foreign target for cash, it may make a Section 338 election. For U.S. tax purposes only, this election treats the acquisition of the target as an acquisition of the target's assets rather than its shares. In the target's country of origin, the tax basis of the assets inside the company stays the same for local tax purposes, and there is no local tax impact. For U.S. tax purposes, the assets of the non-U.S. target are stepped up to their fair market value. In addition, the target's prior earnings history is wiped out for U.S. foreign tax credit purposes. Any retained earnings in the target are treated as "previously taxed income," thus allowing the U.S. investor to distribute such previously taxed income into the United States with no U.S. income tax consequence. Hence, unless the target's shareholders are U.S. persons, under most circumstances a U.S. investor acquiring a non-U.S. target will immediately make a Section 338 election after the acquisition.

Alternatively, a non-U.S. investor seeking to acquire for cash the shares of a U.S. subsidiary in a U.S. consolidated tax return group might discuss with the target the possibility of making a Section 338(h)(10) election, one usually made when a U.S. selling group has a consolidated net operating loss carryforward. As a result of the Section 338(h)(10) election, the target agrees to take any related gain into its consolidated tax return, where it is typically offset by any consolidated net operating loss carryforwards. As a result, the investor can step up the basis of the assets of the target for U.S. tax purposes in a share purchase under the right circumstances.

As described earlier, a "check-the-box" election by the investor can create significant tax opportunities. A non-U.S. investor seeking to acquire a U.S. target may also have good reasons for using a check-the-box structure. The investor's team also should explore the ability to deduct interest from deal debt, keeping in mind that limits imposed on such deductions will vary from country to country.

Tax-Free Exchanges

For federal tax purposes, the U.S. treats statutory mergers, some share-for-assets deals, and some share-for-share exchanges as tax-free "reorganizations." Each type of U.S. tax-free (more correctly, tax-deferred) reorganization contains specific criteria to which the non-U.S. investor must rigorously adhere to achieve tax-free reorganization status. U.S. federal income tax law attempts to achieve symmetry for both sides to a deal. Taxable transactions result in the investor's ability to achieve fair market value tax basis whether it purchased the target's shares or assets. In a U.S. tax-free reorganization, the investor takes the target's basis in the assets or shares acquired. One exception to this symmetry occurs when selling shareholders are taxable under the "boot" rules of a statutory merger or other tax-free transaction for receiving something other than voting shares.

Some countries do not tax the gain on a shareholder's sale or exchange of its company shares. Those selling shareholders may not prefer shares to cash, all other factors being equal. Only a few countries outside the United States have the concept of a tax-free exchange, although the list is growing. For example, despite some setbacks, there has been progress in European Union member countries.

A tax-free asset acquisition typically differs from a taxable asset acquisition in two ways. From a U.S. federal income tax viewpoint, the basis of the assets acquired may be a carryover from the target rather than a fair market value or step up in basis, as discussed in the case of taxable asset acquisitions. From a state and local tax viewpoint, whether state sales and use taxes apply to the acquisition may depend on the type of tax-free reorganization undertaken. For example, many states have specific sales and use tax exclusions for statutory mergers. However, when the investor does a share-for-asset deal, a state may apply its sales and use taxes, property transfer taxes, and mortgage-recording taxes to the transaction. Part of the inbound investor's due diligence demands a review of such matters on a state-by-state, tax-by-tax basis. As a result, all U.S. tax-free reorganizations should be reviewed at the state level from the viewpoint of whether the investor is acquiring assets or shares as a first step to determining what types of due diligence apply to the transaction.

Although most deals don't live or die as a result of tax issues, thoughtful and searching tax due diligence can minimize tax compliance costs and expedite future tax planning. Such efforts can save money by shifting problems from the investor to the target and by planning that can save taxes down the road—all in all an excellent return on the investor's time and funds spent in the process.

Cross-Border Tax Due Diligence

NO CHECKLIST should be followed slavishly, because what is important and what is not in a given transaction depends on the facts and circumstances of the deal: shares versus asset acquisition, the status of the target and investor, the corporate structure of each, and the transactional deal design, among many other factors. Real-world due diligence adapts to the circumstances of the transaction. Many items below may be on the checklists of other due diligence teams. Therefore, coordinate your requests for data and share data common to more than one team—it will make life dramatically easier for the target and remove a potential irritant in the parties' relationship.

CORPORATE STRUCTURE, GOVERNANCE, AND OPERATIONAL MATTERS

1. Obtain corporate structure chart(s).

2. Obtain or create corporate tax structure chart(s), to the extent different from the legal structure, e.g., hybrid entities by definition under two countries' statutes or the U.S. "check-the-box" rules.   ❑

3. Review corporate equity structure, including classes of shares, voting rights, warrants, options, or other existing equity interests or interests convertible into equity.   ❑

4. Review corporate debt structure, separating related-party debt from third-party debt by entity, and intergroup related-party debt across national boundaries.   ❑

5. Obtain target acquisitions, dispositions, and distribution history. Coordinate efforts with financial accounting due diligence team, investor management, and target on significant acquisitions, dispositions, and distributions by the target within the past three to five years.   ❑

6. If target made acquisitions within past three years, discuss with investor management the scope of review.   ❑

7. List intangible assets: Coordinate with intellectual property due diligence team, investor, and target on identification, location, legal ownership, and beneficial tax ownership (if different from legal ownership) of intangible assets, any intangible asset cost-sharing agreements, and any licenses, both in and out.   ❑

8. Obtain operational flowcharts for key production and distribution functions as well as services to external customers.   ❑

9. Obtain flowcharts for internal/external financing as well as funds flows from external operations, e.g., central treasury function, FX management, and/or operational funds flows. ❏

10. Create a chart that organizes tax obligations by level and type of tax, jurisdiction, years open, and years under examination. ❏

11. Obtain copies of all federal, provincial, territorial, state, local, and foreign tax returns by type of tax for the previous three years (or more if still subject to adjustment on examination). ❏

12. Obtain copies of all correspondence concerning significant tax matters other than examinations with any tax authority, including applications for tax holiday, credit or base status; private letter ruling, opinion of counsel, or Advance Pricing Agreement; election of special purpose tax status (e.g., in the United States S corporation or "check-the-box" entity); election or change of accounting method, especially where prior approval of tax authority was required; or any similar matter concerning the tax treatment of any material transaction involving the target. ❏

13. Review examination reports of all federal, foreign, provincial, territorial, state, and local authorities, including supporting materials, as well as tax refund claims, investigations, examination, and/or disputes for any fiscal year at any level not barred by the applicable statute of limitations. ❏

14. Create a chart of ongoing tax examinations, with level and type of tax, noting extensions of the statute of limitations and date of any report, issued together with alleged tax deficiency by year. ❏

15. Obtain copies of all proposed adjustments to income tax liabilities, together with related copies of the taxpayer's submissions at administrative, appeals, or court levels. ❏

16. Obtain copies of tax liens. ❏

PRIOR SHARE ACQUISITION OF TARGET

1. If over 50 percent of target was previously acquired within the past three years, get details of any loss carryforward limitation calculations. ❏

2. If over 50 percent of the target was previously acquired within the past three years, get details of any tax credit carryforward limitation calculations. ❏

3. If a national tax jurisdiction allowed a basis step-up in share acquisition (e.g., Section 338 election in the U.S.), get the appraisal or valuation report used to allocate tax basis to tangible, intangible, and/or real property assets. ❏

FINANCIAL STATEMENTS

1. Calculate tax reserves for accrued but unpaid taxes, coordinated with financial due diligence team.   ❏

2. Calculate tax reserves for issues on returns previously filed, or to be filed before or shortly after closing, by tax jurisdiction, entity, year, issue, and amount, separately noting balance sheet location and amount of any related accrued interest as well as whether or not recorded net of any national tax benefit.   ❏

PRIOR BUSINESS ACQUISITIONS WITHIN THE INVESTOR REVIEW PERIOD

1. For asset or share acquisitions with a Section 338(h)(10) election in open years, get copies of appraisals to compare to results for tax reporting purposes.   ❏

2. Get documentation supporting deduction or capitalization of acquisition-related expenses.   ❏

3. Review postacquisition changes of accounting methods required by operation of law, regulations, or election, as well as by permission granted from national tax authority on taxpayer request, including inventories, research and experimental expenditures, and fixed assets.   ❏

4. List postacquisition interest expense deductions for potential application of limitations based on national tax law.   ❏

5. Detail prior-acquisition tax deductible goodwill or going-concern amortization, relevant financial accounting detail, and book-tax net difference schedule.   ❏

6. Detail applicable prior-acquisition nondeductible tax goodwill by amount and entity, relevant financial accounting detail, and book-tax net difference schedule.   ❏

7. Detail closing or postacquisition tax basis step-up by operation of national law or election (e.g., U.S. Section 338 election) for non-U.S. share acquisition.   ❏

8. Get details of foreign postacquisition distribution reporting for tax exemption or foreign tax credit impact.   ❏

9. Review treatment of prior acquisition-related compensation issues, e.g., golden parachutes, options, or other possibly nondeductible payments made during open years.   ❏

10. Review treatment of prior acquisition built-in gains or losses in open years.   ❏

11. Review postacquisition changes to any cost-sharing agreement involving any of the previously acquired entities.   ❏

12. List amount and year generated of any of the target's previously inherited tax attributes and related limitations, as well as subsequent utilization in open years, including loss carryovers, credit carryovers, and tax basis of assets.   ❏
13. Obtain prior tax indemnification agreements.   ❏

PRIOR BUSINESS DISPOSITIONS WITHIN THE INVESTOR REVIEW PERIOD

1. For asset sales by any target group member in its country of incorporation, obtain details of gain or loss calculation and capital gain or ordinary income treatment.   ❏
2. For sales by any target group member of assets located outside its country of incorporation, obtain details of foreign taxability, domestic taxability, sourcing of income, and any foreign tax credit impact.   ❏
3. Obtain details of tax basis determination of property other than cash received in dispositions.   ❏
4. For share sales by any target group member of an entity within the member's country of incorporation, obtain details of the gain or loss calculation; capital gain or ordinary income treatment; and in countries allowing consolidated tax returns, treatment of intercompany transactions including deferred gains, adjusted stock basis, and/or excess loss account recognition.   ❏
5. For share sales by a target group member of any entity outside the member's country of incorporation, obtain details of the foreign income or withholding taxability, domestic taxability, sourcing of income, potential conversion of capital gain to dividend or other ordinary income, and any foreign tax credit impact.   ❏
6. Obtain details of compliance with special situations at national tax level, such as the U.S. FIRPTA rules or the Canadian Departure Tax rules.   ❏
7. Obtain documentation of any prior spin-off for compliance purposes as well as potential for aggregation with this transaction by tax authorities and related impact.   ❏

TAX ACCOUNTING ISSUES

1. Check method(s) of income recognition.   ❏
2. In an asset acquisition, review assignable revenue-generating contracts, including term, degree of revenue certainty, associated costs, and termination date with associated revenues or costs and

conditions. Coordinate with appraisal/valuation specialist. ❏

3. Check details of inventory methods, including elections of method (e.g., FIFO, LIFO). ❏

4. Check details of accounting for research and development costs, including elections, as well as coordination with special tax regimes (e.g., U.S. FSC or Possessions Corporations), R&D tax credits (e.g., those of Canada and the U.S.), and foreign tax credits in the U.S. or other countries with similar coordination. ❏

5. Check details of capital recovery for tangible assets, including capital cost allowances or depreciation, elections, and coordination with investment tax credit provisions. ❏

6. Review amortization by type of intangibles, e.g., organization costs, start-up expenditures, or acquired intangibles, separating permanent from timing adjustments. ❏

7. Check details of interest expense "paid to," "accrued but not paid to," or "guaranteed by" related parties by jurisdiction where local deductibility is subject to limitations. ❏

8. Check details of all other interest expense potentially subject to limitations on deductibility. ❏

9. Coordinate with financial accounting due diligence team to check return filing and payment for all national income, social insurance, and unemployment insurance withholding, as appropriate to each jurisdiction. ❏

10. Check other methods of accounting for income or costs, including elections. ❏

TRANSFER PRICING

1. Make descriptions of all intangible assets, specifying separate beneficial ownership, if ownership is different. ❏

2. Obtain contemporaneous documentation from any country requiring it where the target has operations and intercompany transfers. ❏

3. Obtain copies of any cost-sharing agreement(s) among corporate affiliates. ❏

4. Coordinate with any transfer pricing specialist on due diligence team. ❏

5. Integrate operational flowcharts (Corporate Structure–Number 8) and transfer pricing tax reserves (Financial Statements–Number 2) with items above for analysis of investor exposure and/or opportunity. ❏

CONTROLLED FOREIGN CORPORATIONS ("CFC" OR "ANTI-DEFERRAL" REGIMES)

Based on the CFC rules of target's country of incorporation, as well as any foreign holding company whose country of incorporation also has CFC rules:

1. Document transaction flow among members where CFC rules may create income taxable to the shareholder without any cash distribution, e.g., "tax haven" rules of some EU countries or impact of U.S. "check-the-box" rules.   ❏

2. Review supporting details for potential application of CFC rules, including amounts, treatment on relevant tax returns, and coordination with tax reserves.   ❏

3. Review details of subsequent distributions from CFC income where deferral was lost (e.g., "previously taxed income"), including income recognition or exemption, as well as foreign tax credit considerations in relevant national tax jurisdiction.   ❏

SOURCING OF INCOME

1. Review details of foreign source income by category (U.K.), by basket (U.S.), and by type of transaction or other country-relevant criteria.   ❏

2. Review details by entity of any active operating foreign source income for consideration of exposure to foreign country Permanent Establishment nexus for taxation.   ❏

3. Review details of expenses reducing foreign source income based on country criteria.   ❏

4. Review prior foreign losses deducted in domestic return with recapture/source conversion potential, e.g., sale of foreign branch assets that previously generated losses or U.S. "dual consolidated loss" rules.   ❏

5. Review details of calculation for countries that exempt foreign source income.   ❏

FOREIGN TAX CREDITS (FTC)

1. Coordinate with due diligence teams in non-U.S. jurisdictions to obtain detail of non-U.S. taxes paid that were, are, or will be claimed as foreign tax credits.   ❏

2. Obtain details of distributions that generate foreign tax credits, including, for example, U.S. post-1986 pools or individual pre-1987 layers of earnings and profits as well as related FTC chain distribution effects to third-tier affiliates or below to sixth tier.   ❏

3. Obtain details of FTC calculations under relevant country rules for all open years. ❏

4. Obtain details of undistributed earnings and foreign taxes paid under the relevant country's FTC rules. ❏

CONSOLIDATED TAX RETURNS

1. Review consolidated tax returns filed in all countries and for all target group entities. ❏

2. Review details of special consolidated items, including deferred gains, intercompany transactions, member share basis adjustments, allocation of tax liability (including copy of any tax-sharing agreement), and excess loss accounts. ❏

EMPLOYEE BENEFITS

1. List details of all companies, businesses, or employees that are, or may be, subject to Aggregated Group Rules under appropriate national tax and/or labor laws, including the following:

    A. Controlled Group of Corporations, identifying shareholders and degree of interest or value owned in each entity for both parent-subsidiary and brother-sister groups ❏

    B. Affiliated Service Groups, including A, B, and management service organizations or local non-U.S. equivalent ❏

    C. Total number of leased employees ❏

2. Review plans, programs, or other arrangements, written or oral, of aggregated group members and other related employees under local national rules (e.g., ERISA and non-ERISA). ❏

3. Review details of each qualified pension and/or profit-sharing plan of an actual or potential Aggregated Group Member or other appropriate local national grouping, including the following:

    A. Current plan document and amendments ❏

    B. Current trust agreement and amendments ❏

    C. Favorable Determination Letters from national tax authorities ❏

    D. Most recent filing application, including all attachments on any current Favorable Determination Letter from a national tax authority ❏

    E. Current Summary Plan Description ❏

    F. Most recent federal plan tax returns filed for past three plan years (and note if any plan tax return was not filed in the U.S. for any plan year beginning on or after January 1, 1988) ❏

    G. Any actuarial reports for the most recent three plan years ❏

H. Any collective bargaining agreement for single-employer
plans   ❏
I. Insurance agreements   ❏
J. Other instruments, documents, or other written instructions
under which the plan is maintained or operated   ❏
K. Nondiscrimination testing, if applicable, for last three years
for which federal plan tax returns have been filed   ❏
L. Current administrative forms and procedures (qualified
domestic relations order procedures, notices and information
for qualified joint-and-survivor annuities, etc.)   ❏
M. Any fiduciary responsibility insurance   ❏
N. Fidelity bonds   ❏
O. Funding policy statement   ❏
4. Review details of each welfare benefit plan, whether or not
formed under specific national tax or labor law (e.g., ERISA and
non-ERISA benefit plans), including any:
A. Third-party administration agreements with respect to the
plan   ❏
B. Managed care agreements   ❏
C. Preferred provider agreements   ❏
D. Board resolutions adopting plan   ❏
E. Items A, B, E, F, I, K, and L of Number 3 above   ❏
5. Review details of each multiemployer pension plan of an actual
or potential Aggregate Group Member or similar grouping under
local national law, including the following:
A. Applicable collective bargaining agreement   ❏
B. Withdrawal liability reports, if available   ❏
C. Items A, B, E, F, G, and L of Number 3 above   ❏
6. Review details of any retirement plan not established under a
country's national tax and/or labor law rules, e.g., a nonqualified
plan, including plan documents, arrangements for funding the
plan, and all related employee communications or agreements.   ❏
7. Review details of employee benefit plans not formed under specific provisions of national tax and/or labor law (e.g., non-ERISA
plans), including copies of the plan document and summary, all
employee communications, and the federal plan tax returns filed
for the last three years, if required.   ❏
8. Identify pending employee benefit investigations or examinations
being conducted by national authorities or government-related
entities (e.g., Pension Benefit Guaranty Corporation), including all
relevant correspondence.   ❏

9. Obtain documents and details of executive compensation arrangements maintained or operated for any of the following:

    A. Insured medical reimbursement plan ❏

    B. Qualified or nonqualified share option plans ❏

    C. "Top hat" plans ❏

    D. Golden parachutes ❏

    E. Any other arrangement particular to officers or senior management ❏

10. Obtain personnel policy manual for each potential or actual Aggregation Group Member or similar manual under the national rules of all jurisdictions in which the company employs persons covered by the manual's provisions. ❏

OTHER PROVINCIAL, TERRITORIAL, STATE, AND LOCAL TAX DUE DILIGENCE

1. In addition to copies of all income tax returns for the past three years and access to all other tax returns filed for the past three years, obtain or develop a separate schedule (for each type of tax below) of all jurisdictions where one or more group members had any of the following:

    A. Employees, property (including leased premises), or receipts but did not file an income tax return if the jurisdiction had an income or franchise tax ❏

    B. Sales, particularly Internet sales, to a different jurisdiction but did not file value-added tax returns for the recipient's tax jurisdiction ❏

    C. Employees, property, or sales in a particular jurisdiction by the same company but the entity did not file sales and use tax returns ❏

    D. Internet sales to a jurisdiction in which the e-business seller had no employees or property but a related party did and accepted returns of prior e-business company sales, where the e-business did not file sales and use tax returns ❏

    E. Transported purchased goods into or installed purchased equipment or parts assembled into an object or fixture for self-use or self-service support in a different jurisdiction from the one in which goods were purchased but did not file use tax returns in the jurisdiction to which taken ❏

2. Develop a schedule of relevant provincial, territorial, state, and local income or franchise tax apportionment factors, including payroll, property, and receipts among others, noting double-weighted factors where appropriate.   ❏

3. Document the debt/equity structure within each group in a country (based on a review of Corporate Structure–Number 4 above).   ❏

4. Detail the existence and function(s) of nonfederal or foreign intangible property holding company for provincial, territorial, state, and/or local tax purposes.   ❏

5. Check the use of special purpose entities, such as S corporations, LLP or LLC, and/or "check-the-box" companies in the U.S. and their impact on provincial, territorial, state, or local taxes, noting any jurisdiction and relevant type of tax where special purpose entity treatment below federal level is different (based on a review of Corporate Structure–Number 2 above).   ❏

6. Assess the impact of a Section 338/338(h)(10) election for nonfederal income tax purposes.   ❏

7. List provincial, territorial, state, and local income tax attributes acquired, including loss or credit carryovers; tax basis of assets; and limitations on their use in the specific jurisdiction, in light of the transaction form used to acquire the target.   ❏

8. Create a schedule of capital structure and application to target for capital taxes, subsidiary capital transactions, and net worth taxes.   ❏

9. Create a schedule of real property by location, including book value and accumulated depreciation and cost segregation of personal property from real property   ❏

10. Confirm real estate tax payments with accounting due diligence.   ❏

11. Detail by location real property transfer tax rates, methods, and time for filing.   ❏

12. Cross-check nonfederal income tax, sales and use tax, and property tax filings for nexus compliance issues.   ❏

13. Check use tax compliance for large out-of-jurisdiction purchases brought into different jurisdiction where target is already filing sales tax or equivalent returns, e.g., GST in Canada or property moved from Maryland to Pennsylvania.   ❏

14. Check resale certificates filed for property purchased and resold by target for sales and use tax purposes.   ❏

15. Check resale certificates from others to target for target sales where recipients claim resale exemptions from sales and use tax.   ❏

16. Check VAT filings and reconciliations supporting purchases of goods or services and revenues from sales of goods or services performed.   ❏

17. Check details of VAT exemptions claimed, e.g., exports.   ❏

18. Based on personal property locations, in an asset transfer, check each jurisdiction's application of "bulk sale" rules to the proposed asset transfer.   ❏

CONTINUOUS IMPROVEMENT

1. Discuss potential tax problems or opportunities with other due diligence teams as necessary.   ❏

2. Review all tax problems or opportunities with the investor on the investor's schedule, with the exceptions as appropriate under circumstances previously set by or agreed to with the investor   ❏

PRE-CLOSING

1. Coordinate with financial accounting due diligence team to verify all pre-closing taxes due paid to appropriate tax authorities in any country, including income, payroll, social insurance, unemployment, sales and use, VAT, capital, and property.   ❏

2. Based on prior due diligence and coordination with investor management, draft tax indemnification agreement.   ❏

7 People and Organizational Due Diligence

CYNTHIA N. WOOD, PH.D.
RICHARD C. PORTER

I N 1990, GE ACQUIRED a majority interest in Tungsram, the inventor of the tungsten filament for incandescent lights and one of the oldest, most internationally recognized companies in Hungary. But it took four years before GE fully acquired Tungsram and ultimately renamed it GE Lighting Tungsram. Even though GE is one of the world's most experienced deal makers, management was caught off guard by conditions at Tungsram and required more time than expected to assimilate the company and meet strategic objectives.

What led to this protracted period of adjustment and delay in integrating Tungsram with GE? Tungsram managers were reluctant to accept individual responsibility for problems. There was a strong tendency to blame others for problems and to say that they could not be fixed. At GE, on the other hand, managers were rewarded for individualism and self-confidence. They were expected to solve problems efficiently.

In addition, management controls and practices at Tungsram were weak by GE standards. Communication was informal. Perhaps even more important, Tungsram employees were accustomed to being taken care of from cradle to grave. Their children attended company-run schools; they lived in company-owned housing; they socialized at company-sponsored sports events; and they were accustomed to very few layoffs. At GE, however, the primary concern was providing an appropriate return to stockholders.

If even experienced deal makers like GE, which made more than two deals per week at one point, tend to overlook the powerful impact of organizational issues, it is not surprising that other less experienced companies make similar mistakes. Some companies, for example, think that financials tell everything, while others are uncomfortable with the so-called soft side of due diligence. The result in both cases is that many very promising deals fail to meet expectations altogether or require more time and resources to achieve the anticipated return on investment.

Thorough organizational due diligence can ensure that "soft" issues don't lead to hard times. An effective organizational due diligence requires understanding the deal's strategic objectives; the target's national and organizational culture; its overall structure; its communication patterns and processes; its mission, vision, and values; its people issues; and the individual functional areas of its organization.

General Considerations

Strategic Objectives

As discussed in Chapters 1 and 2, the primary consideration in preparing to conduct due diligence should be the strategic objectives of the deal. They should serve as the overall framework for the scope and depth of the due diligence effort. For example, the number of mergers and acquisitions in the food industry has increased over the past decade as companies have divested nonstrategic units and replaced them with purchases that better matched their core competencies. With an annual growth rate of nearly 2.2 percent, the domestic processed food market is mature. Consequently, manufacturers are using acquisitions and divestitures to boost growth and market share. In most cases, the deals' strategic objectives are to increase the acquirer's share of a specific market or to obtain new products with a high potential for growth.

Consider the cross-border case of Unilever. Through the 2000 purchases of Slim-Fast Foods for $2.3 billion, Ben & Jerry's for $326 million, and Best Foods for $20.3 billion, Unilever moved from fourth to second among global food manufacturers. Those purchases also gave Unilever more favorable positions in the high-growth diet foods and specialty ice cream markets. In all three cases, due diligence needed to closely examine the target's product development, sales, and marketing functions. In the case of Ben & Jerry's, which has a unique corporate culture, due diligence also had to focus on the issue of corporate cultural compatibility and the willingness of Ben & Jerry's executives to become part of a very different organizational environment.

Type of Deal

The type of deal contemplated also influences the nature of the due diligence. A company planning a joint venture with majority ownership needs very thorough due diligence, whereas a company entering into a joint venture with minority ownership might be willing to have a more hands-off relationship and, thus, conduct a much less detailed analysis.

Acquisitions with full integration and those with a more arm's-length relationship both require detailed due diligence. For acquisitions in which full integration is planned, however, the buyer should conduct a particularly thorough examination that includes extensive organizational due diligence. In addition, particular attention should be given to the full integration of information systems and work processes. Many organizations also find it useful to identify key personnel whom they wish to retain after full integration has been achieved.

When preparing to conduct M&A due diligence, one of the primary considerations shaping the focus of the analysis is whether the deal is a "merger of equals": a deal in which the two organizations involved announce that they intend to proceed as equal partners in the formation of a new entity. In such a case, the due diligence team must pay particular attention to management, personnel, and organizational issues. If an announcement is made, for example, that personnel selection will be evenhanded across organizational boundaries, but an imbalance in favor of one entity develops, then significant problems in integration may develop. Both the DaimlerChrysler/Mercedes-Benz and the Homedco Group/Abbey Healthcare deals were initially portrayed as "mergers of equals" but subsequently experienced difficulties because employees felt betrayed and many eventually left.

In an acquisition, the due diligence team must examine the types and depth of management expertise available in both organizations and provide data for determining who will be on the new management team. Information should also be collected for use in selecting a new name for the organization and properly positioning product lines in the market.

When conducting due diligence involving virtual organizations and strategic alliances, which are increasingly used to take advantage of time-sensitive marketing opportunities, particular attention should be paid to the interface of key information systems and market positioning. An example of such an alliance is the one among IBM, Motorola, AT&T, and Loral, which collaborated to develop a new PC chip.

Composition of the Organizational Due Diligence Team

Putting together an effective due diligence team requires careful attention to the specialized types of expertise required. In cross-border transactions, due diligence teams should include not only legal and financial experts but also the following:

♦ **Human resources specialists** who have a strategic view of the organizations involved.

♦ **Functional area managers** with both technical expertise and the ability to think strategically.

♦ **Individuals with knowledge of the national culture** where the deal is to take place. These individuals are especially important because it is very easy to become so engrossed in the technical minutiae of the deal that not enough attention is paid to the big picture of the environment surrounding the deal.

♦ **Representatives of the "other side"** who can identify data sources, make critical introductions, and help interpret organizational peculiarities. These individuals are critical in situations in which there is widespread organizational distrust of the due diligence process and reluctance to cooperate.

In addition to technical expertise, cultural understanding is also important when organizing the due diligence team. In Japan and Korea, for example, attorneys are seldom employed in due diligence because most Japanese business managers have some legal training and are considered qualified to conduct due diligence. In Korea, due diligence is usually conducted by only accounting firms. In Saudi Arabia, the limitations placed on female travelers may make it nearly impossible for them to accomplish much. All individuals assigned to the due diligence team should be prepared to stay until the completion of the process. The reassignment of personnel is considered a major breach of business etiquette in some countries, such as Brazil, where people and personal relationships are highly valued.

Impact of Organizational Experience and Cultural Milieu

The investor's prior experience and the facts of the proposed transaction affect the types of data that the investor collects and the data collection techniques it uses. If the organizations involved in the deal are similar and the investor has prior experience in the country and market area, a less detailed due diligence may be appropriate. If, however, the investor has little prior experience in a country or market, a more extensive due diligence is essential. GE's due diligence for the Tungsram deal, for example, failed to take into account all the implications of conducting business in a country emerging from a planned economy. Accounting and management practices were different; there were multiple sets of financial records; and company employees and consumers had very different expectations of organizational performance.

In some countries, typical so-called Anglo-Saxon due diligence processes as conducted in English-speaking countries are considered intrusive and threatening. In Russia and China, for example, there may be one set of company records for outsiders and another for insiders. There also may be legal restrictions affecting the disclosure of sensitive company information, particularly if the company is engaged in an industry deemed essential to national defense.

In Japan, Anglo-Saxon-style due diligence may be viewed as a sign of mistrust. Consequently, Japanese executives are typically reluctant to participate in a detailed disclosure until mutual trust has been established. Indeed, in Japan and many other Asian countries, the deal may be embodied in the establishment of a harmonious working relationship rather than in legal documents. This emphasis on mutual trust and long-term relationship building is also prevalent throughout Asia and Latin America.

The timing of due diligence is also affected by cultural and legal considerations. As previously discussed, in most countries in which Anglo-Saxon-style due diligence is the norm, due diligence processes are based on the concept of "buyer beware." Consequently, Western businesses generally prefer to conduct some due diligence before the formal agreement to a deal and then complete a more thorough analysis after a letter of intent has been signed. In most cases, satisfactory completion of the due diligence is a condition for closing the deal. In other countries, however, where establishing mutual trust early is paramount, due diligence is not conducted until after a deal has been concluded, and even then the process may be quite protracted. The due diligence process in Japan can involve months of negotiations with both the target company and the Japanese government. The Japanese business system emphasizes harmony and hierarchy; hence the need to build many relationships before obtaining information.

Negotiations

When beginning the due diligence process, it is important to establish what will be done, when it will be done, and who will do it. Even the seemingly straightforward development of a task list, however, is subject to cultural considerations. The investor must determine what information is absolutely essential and what would be useful to know but would not preclude a deal.

To help establish mutual trust, the investor may need to be sensitive to the cultural implications of the due diligence process and set aside certain information requests until later in the deal or even until the deal has been consummated. In planning face-to-face meetings with the target, the due diligence team should take into consideration cultural factors affecting how the meetings will be conducted. In some countries, like China, only the most senior members of the team actually communicate, and participation at meetings by subordinates is considered inappropriate. In other countries, junior members of the team deal with specific technical tasks, whereas senior members conduct top-level strategy discussions. In many Latin American and Asian countries, there should be no expectation of conducting business at the first or even the second sessions. When meeting with Russian businesspeople, the due diligence team should be prepared to present a unified front and to deal with extensive delaying tactics, including emotional outbursts. Delaying tactics are also common in discussions with Chinese businesses, but any show of emotion or loss of composure is taboo.

Throughout the negotiations, particular attention should be paid to what is being said and how it is being said. In many Asian countries and in India, for example, there is a reluctance to say *no* because it suggests a lack of harmony with others and is considered impolite. Indeed, the various words used for *yes* have many other connotations than *yes* does in the West. An Asian negotiator may seemingly say *yes* when what he means is "I understand what you said." Similarly, an Asian negotiator may say "Perhaps" or "We'll think about it" when the real intent is *no*. Consequently, Western negotiators should take care to phrase questions carefully and to probe for verification of the intent of what was said.

Key Components of Organizational Due Diligence

Organizational Performance Measures

In the current business environment of rapid change, businesses and analysts increasingly rely on nonfinancial metrics to help assess an organization's performance and prospects for the future. Although the precise measures vary from industry to industry, typical ones include customer retention, market share, innovation, and employee empowerment. In high-tech and service industries, which are heavily reliant on intangible assets, these nonfinancial metrics are especially important. Such industries tend to focus on knowledge and skills-based measures, such as employee knowledge, training and development, and knowledge transfer. Employee retention is also an important factor.

Nonfinancial metrics are an important source of information for investors and due diligence teams. Unlike financial measures, which focus on past performance, they are forward-looking. When beginning a project, the due diligence team should determine whether the target has nonfinancial performance measures such as those referred to in Robert S. Kaplan and David P. Norton's Balanced Scorecard methodology and whether such metrics have become part of the organizational culture. As shown in *Table 7.1*, typical measures can be grouped into three broad categories: those relating to customers, employees, and internal business processes. Additional information on how these performance measures relate to various components of the due diligence process is provided in later sections.

TABLE 7.1

Nonfinancial Performance Measures

Category	Metric

Customers	◆ Retention
	◆ Value proposition
	◆ Satisfaction
	◆ Market share by product/service line
	◆ Image of products and services
	◆ Understanding of customer segments within markets
	◆ Global capability
	◆ New product development
	    Efficiency
	    Cycle time

Employees	◆ Innovation
	◆ Ability to attract new employees
	◆ Ability to retain employees
	◆ Training and development related to strategic initiatives
	◆ Succession planning
	◆ Knowledge transfer processes
	◆ Skills coverage of strategic areas
	    Current
	    Provisions for the future
	◆ Performance-based compensation
	◆ Teamwork
	◆ Access to strategic information needed to do jobs

Internal Business Processes	◆ Time
	◆ Cost
	◆ Quality
	◆ Customer perceptions and satisfaction
	◆ Process documentation
	    Up-to-date
	    Interface with other processes

Cultural Factors

Culture is one of those "soft" factors that is frequently overlooked during the due diligence process. Unfortunately, this oversight may be the single most important reason for the high failure rate of cross-border deals. After a deal, employees may find that behavior that once was rewarded is no longer considered appropriate within the newly merged or aligned business culture. There are new values and norms; communication patterns change. The 1995 merger of Electronic Data Systems (EDS) and A. T. Kearney provides a classic example. EDS was a very hierarchical, technology-driven organization, while Kearney was the typical entrepreneurial, ego-driven consulting firm. After the merger, the EDS staff reportedly resented what some considered the arrogance of the Kearney consultants, while the Kearney staff was not enthusiastic about selling information technology services. There was resistance on both sides to the creation of a new culture. GE, Chrysler, Daimler-Benz, Guinness, and Unilever are other well-known organizations that have been involved in deals that delivered less than satisfactory results because of inattention to potentially conflicting cultural factors.

Culture has at least two components: national and corporate.

NATIONAL CULTURE. National culture refers to the unique norms, values, and beliefs to which a group of people generally adhere. Cultures differ, for example, in the ways they solve problems, view time, deal with the external world, and perceive themselves and others. National culture may be very strong and yet difficult to define. It is estimated that less than 15 percent of a national culture is readily observable. It is such an innate part of each individual, however, that cultural bias in favor of one's own experience can cause unexpected problems. For example, during the 1980s, Finnish companies acquired a number of factories in Sweden and sent Finnish managers to run them. Several years later, the Finnish managers were startled to discover that their Swedish employees referred to their management style as "management by cursing and swearing." The Finnish managers had erroneously assumed that 700 years of shared history meant that they also shared a common culture with Sweden.

While cultural norms are deeply embedded in the national psyches of all nations, greater exposure to other cultures through travel, television, and the Internet is causing traditional national cultural norms to shift rapidly. Young urban Chinese, for example, are becoming more individualistic and less concerned about collective values. Many Muslim nations, not just those containing minority elements sympathetic to terrorism, are concerned about creeping Westernization and the subsequent loss of traditional values and cultural norms. Consequently, the challenge for global enterprises is to determine precisely how much sensitivity to national cultural differences is required in both organizational settings and marketing campaigns.

When undertaking the analysis of national cultural factors and their implications for a deal, the due diligence team should examine the following factors that have particular significance for the success of cross-border deals:

♦ **Time.** Is time viewed as a continuum or as a resource that must be used carefully? In cultures where time is viewed as a continuum, there is little emphasis on promptness, and personal matters are considered just as important as business.

♦ **Task orientation versus relationship building.** This difference is related to a culture's perception of time. In cultures where time is viewed as a continuum, there tends to be more emphasis on relationship building. In those cultures where time is viewed as a resource, individuals tend to be more task oriented.

♦ **Free will versus fate.** In most Western cultures, individuals believe that they can control what happens to them ("Where there's a will, there's a way"); planning is considered important. In many Eastern cultures, however, a philosophy that everything is determined more by fate is more prevalent.

♦ **Leading versus following.** Western companies typically encourage employees to show initiative. In some non-Western countries (to some degree India, for example), that is not always the case. Traditional convention has fostered an environment in which Indian employees tend to do what they are told, even if they know the instructions are incorrect. They are accustomed to having their managers make all decisions and accept responsibility for everything. Consequently, many talented employees in such a culture may avoid leadership positions because of the accompanying pressure.

♦ **Reward systems.** In most Western cultures, rewards are generally linked to merit; there are performance appraisal systems, and hiring is linked to perceived ability to perform on the job. In other cultures, however, rewards and success are linked to family connections.

♦ **Face versus open feedback.** In most Western cultures, performance appraisal systems are used to provide regular feedback on job performance; public praise is frequently considered good. In other cultures, however, individual feedback and praise result in loss of face for the recipient. Feedback must be given indirectly.

CORPORATE CULTURE. Corporate culture refers to the common set of values, traditions, and beliefs that influences organizational behavior. Corporate culture provides unwritten rules that help employees know how to behave and what they must do in order to succeed. Strong corporate cultures also have the ability to influence a company's success or failure. In the current U.S. economy, for example, companies with a corporate culture emphasizing cost-effectiveness and stakeholder value are more likely to succeed than those emphasizing more unconventional values such as novelty and fun (traditions which some organizations came to herald as values in the dot-com heyday).

When undertaking the cultural component of an organizational analysis, the due diligence team should take the following factors into consideration. Taken together, these factors can be used to compile an accurate description of a company's collective personality.

♦ **Self-image.** How does the company describe itself? Is it self-confident, flamboyant, conservative, innovative? Information on a company's self-image can be found in annual reports, brochures, press releases, and interviews with employees. Sometimes an analysis reveals that a discrepancy exists between the official company image and the unofficial one perpetuated by employee interaction.

♦ **Attitude toward risk and reward.** A company's compensation system provides an excellent snapshot of its culture. Risk-taking organizations generally have high levels of compensation at risk (modest salaries and large bonuses, stock purchase and stock option plans, and the like), while conservative cultures compensate conversely. Team-oriented cultures tend to reward team rather than individual performance.

♦ **Traditions.** What does the company view as important enough to pass from one generation of managers to the next? Celebrations of success provide another way of verifying what is important to an organization and its self-image. Information on traditions and celebrations usually can be obtained from interviews and corporate publications.

♦ **Requirements for "getting ahead."** Part of the company's risk and reward philosophy may be observed in policy and procedures manuals that provide official information on how to move from one level of the organization to another. Interviews with employees will provide additional details about what actually happens.

♦ **Decision-making processes.** Are these processes structured or unstructured; quick or slow; based on consensus building or unilateral?

♦ **Communication processes.** Are they open or closed; formal or informal? (We'll discuss this later in the section on communications.) Both decision-making and communication processes provide information on the company's ability to operate effectively in a dynamic environment and its willingness to empower employees to make decisions.

♦ **Commitment to employee development and safety.** Employee development and safety practices indicate how a company views its employees. Those organizations with comprehensive development and safety programs and low accident rates have major pluses going for them. The converse is also true. A review of HR records will provide statistics on accidents and also show the emphasis on training in safe work practices. HR and departmental personnel records also will provide information on the emphasis placed on employee development.

♦ **Emphasis on people versus tasks.** In some countries, relationships with people are considered much more important than the immediate completion of scheduled tasks. In Latin American countries and Saudi Arabia, for example, it is not considered rude to interrupt scheduled meetings to deal with unexpected personal or personnel issues.

♦ **Labor relations policies and philosophy.** In Russia and other countries emerging from a long history of centrally planned economies, it is not unusual for large companies to continue to provide extensive services, such as housing, day care, and recreational activities, for employees. In Japan, until recently, employees typically joined a company after graduation and expected to remain there until retirement.

♦ **Community involvement and concern about social responsibility.** Does the company support local charities and encourage employees to become involved in their communities? Does the company have a statement of social responsibility that reflects concern for key global issues? New-employee orientation programs and HR records are both useful sources of information.

♦ **Degree of cultural diversity.** Does the workforce include both men and women of many different cultural groups? Is diversity valued and supported? Cultural diversity may be an effective indicator of an organization's ability to operate in a global market. Records of hiring practices and policies can be found in HR.

♦ **Lifestyle indicators, such as management perquisites, distinctions made between organizational levels, the working environment, and travel and entertainment practices.** These factors provide another view of what the company considers important and how it treats employees. HR records provide a valuable source of information.

♦ **Corporate values.** The company's view on its mission and vision reflects its corporate values and provides useful information on how its employees will behave under difficult circumstances.

Throughout its cultural analysis, the due diligence team must continually weigh the amount of adaptation required to demonstrate cultural sensitivity. Today's increasing emphasis on global business means that there is also more widespread familiarity with other cultures. Most global businesses have found it important for two cultures to meet halfway, not for one to dominate the other. Companies with experience in international M&A tend to recognize that the buyer and target always have much to learn from each other. These organizations view cultural differences as opportunities to improve effectiveness, not as insurmountable obstacles.

Mission, Vision, and Values

For the integration of two businesses to succeed, the resulting organization must have a clear statement of purpose and guidelines for behavior. When a "merger of equals" is anticipated, the creation of a new mission is advisable. It must incorporate the major elements of the merging entities while also reflecting the market positioning and identity of the newly created organization. When a larger organization acquires a smaller one and complete integration is not planned, then the acquired organization may be allowed to keep its mission if linkages to the acquirer are established. In this case, the target is treated as a division of the acquirer.

A company's mission and vision typically provide a statement of the company's purpose; general types of products and services offered; markets served; broad goals; general philosophy; and competitive strengths. The values statement offers guidelines for personal and organizational behavior. Typical values statements include themes such as agility, honesty, innovation, trust, and respect for others.

The due diligence team's task is to collect and analyze data concerning the target organization's mission, vision, and values and their similarity and dissimilarity to those of the buyer. The results of the due diligence analysis then can be used to identify potential cultural and values clashes that might hinder integration and the achievement of overall goals. Strongly held values, for example, can be a warning sign of potential cultural incompatibility. A case in point is suggested in the integration of U.S. Ben & Jerry's into Dutch-British Unilever since its acquisition in 2000. Will Ben & Jerry's be able to maintain its distinctive values concerning social action, which have clearly contributed to the company's success? Press reports have indicated that as a global corporation, Unilever has had some concerns about Ben & Jerry's continued funding of a number of antiglobal trade groups as part of its outreach program.

In countries where the development of mission, vision, and values statements is standard business practice, the team can use them to learn about the target company's expectations for interaction with competitors, treatment of consumers and employees, behavior during crises, and social responsibility in the local and global community. When conducting research for deals in countries with a strong traditional belief in fate or a history of central economic planning, however, the due diligence team may not find such meaningful information. Mission and vision statements may be lacking or may simply be pro forma statements with no actual impact on operations.

Mission, vision, and values statements are generally available in annual reports, new-employee orientation programs, strategic plans, and promotional materials. Some companies post mission statements in prominent locations and give copies to employees and customers. Websites are also useful sources of information.

Because of the importance of corporate mission, vision, and values statements as indicators of corporate behavior, the due diligence process should not only identify them but also determine whether they are in fact integral to the organization's culture and operating procedures. Whereas some companies do little more than treat such statements as promotional slogans, many others value their integration and make them part of their values system.

Key questions the due diligence team should ask when considering integration strategies include the following:

♦ Are the mission, vision, and values included in the new-employee orientation program?

♦ Do most employees know the mission, vision, and values?

♦ Is there a regular process for updating the mission, vision, and values?

♦ Are the values reflected in the company's performance-appraisal process?

♦ Are the values congruent with the observed corporate culture?

Even more important, the due diligence team should review past and present corporate behavior to determine whether there are discrepancies between stated values and actual behavior.

Communications Patterns and Processes

Communication processes are indicators of corporate effectiveness and efficiency. In typical Western companies, they also affect morale and public image. Johnson & Johnson, for example, is perceived as having very open communications with employees. The company credo states that "employees must feel free to make suggestions and complaints." This same emphasis on open communication extends to customers and helped the company deal with a product-tampering scare without significant loss of consumer confidence.

While communication processes are an integral part of a company's culture, they also are influenced by the surrounding national culture. The due diligence team's task is to describe the various types of communication processes present in an organization and determine whether they are effective and whether they will mesh well with the buyer's organization.

In describing organizational communications, the due diligence team should consider whether they are informal or formal, and open or guarded. Unless these tendencies are identified and their implications considered, individuals from the two companies will have difficulty working together effectively. American organizations tend to have very open, informal patterns of communications. Managers pride themselves on having an "open door" policy that encourages interaction with employees. Subordinates often feel free to speak up at meetings, even when senior company officials are present. Managers, in turn, often give very direct feedback to employees, sometimes even when others are present.

Many European companies, however, have much more formal communication patterns. More information is put in writing, and junior employees generally do not speak as freely at meetings. The precise wording of memos is considered very important. In Asian companies, negative feedback is never given in public; even in private it is often given very indirectly so that the employees do not lose face. Daimler-Benz and Chrysler, for example, experienced considerable difficulty at the beginning of their "merger of equals" because they initially discounted the importance of such disparities in communication. Employees at Chrysler were proud of their informal work environment and ability to make decisions quickly. At Daimler-Benz, bureaucracy was a well-known impediment to innovation and improved speed to market for new products.

The merger of Upjohn and Pharmacia AB of Sweden also has been troubled by differences in communication styles. In this case, the American company was accustomed to frequent and very detailed written reports, which the Swedish company resented having to prepare. Employees at Pharmacia AB expected to work in small teams that had considerable autonomy, whereas the Americans were most comfortable with a very hierarchical decision-making process.

The leadership styles of senior managers and patterns of conflict resolution should also be examined and the potential impact of cultural and personal differences noted. There were concerns that the Morgan Stanley/Dean Witter deal would experience difficulties because of the radically different leadership styles of the two CEOs. Personal chemistry is important.

In the United States, a participative leadership style is generally considered desirable. By contrast, in Indonesia, India, and Mexico, for example, leadership is more paternalistic, but the achievement of group consensus is still considered important. In Saudi Arabia, leadership is linked to lineage and social status, whereas in Singapore and other Asian countries, age and seniority are considered important for leadership. Note, however, that throughout this review of communication processes, the due diligence team should be aware that globalization is gradually lessening many of the differences in leadership styles. Many managers have been educated in other countries and have worked in a variety of national settings, thus providing them with increased familiarity with and understanding of other leadership and communication styles. In Mexico, for example (perhaps as a result of NAFTA), employees are becoming much less passive and senior managers are becoming less concerned about authority and status, thus resulting in a leadership style closer to that used in the United States.

When examining the communication processes of a target organization, the due diligence team should review both internal and external communication processes. The following tables summarize types of processes that should be analyzed and what the due diligence team should look for in each case. As the due diligence team examines each type of communication, it should constantly consider whether there are major incongruities with the buyer's communication patterns and what the potential implications may be for the deal's success.

The due diligence team should also note cultural factors that may prevent the implementation of specific types of communication processes that have proven successful in the buyer's organization but that may not be effective in the target. For example, over the strong objections of Tungsram's unions, GE followed its customary practice of installing a hotline that employees could use to anonymously report ethics violations. GE failed to understand that the hotline reminded Hungarians of the hated snitching on friends and neighbors that they were forced to participate in under the Communist regime.

As *Table 7.2* details, when examining external communication processes, the due diligence team should examine messages for consistency:

♦ Do the annual report, marketing brochures, and press releases tell essentially the same story?

♦ Is the company's image consistent?

The team also should consider interviewing key external stakeholders to provide additional input on the effectiveness of the corporate identity program and key communication processes and communication tools.

TABLE 7.2

Indicators of External Corporate Communication Processes

Type of Communication	What to Look For
Press releases	♦ Information on corporate achievements ♦ Information on key managers ♦ How the company manages problems and potentially difficult situations ♦ The company's unique "spin"
Annual report	♦ Basic financial and management information ♦ Product and market information ♦ Strategic positioning ♦ Mission, vision, and values
Brochures and other marketing materials	♦ Corporate image and its congruence with strategic intent and reputation ♦ Adherence to corporate values
Communications with suppliers	♦ Quality of supplier relations ♦ Adherence to stated corporate values
Communications with distributors	♦ Quality of distributor relations ♦ Adherence to stated corporate values
Communications with customers	♦ Guidelines for product recalls ♦ Information on product safety ♦ Contingency plan for dealing with potential product contamination during biological terrorism
Corporate identity program	♦ How the organization perceives itself and wants others to view it ♦ What the organization considers important

Throughout the examination of the target's communications, the team should note processes that are especially effective and consider how they can be used during integration. These tools appear in *Table 7.3*.

People Issues

Employees are many of a company's most important assets. In the case of companies with modest amounts of fixed assets, like advertising agen-

TABLE 7.3

Indicators of Internal Corporate Communication Processes

Type of Communication	What to Look For
Newsletters	◆ Openness of communication ◆ What is important to management and employees ◆ What is celebrated

Bulletin boards
  Traditional
  Electronic
	◆ Openness of communication, including job postings and celebration of successes
	◆ Communication of information concerning safety and legal requirements

Letters to employees	◆ How management shares information, especially very important facts ◆ General tone of communication, including informality versus formality
Management by walking around	◆ Openness of communication between managers and employees ◆ Informality versus formality of organization
Strategic and operational plans	◆ Incorporation of planning into ongoing management activities ◆ Inclusiveness and openness of planning process ◆ Use of planning to communicate critical changes in strategic direction ◆ Mission and vision

Meetings
  All hands
  Departmental
  Board
	◆ Formal versus informal
	◆ Efficient versus inefficient
	◆ Inclusive versus exclusive
	◆ Decision-making style
	◆ Conflict resolution style
	◆ Time-management style

Performance appraisal systems	◆ Linkages between strategic plan and evaluation of results on individual level ◆ Linkages between values and evaluation of individual behavior and performance

TABLE 7.3 (continued)

Type of Communication	What to Look For
	◆ Openness (Western style) of appraisal process ◆ What the company considers important
New-employee orientation programs	◆ What new employees must know to succeed ◆ How the company wants to be seen by others
Quality circles	◆ Problem-solving processes ◆ Conflict resolution techniques ◆ Emphasis on teamwork
Hot lines	◆ Processes for dealing with customer complaints ◆ Processes for dealing with employee complaints ◆ Number and types of complaints typically resolved
Employee attitude surveys	◆ Morale problems ◆ Adherence to corporate values ◆ Cohesiveness of corporate culture ◆ What employees consider important: what's working well and what needs improvement

cies or other consulting organizations, they *are* the company. Loss of key performers or those with sensitive client relationships can quickly destroy any added value anticipated from the deal. In the heady days at the end of the twentieth century, it was not unusual in the financial sector for whole teams to walk out at the time of an acquisition unless they were given very large financial incentives to stay. The due diligence team must assess the possibility of this prospect and devise a plan based on the risk. Unfortunately, within twelve to eighteen months, it is not uncommon for buyers to lose the target's senior management team and many of its most talented technical personnel. The buyer may suffer defections as well. The result is a slower rate of integration and achievement of initial goals for the deal. This loss of personnel may also result in confusion and loss of customer confidence.

The due diligence team's efforts in conducting a thorough profiling of the target's personnel can be invaluable. A comprehensive review completed early in the due diligence process enables the buyer to make a timely announcement of the members of the senior management team,

TABLE 7.4

Profiles of Key Management Personnel

Type of Information	Source	Why Important
Personal profiles Name Position Education Length of time with company Ethical issues	◆ Résumés ◆ Personnel files	◆ General background information ◆ Identification of any ethical issues that might be significant in the new organization
Unique skills and talents Technical Managerial Other potentially useful skills not related to current position	◆ Résumés ◆ Performance appraisals ◆ Interviews	◆ How can enhance effectiveness of new organization ◆ Identification of highly specialized skills critical to success of the enterprise
Inclusion in fast-track promotion programs and succession planning	◆ Personnel records	◆ Indicator of perceived value to organization
Attitude toward advancement	◆ Interviews ◆ Performance appraisals	◆ Indicator of willingness to grow and assume responsibility ◆ Willingness to relocate to overseas offices
Historical data on experience and background	◆ Résumés ◆ Personnel files ◆ Interviews	◆ General background information
Areas of responsibility In the current organization With previous employers	◆ Résumés ◆ Personnel files ◆ Interviews	◆ Identification of talents and experiences useful to new organization
Compensation history ◆ Current and previous compensation agreements ◆ Consulting agreements ◆ Golden parachutes ◆ Union or collective bargaining contracts ◆ When contracts due for renewal	◆ Personnel records	◆ Compatibility of compensation systems of both organizations

TABLE 7.4 (continued)

Type of Information	Source	Why Important
Perceived intent to remain with the company	◆ Interviews with individual and immediate supervisor	◆ Essential for staffing new organization
Compatibility of key managers with the acquiring organization	◆ Interviews	◆ Congruence of leadership styles and personal chemistry
Reputation ◆ Internal ◆ External	◆ Interviews with peers and subordinates ◆ Interviews with customers ◆ Interviews with suppliers	◆ "Soft" informationproviding additional input on leadership and management styles

personnel who will be terminated, and the plan for integrating all other staff into the new organization. As a result, fewer key personnel are likely to leave the organization, and morale is less likely to plummet.

Two primary tasks of the due diligence team, therefore, are to prepare profiles of key management personnel and to conduct a staffing analysis. *Table 7.4* summarizes the types of information typically included in management profiles. Sources for key information also are included. Although much of the required information is available in personnel and other human resources files, the due diligence team should not overlook interviews as critical sources of information. They can help clarify perceptions and provide additional details concerning leadership and management styles. Interviews are also useful in learning more about unique skills and talents, information that is especially important in companies with few tangible assets.

If the due diligence team spots unhappy target company executives, it also can be worthwhile to have a senior executive from the buyer invest some time in talking with these executives to try to raise their level of comfort with the changes that are likely to occur following the deal. There are, however, legal risks in certain countries. For example, companies acquiring in the United States must be careful not to give reassurances to only the younger members of a particular group—for example, the sales force—as this could result in a later age discrimination class lawsuit if it is only the older individuals who are let go. One president of a beverage company unfortunately stood up in an all-company meeting and said, "We are determined to build a young, dynamic workforce." These words duly came back to haunt him in court.

A staffing analysis should be conducted for each organizational unit. *Table 7.5* on the following page summarizes the key information that the due diligence team should compile.

While conducting the staffing analysis, the due diligence team should review key executives' reputations within both the organization and the business community. The team also should determine the host country's definitions of "nationals," "residents," and "nonresidents," as well as the documentation required for each group. Some countries require work documents and residency visas. Others restrict the movement of foreign nationals and do not allow them to serve on corporate boards. Many countries have restrictions on the employment of expatriates. Some countries restrict the use of expatriates in certain industries considered critical to national security or economic development. Other countries place quotas on expatriate labor and require companies to have a plan for training nationals to replace expatriates within a certain time frame.

Overall Organizational Structure

The main purpose of organizational due diligence is to examine the target's existing organizational structure and determine its implications for the future effectiveness and efficiency of the deal. In organizing the due diligence effort, the team should keep in mind whether the buyer intends to fully integrate the target into its organizational structure or maintain it as a separate entity. *Table 7.6* summarizes the types of information that should be collected, where the data generally can be found, and some general implications.

Many due diligence teams like to examine the organizational structure and the organizational culture at the same time. The structure frequently has an impact on the culture and vice versa. A company with a hierarchical structure, for example, will have a very different culture and way of doing business from one with a flat structure. The merger of two such different entities generally requires more time, planning, and ongoing employee communication to ensure that the deal meets its overall goals for performance.

TABLE 7.5

Staffing Analysis

Type of Information	Source	Why Important/Use
Level of staffing by function and location ♦ Level of staffing ♦ Current ♦ Anticipated for next 3–5 years ♦ Employee relations problems	♦ HR files ♦ Interviews	♦ Identify potential economies ♦ Identify potential strengths and weaknesses ♦ Identify legal liabilities and related expenses
Types of expertise available ♦ Management ♦ Technical ♦ Global work experience and perspective ♦ Strategic knowledge of market ♦ Unique skills or knowledge	♦ HR files ♦ Interviews with key personnel and HR executives	♦ Identify unique skills not in the buyer's organization ♦ Analyze areas of overlapping expertise
Types of expertise needed but not available ♦ Management ♦ Technical ♦ Global work experience ♦ Unique skills or knowledge	♦ HR files ♦ Interviews with key personnel and HR	♦ Identify unique skills not in the buyer's organization ♦ Identify areas of overlapping expertise
Key personnel to be retained ♦ Management ♦ Technical	♦ Analysis of all related due diligence	♦ Assist with postmerger integration and achievement of strategic objectives
Key personnel to be terminated ♦ Management ♦ Technical	♦ Analysis of all related due diligence	♦ Assist with postmerger integration and achievement of strategic objectives
Compliance with employee welfare regulations. Example: In the United States, EEOC, NLRB, ERISA, OSHA	♦ HR records	♦ Verify knowledge of new legal requirements and potential impact ♦ Identify unexpected liabilities and expenses

TABLE 7.6

Key Components in Reviewing Organizational Structure

Data Required	Source	Why Important
Overall corporate organizational structure ♦ Recent changes, acquisitions ♦ Planned changes ♦ Reporting relationships ♦ Organizational focus: products, markets, matrix ♦ Shareholder list	♦ Organization chart ♦ Articles of incorporation ♦ Bylaws ♦ Shareholder agreements ♦ Minutes of the Board of Directors	♦ Determine organizational focus: products, markets, regional, global ♦ Identify unresolved shareholder and structural issues ♦ Identify types of management control ♦ Assess potential compatibility with buyer
Responsibilities of each major functional area and key leadership positions with them ♦ Formal and informal procedures ♦ Coordination of work across functional lines ♦ Key business success measures ♦ Interface with regulatory agencies, labor groups	♦ Position descriptions ♦ Reporting relationships ♦ HR and OD (organizational development) policies ♦ IT systems and interfaces ♦ Fiscal systems and policies	♦ Determine levels of authority and responsibility ♦ Determine management controls and decision-making processes ♦ Identify ability of different organizational levels to set policy and bargain with labor
Coordination of work between functional areas ♦ Ongoing conflicts ♦ Conflict resolution processes ♦ Reporting processes and flow of routine information	♦ Interviews ♦ Employee surveys ♦ Work flow analysis ♦ Functional area and departmental missions/charters	♦ Assess labor and morale problems affecting effectiveness and efficiency ♦ Identify changes needed in evaluation and reward processes ♦ Determine need to re-engineer processes
Morale and work environment within organizational areas	♦ Organizational climate surveys ♦ Interviews	♦ Identify labor problems ♦ Review leadership issues ♦ Assess reporting and structural issues

Facilities for each functional area, including current and planned
♦ Buildings
♦ Work spaces
♦ IT systems
	♦ On-site analysis
	♦ Equipment and facilities inventories
	♦ Strategic plan
	♦ Environmental studies
		♦ Assess capacity
		   —Overcapacity
		   —Undercapacity
		♦ Identify duplication of facilities with buyer

TABLE 7.6 (continued)		
Data Required	**Source**	**Why Important**
♦ Telecommunications ♦ Plant equipment, including age and appraisal ♦ Environmental issues		♦ Review compatibility of IT and other major systems ♦ Assess age of technology and ability to meet future needs ♦ Assess environmental compliance costs
Community relations for each location	♦ Strategic plan ♦ HR records ♦ Press releases ♦ Newspaper articles ♦ Interviews with community leaders	♦ Verify corporate reputation ♦ Identify potential PR problems

Functional Areas

There is a tendency for due diligence teams to examine a target's overall organizational structure but not spend enough time analyzing the unique capabilities of each functional area. Consequently, many buyers receive unpleasant surprises after a deal is completed. One British company, for example, did not fully explore the financial and legal liabilities related to compliance with environmental regulations affecting a production facility owned by a company it acquired. The problem was much more severe than anticipated and required considerable time and expense to resolve. Another multinational company failed to understand the complexity of combining sales and marketing functions in two seemingly similar markets. A more thorough due diligence effort would have revealed key cultural and operational differences. Accounting and information systems also pose problems for the success of many mergers.

The following subsections provide guidelines for conducting thorough organizational due diligence of major functional areas.

Information systems. Information systems are becoming increasingly critical for the success of mergers, especially cross-border ones. Companies rely on rapid access to accurate, up-to-date information for decision making. Electronic mail, facsimile transmissions, electronic conferencing, and websites are now essential for conducting routine internal business, as well as interacting with customers and suppliers.

Manufacturing organizations are increasingly using e-commerce to improve supply chain management, and these mechanisms and their security are likely to become ever more important.

Information systems are both expensive and time-consuming to update; system integration is often very difficult for two organizations to achieve. Before beginning the due diligence process in this area, the team should, as stressed previously, take care to consider the initial organizational goals of the planned deal—complete integration, partial integration, or very little integration—because each requires a different level of systems integration. The team should also review the people and organizational portion of the due diligence to determine the following:

♦ Those individuals in the target organization who have unique information-systems-related expertise and who are widely respected enough to serve as champions of an integration initiative.

♦ The impact of organizational structure on potential systems integration. For example, organizations that are highly decentralized tend to have difficulty standardizing information systems.

To be effective, potential systems champions must be willing to remain with the new organization for quite some time. Other broad issues that the due diligence team should examine include the following:

♦ Whether the target values information technology

♦ How information technology can support the planned deal

♦ The extent to which IT architecture supports business strategy

♦ The types of information required for the new organization

♦ How and with whom information will be shared

♦ Requirements for system security

♦ What the information technology strategy for the new organization is

♦ The need to migrate from antiquated legacy systems to state-of-the art platforms, applications, and technologies.

Table 7.7 summarizes five major categories of information that the due diligence team should examine in detail.

Finance. Due diligence teams typically collect substantial financial information. They tend to overlook, however, the issues related to the integration of multiple financial functions. As in the case of information systems, the degree of organizational integration that the buyer and target expect to achieve is an important consideration for the due diligence team.

TABLE 7.7

Information Systems Due Diligence

Type of Information	Source	Why Important/Use
Hardware and software ◆Owned ◆Leased ◆Location ◆Use ◆Age ◆Reliability ◆Estimated capacity ◆Systems security, especially in locations where terrorist attacks are likely	◆ Information Technology (IT) department documentation ◆ Functional area records ◆ System documentation	◆ Determine whether equipment and software are obsolete ◆ Identify potential strengths and weaknesses ◆ Identify potential compatibility with equipment and software of buyer ◆ Determine implications for additional acquisitions in same market area ◆ Identify unique systems capabilities ◆ Determine if fire walls and other security measures are sufficient to withstand systems attacks
Communications capabilities and networks ◆Types of voice and data communications systems used ◆Availability of local area or wide area networks ◆Number and location of terminals and microcomputers allowing network access ◆Web-based services	◆ IT department documentation ◆ Functional area records ◆ Interviews with IT and functional personnel ◆ Interviews with support users	◆ Determine whether equipment and software are obsolete ◆ Identify potential strengths and weaknesses ◆ Assess potential compatibility with buyer's equipment and software ◆ Determine implications for additional acquisitions in same market area ◆ Identify unique systems capabilities ◆ Determine if fire walls and other security measures are sufficient to withstand systems attacks
Technical support ◆Technical documentation ◆Vendor agreements ◆Training, including plans for technical systems personnel and users ◆In-house support ◆Standards for systems development and operation	◆ IT department ◆ Interviews with IT and functional area personnel	◆ Quantify adequacy of technical support for current needs, including staffing and technical expertise ◆ Verify ability to provide support during transition ◆ Determine ability of vendors and in-house support groups to meet anticipated demand ◆ Assess potential strengths and weaknesses ◆ Identify unique capabilities

TABLE 7.7 (continued)

Type of Information	Source	Why Important/Use
Business requirements and associated systems support needed ♦ Buyer ♦ Target	♦ Strategic plans ♦ Objectives of deal	♦ Identify potential areas of common systems development and processing ♦ Determine basis for systems integration plan ♦ Identify ways to link systems integration to strategic business objectives ♦ Estimate time needed for systems integration
Compatibility of existing systems	♦ Review and analysis of all data collected and examination of strategic objectives of deal	♦ Determine need for new systems development or modification ♦ Identify potential areas of common development and processing ♦ Establish basis for systems integration plan ♦ Estimate systems integration time
Information systems organizational structure ♦ Role of CIO ♦ Reporting	♦ Corporate organization charts ♦ Job descriptions ♦ Interviews	♦ Determine if the IS function is strategically positioned ♦ Determine if the CIO plays a strategic role in the organization

Table 7.8 summarizes key finance-related items that the due diligence team should examine.

Throughout each component of the financial function due diligence, the team should keep in mind the dual needs for operating efficiency and adequate controls to support future growth. The team should also consider whether information systems are adequate to support the need for financial information.

Sales. The target's sales function can be especially important to a buyer with little expertise in the global marketplace because it allows the buyer to expand its operations while also gaining valuable expertise. For example, through a series of acquisitions, a European beverage company gained access to U.S. distribution channels in the spirits market. In such a case, the buyer generally allows the sales function to continue as a stand-alone entity; integration is not a critical initial consideration. More

TABLE 7.8

Financial Function Due Diligence

Type of Information	Source	Why Important/Use
Budgets ♦ Types ♦ Frequency ♦ Distribution ♦ Use ♦ Time Frame ♦ Integration of budgeting into daily operations ♦ Process flowcharts	♦ Finance function ♦ Other functional areas ♦ Interviews	♦ Assess adequacy and timeliness of information ♦ Create interface of budgeting and other processes ♦ Assess effectiveness and efficiency of process ♦ Determine need for adaptation of existing process or development of new one ♦ Determine how to make changes without interrupting information flow
Plans ♦ Frequency ♦ Distribution ♦ Use ♦ Time Frame ♦ Integration of budgeting into daily operations ♦ Process flowcharts	♦ Finance function ♦ Other functional areas ♦ Interviews	♦ Identify potential philosophical and cultural differences ♦ Assess adequacy and timeliness ♦ Assess effectiveness and efficiency of process ♦ Assess need for adaptation of existing process or development of new one ♦ Determine how to make changes without interrupting information flow
Operating procedures	♦ Finance function documentation ♦ Interviews	♦ Assess adequacy ♦ Facilitate integration ♦ Determine adherence to procedures ♦ Assess familiarity of personnel with procedures ♦ Determine need for development of common operating procedures ♦ Determine how to make changes without interrupting information flow
Reports ♦ Internal and external consistency ♦ Frequency ♦ Distribution ♦ Process flowcharts	♦ Finance function ♦ Interviews	♦ Identify potential financial and control issues ♦ Evaluate familiarity of personnel with reports and their purpose ♦ Quantify effectiveness and efficiency of reporting processes ♦ Determine need for development of common reports and intervals

TABLE 7.8 (continued)

Type of Information	Source	Why Important
		◆ Evaluate how to make changes without interrupting information flow
Cost processes ◆ Process flowcharts	◆ Finance function ◆ Interviews	◆ Identify potential financial and control issues ◆ Determine familiarity of personnel with processes ◆ Assess adherence to processes ◆ Evaluate effectiveness and efficiency of processes ◆ Determine need for adaptation of existing processes or development of new ones ◆ Determine how to make changes without interrupting information flow
Credit and collection processes Process flowcharts	◆ Finance function ◆ Interviews	◆ Identify potential financial and control issues ◆ Determine familiarity of personnel with processes ◆ Assess adherence to processes ◆ Evaluate effectiveness and efficiency of processes ◆ Determine need for adaptation of existing processes or development of new ones
Guidelines for disclosure of information	◆ Finance function ◆ Interviews with key managers	◆ Identify legal considerations ◆ Identify cultural implications ◆ Identify potential difficulties in integration
Staffing ◆ Current and projected levels ◆ Skills and expertise	◆ Finance function ◆ Interviews ◆ HR files ◆ Training and development plans	◆ Assess adequacy of staffing levels ◆ Assess potential for staff reduction ◆ Assess need for reinvestment in training and development ◆ Identify unique skills and expertise of strategic importance
Organizational structure ◆ Role of CFO ◆ Reporting	◆ Organization charts ◆ Job descriptions ◆ Interviews	◆ Determine degree to which target is finance-driven

TABLE 7.9

Sales Function Due Diligence

Type of Information	Source	Why Important
Sales systems and techniques ♦ Sales approaches used for each product line, catalogs, the Internet, company-owned stores, sales representatives, external distributors, etc. ♦ Sales strategies ♦ Lead development and tracking ♦ Customer calls ♦ Closing sales ♦ Order placement ♦ Complaint resolution ♦ E-commerce ♦ Compensation	♦ Sales department flowcharts ♦ Sales department policies and procedures ♦ IT department ♦ Interviews with customers ♦ Strategic plan	♦ Determine efficiency and effectiveness of processes and interaction with other processes ♦ Determine access to domestic and international markets ♦ Determine opportunities for synergy ♦ Determine types of technology used, their effectiveness, and compatibility with the buyer's technology ♦ Assess efficiency in dealing with complaints ♦ Identify E-commerce effectiveness, including security provisions ♦ Determine if compensation is competitive and compatible with buyer's program ♦ Identify differences in strategic vision that may affect postdeal success
Warehousing and shipping operation ♦ Information systems ♦ Automated systems	♦ Sales department ♦ IT department	♦ Identify adequacy of information systems to provide controls ♦ Determine ability of systems to interface with buyer's systems
Government regulations	♦ Sales department ♦ Corporate counsel	♦ Identify obstacles to achieve objectives ♦ Identify recurring problems
Customer service ♦ Resolution of complaints ♦ Number and type of complaints	♦ Sales department ♦ IT department	♦ Identify recurring problems with specific products ♦ Identify recurring problems
Key accounts ♦ Account volume ♦ Types of purchases ♦ Unique requirements ♦ Pricing sensitivity	♦ Sales department	♦ Identify sales priorities: increase market share or increase profit, etc. ♦ Set strategy for reassuring key accounts ♦ Determine how to deliver value after deal
Products and services ♦ Descriptions of products/services ♦ Descriptions of typical users	♦ Brochures and other promotional items ♦ Strategic plan ♦ Sales department	♦ Identify appropriate staffing levels ♦ Identify strengths and weaknesses of product lines

TABLE 7.9 (continued)

Type of Information	Source	Why Important
♦ Legal liabilities related to products ♦ New products being developed ♦ Government regulations	♦ Corporate counsel	♦ Identify areas of duplication with the buyer's product line ♦ Identify potential areas of synergy ♦ Identify continuing gaps in market coverage ♦ Identify potential conflicts between buyer's and target's products ♦ Identify unanticipated, costly legal issues
Forecasting techniques for each product line	♦ Sales department	♦ Identify how forecasts are used ♦ Determine accuracy of forecasts for the past 5 years ♦ Identify best practices
Staffing ♦ Current and projected needs ♦ Hiring processes ♦ Turnover ♦ Management expertise ♦ Organization structure	♦ Sales department ♦ HR	♦ Identify unusually high personnel turnover and related problems ♦ Re-affirm definition of corporate culture and treatment of people ♦ Identify "stars" who should be retained ♦ Determine the compatibility of the existing organization structure with plans for the new organization
Product knowledge of staff ♦ Knowledge ♦ Training processes	♦ Sales department ♦ Interviews with staff and customers	♦ Determine staff's product knowledge ♦ Identify best practices for transfer of product knowledge to new recruits ♦ Make plans for remedial training, if needed
Training and development ♦ Sales techniques ♦ Customer service ♦ Supervision ♦ Management ♦ Cost of training	♦ Sales department ♦ HR	♦ Identify best practices that should be preserved ♦ Identify need for remedial training ♦ Re-affirm definition of corporate culture and treatment of people: sink or swim culture, etc.

commonly, however, buyers choose to pursue full integration of the target's sales function with theirs. In both cases, the information provided by the organizational due diligence team is essential for ensuring that necessary economies of scale arc achieved and that key sales accounts are retained. *Table 7.9* summarizes critical information that this team must collect and how that information can be used.

When reviewing the staffing of the sales function, the due diligence team should also conduct a thorough analysis of the strengths and weaknesses of key managers. This analysis is especially important if the buyer intends to integrate its sales team with the target's. The analysis should include each manager's knowledge of key products, markets, and customers; relationships with key customers and reputation within the industry; ability to make accurate forecasts and achieve goals over a long period of time; ability to work across functional lines and develop positive working relationships within and outside the company; ability to hire and train potential winners for the sales team; and overall commitment to the organization's goals.

In conducting sales due diligence, the team should be especially careful to avoid culturally induced myopia when analyzing data. There can be a tendency for some due diligence team members to assume that what works in their country or company will work in the target's as well. Unfamiliar legal restrictions on product development and distribution, for example, may be overlooked, thus causing delays in achieving the deal's objectives.

Marketing. In the current atmosphere of globalization and industry consolidation, many companies are setting organization-wide marketing strategies at the corporate level but returning many other marketing functions to units closer to the markets served. Companies also are using outsourcing to increase flexibility and cost-effectiveness. This approach enhances knowledge of local needs and provides a quicker response time to changing regional/local market conditions. However, unless a buyer has a clear understanding of the strategic advantages of centralization versus decentralization for its situation prior to attempting postmerger integration, considerable time and money can be wasted. The organizational due diligence team's analysis of the target's marketing function is vital for sound decision making. In such cases, the team should focus on the similarities and differences between the markets served by the buyer and the target, as well as the potential added value of marketing support services and staffing. *Table 7.10* outlines key areas of analysis and some implications of each area.

As noted in other contexts in this chapter, the organizational due diligence team should pay particular attention to cultural issues affecting

TABLE 7.10

Marketing Function Due Diligence

Type of Information	Source	Why Important/Use
Market characteristics ♦ Maturity ♦ Seasonality of products ♦ Image and marketing campaign associated with each product line ♦ Market share by product line ♦ Impact of industry consolidation ♦ Areas of conflict in markets served ♦ Legal issues ♦ Cultural differences ♦ Strategies for each product line	♦ Marketing department —Regional —Corporate ♦ Strategic plan ♦ Interviews with key executives ♦ Advertising campaigns and other marketing materials, such as websites	♦ Determine if target company will help increase stability of buyer, e.g., because not all products are maturing at the same time or because products with year-round demand will balance those with seasonal demand ♦ Review laws affecting advertising and promotion by country; identify differences and their implications in advance ♦ Identify cultural taboos that forbid specific marketing strategies in some countries, so that marketing campaigns and standardized images can be adjusted ♦ Determine effectiveness of marketing strategies for each product line and ability to meet changing requirements ♦ Assess compatibility of buyer's and target's strategies
Support services ♦ Advertising ♦ Research ♦ Public relations ♦ Printing ♦ Publications ♦ Technology available to support marketing function	♦ Marketing department ♦ HR ♦ Interviews ♦ Samples of vendor work ♦ Samples of press releases ♦ Information technology department	♦ Assess quality and cost-effectiveness ♦ Determine if outsourcing or in-house functions would be more effective ♦ Identify areas of overlap with the buyer's marketing function ♦ Identify areas of excellence that should be used to support the new organization ♦ Identify need for new IT systems or new interfaces with the buyer's systems
Staffing ♦ Unique areas of expertise available ♦ Reputation within field ♦ Turnover ♦ Geographic location	♦ Marketing department ♦ HR	♦ Determine ability of staff expertise to support buyer's strategy ♦ Determine staffing duplication and opportunities for synergy ♦ Identify key staff to be retained and those to be terminated

global marketing and advertising strategies. As an example, France is the world's largest consumer of baby foods, including breakfast cereals. The love of cereals, however, does not extend to French adults; only 17 percent of the French eat cereal for breakfast, and most of those who do are children. Until recently, American breakfast cereal companies found that they could not assume that French adults would put milk on their cereal. Indeed, many preferred orange juice.

In Saudi Arabia, there is a large market demand for women's lingerie, but advertising it is considered unethical. In addition, most traditional Western direct marketing strategies are not widely used there because personal relationships are considered so important. Religious precepts regarding gender segregation also make some forms of direct marketing unacceptable. These same precepts mean that separate stores exist for men and women.

Legal issues can be especially complicated. Only four of fifteen EU countries do not consider advertising aimed at children harmful. Sweden and Norway forbid all advertising targeted to children under age twelve. The United Kingdom, however, has a very high level of advertising targeted to children; only the United States and Australia have more. The direct and indirect advertising of tobacco products in France is strictly prohibited. In a recent court case, for example, photos of Formula 1 cars and drivers wearing ads for tobacco products were considered indirect advertising and therefore illegal.

Manufacturing. It is not uncommon for a buyer to select a target primarily for its unique manufacturing technology or expertise. In the food manufacturing business, there have been numerous recent mergers and acquisitions driven by the search for new, more efficient manufacturing processes. A food and drinks company, for example, recently acquired a small company because it had a unique packaging technology that would work well with the buyer's products.

When conducting an analysis of manufacturing functions, the due diligence team must keep in mind the deal's overall objectives for value creation through cost reduction or expansion into new markets. The geographic location of the target's manufacturing facilities and their efficiency can be especially important as well. If the target's manufacturing facilities are in a low-cost, conveniently located area that's at low risk for terrorism or other potential dangers, then optimizing their use will be

TABLE 7.11

Manufacturing Function Due Diligence

Type of Information	Source	Why Important/Use
Facilities ♦ Capacity ♦ Potential for expansion ♦ Potential cost reductions ♦ Age and condition of equipment and technology ♦ Maintenance budgets ♦ Environmental regulations, including areas of noncompliance ♦ Health and safety regulations ♦ Product safety and government controls	♦ Strategic plan ♦ Visits to facilities ♦ Interviews with plant managers, IT department, corporate counsel	♦ Identify whether currently operating over- or undercapacity and implications for deal's objectives ♦ Identify duplicate facilities and whether they are more cost-effective than the buyer's ♦ Determine if unanticipated investment in technology upgrades is required ♦ Determine if expansion is cost-effective ♦ Quantify the cost implications of compliance with regulations
Manufacturing planning processes ♦ Production planning ♦ Materials ordering ♦ Order entry ♦ Quality control ♦ Relationship of sales forecast to production plan	♦ Interviews with plant managers and other key personnel ♦ Interviews with IT personnel	♦ Develop indicators of overall plant efficiency ♦ Determine need for unexpected investment to enhance efficiency ♦ Define type of manufacturing environment—rigid or flexible—and ability to meet buyer's needs ♦ Determine the ability of the planning and ordering functions to work together ♦ Determine need for and feasibility of interface with buyer's systems
Manufacturing operations ♦ Technology ♦ Processes ♦ Inventories —Raw materials —Work-in-process —Finished goods ♦ Setup or changeover times ♦ Move to automation	♦ Interviews with plant managers, engineers, and IT personnel ♦ Plant data, such as cycle time, cost per unit of output, first-run yield, ratio of throughput time to value-added time	♦ Identify core manufacturing competencies ♦ Determine if the technology is state-of-the-art or will require upgrading ♦ Compare plant data to industry standards to determine competitiveness ♦ Determine if interface with the buyer's systems is necessary and feasible ♦ Assess the effectiveness of process control, including automation and integration

TABLE 7.11 (continued)

Type of Information	Source	Why Important/Use
Purchasing and suppliers ◆ Just-in-time inventory ◆ Partnerships with key suppliers ◆ Process for reviewing supply base	◆ Plant records ◆ Interviews with plant managers, IT personnel, and key suppliers	◆ Quantify the effectiveness and efficiency of these functions ◆ Identify best practices, such as reduced inventories of raw materials and finished products, supplier partnerships, automated direct store delivery, and continuous replenishment, to be used company-wide
Staffing ◆ Plant managers ◆ Middle and supervisory level personnel ◆ Production workers ◆ Engineers ◆ Maintenance personnel, etc. ◆ Training ◆ Location of engineers and other key personnel	◆ HR records ◆ Interviews with plant and HR personnel ◆ Personnel and climate surveys	◆ Identify appropriate staffing levels and whether overtime is routine, thus indicating staffing and cost issues ◆ Determine if managers have the appropriate management and technical skills for their jobs ◆ Determine if there is a plan for regularly upgrading personnel skills ◆ Identify employee relations problems, such as poor working relations with collective bargaining units ◆ Determine level of employee empowerment
Improvement initiatives ◆ Training and development ◆ TQM ◆ Re-engineering ◆ Problem-solving teams	◆ Plant documents ◆ Interviews with plant personnel	◆ Evaluate organization's ability to grow and change to meet new market demands
Emergency preparedness ◆ Terrorist attacks ◆ Disaster recovery ◆ Contamination of products with biological agents	◆ Plan documents ◆ HR ◆ Corporate staff	◆ Evaluate readiness for dealing with potential terrorist attacks and natural disasters

highly desirable. A thorough analysis of the target's manufacturing function is essential for ensuring that the deal has the potential to meet the buyer's strategic objectives and that there are no hidden liabilities. *Table 7.11* details key areas that the due diligence team should examine.

As the due diligence team conducts its analysis, it should highlight actions that can be taken to reduce manufacturing costs and enhance synergy between the buyer's and target's operations. Duplicate capabilities and excess capacity should be earmarked for elimination. For example, a European food and beverage company recently purchased a manufacturer of non-cola drinks. Organizational due diligence confirmed that the target had no special expertise in manufacturing but was highly skilled in new-product development and marketing. Consequently, after the deal was completed, the buyer transferred all of the target's manufacturing operations to another division that was highly skilled in manufacturing.

The due diligence team also should carefully review relevant environmental regulations to ensure that they are understood and that all facilities are in compliance. This is especially important in cross-border deals involving the environmental regulations of several countries. A European beverage company, for example, bought manufacturing facilities in the United States only to discover that there were serious legal and financial liabilities related to water pollution. A more thorough due diligence could have identified the areas of noncompliance and their implications. (For topics relating to liability issues, see also Chapter 5.)

Human resources. Companies tend to downsize their human resources (HR) function whenever there is a consolidation, whether through merged operations or some other structural change in the organization. Some HR functions, such as management development and training, may be scaled back while others are decentralized. Current trends in globalization also often lead to increased decentralization of HR functions. Global organizations increasingly are decentralizing everything except corporate-wide policy development, HR information system development, certain company-wide training and development initiatives deemed essential for strategy implementation or culture change, and succession planning for top-level positions. The purpose of such decentralization is to more effectively attract, develop, and retain high-potential performers in all global markets, not just the home market.

The task of the organizational due diligence team is to examine the HR function of the target company and determine whether it offers value. For example:

♦ Does the department typically meet its performance objectives, and are they linked to key corporate initiatives?

♦ Does the department have its own planning process, and is it integrated into the corporate process?

TABLE 7.12

Human Resources Function Due Diligence

Type of Information	Source	Why Important/Use
Corporate policies and procedures ♦ Vacation ♦ Other types of leave ♦ Holidays ♦ Work hours ♦ Expatriate management ♦ Legal requirements ♦ Compensation and benefits ♦ Training and orientation programs ♦ Support programs for spouses and families ♦ Security ♦ Repatriation	♦ Employee handbooks ♦ HR department files ♦ Interviews to discuss application of policies	♦ Determine if policies are congruent with buyer's and if they are company-wide or adjusted to meet local practices ♦ Identify unique legal requirements by country and their impact ♦ Identify any areas of noncompliance with legal requirements
Benefits programs ♦ Health insurance ♦ Life insurance ♦ Travel insurance ♦ Disability insurance ♦ Retirement plans ♦ Profit sharing ♦ Bonuses ♦ Stock options ♦ Tuition reimbursement ♦ Computer purchase ♦ Regional benefits	♦ Plan trust documents, including amendments ♦ Interviews to discuss application of programs	♦ Identify unanticipated liabilities and unique liabilities triggered by an acquisition ♦ Determine cost of programs and effectiveness in enhancing retention ♦ Determine congruence of programs with buyer's ♦ Identify areas where adjustments will have to be made and the associated costs ♦ Identify best practices that should be considered for corporate-wide adoption
Compensation ♦ Executive ♦ Deferred ♦ Corporate guidelines ♦ Local differences	♦ Corporate and regional HR departments ♦ Interviews to discuss application of programs	♦ Identify local variances from corporate guidelines ♦ Determine if compensation is standard for industry ♦ Determine congruence with buyer's compensation
Hiring practices ♦ Corporate guidelines ♦ Local practices Succession planning process	♦ HR policies and procedures ♦ Interviews with corporate and regional managers ♦ Corporate and regional HR departments ♦ Interviews to discuss application of process	♦ Determine effectiveness of practices: cost and retention ♦ Identify potential cost savings through enhanced hiring ♦ Determine if process is in place and working ♦ Determine if information systems must interface and are compatible

TABLE 7.12 (continued)

Type of Information	Source	Why Important/Use
Training and organization development ♦ Recurring programs, such as employee orientation and managerial skills development ♦ Special strategy-linked programs, such as values and culture ♦ Leadership programs	♦ Corporate and regional HR department files ♦ Interviews with HR personnel and training program users	♦ Identify effectiveness and associated costs, especially for recurring programs ♦ Determine degree of corporate commitment to training and development ♦ Determine best practices that should be implemented corporate-wide ♦ Identify opportunities for synergy and cost savings
Performance evaluation processes ♦ Overall process flow ♦ Allowable variations based on local culture ♦ Linkage of process to corporate strategies	♦ Corporate and regional HR departments ♦ Employee handbooks ♦ Interviews with process users	♦ Identify effectiveness ♦ Quantify uses of process ♦ Identify unanticipated costs associated with process ♦ Determine if process should be maintained or buyer's process should be implemented
Human resource information systems ♦ Uses ♦ Types of systems used ♦ Level of satisfaction	♦ Interviews with HR staff and other system users ♦ Interviews with IT staff	♦ Determine ability of system to support current business strategies and to expand ♦ Determine if system should interface with the buyer's and if interface is cost-effective
Communication initiatives ♦ Hotlines ♦ Newspapers ♦ Quality circles ♦ Employee surveys ♦ Community relations	♦ HR files ♦ Interviews with HR and other functional area personnel	♦ Assess level and effectiveness of communications within the corporation ♦ Identify best practices ♦ Identify recurring issues
HR organization structure and staffing	♦ HR personnel files ♦ Interviews with HR personnel and managers from functional areas	♦ Identify the reporting relationship of the HR function ♦ Evaluate the role of HR head in developing and implementing corporate strategy ♦ Determine if staffing level is adequate ♦ Determine if individuals have appropriate types of skills and prior experience ♦ Identify individuals with unique and strategically important expertise ♦ Identify key personnel who should be retained

♦ Is the department regularly involved in the development, implementation, and evaluation of corporate strategies?

♦ What are the internal and external reputations of the department? Are they consistent?

Table 7.12 details key areas that should be reviewed and explains why they are important. As noted in the table, in our post-9/11 environment it has become imperative for the HR function of most organizations, and especially global ones, to have contingency plans in place for dealing with natural disasters, political instability, and terrorist attacks at home and abroad.

The due diligence team's examination of the HR function is often overlooked, but it is especially critical to the success of a deal. Policies and procedures, as well as company benefits, can provide considerable information that can be used to substantiate previously developed profiles of the corporate culture, overall competitiveness, and organizational effectiveness.

There are also numerous potentially hidden costs, legal liabilities, and cultural stumbling blocks associated with the HR function that should be identified before a deal is completed. The due diligence team should be aware that in certain countries there are legal requirements concerning the ascertainment of the following:

♦ Outstanding employee grievances, particularly those that have the potential to develop into class-action lawsuits

♦ Special employee deals or contracts that either must be honored or, worse, could trigger golden parachutes if a deal goes through

When considering wholesale changes to either the HR team or to employee terms and conditions of employment, the due diligence team should weigh the message that will be sent to the target's employees. In recent years, most companies have publicized the message that "our employees are our most important asset." Any goodwill that had been carefully developed could be quickly squandered by precipitous action.

The due diligence team should be especially vigilant for signs of cultural imperialism in the HR function. Warning signs include the tendency to hire few local nationals; failure to adjust job competencies to reflect local conditions; and large differences in compensation for expatriates and local nationals.

Cross-Border Organizational Due Diligence Process

GENERAL CONSIDERATIONS

1. The **strategic objectives** of the deal should serve as a framework for the due diligence process.

2. The **type of deal** also affects the level and emphasis of the due diligence.
- ❏ Acquisitions with full integration
- ❏ Acquisitions with "arm's-length" relationships
- ❏ Mergers
- ❏ Various types of strategic alliances

3. The **composition** of the due diligence team requires careful consideration of the types of specialized expertise required.
- ❏ Human resources specialist
- ❏ Functional area managers
- ❏ Individuals with knowledge of the national culture
- ❏ Legal experts
- ❏ Financial advisers
- ❏ Outside consultants
- ❏ Representatives of the target

4. The **prior experience** of the company conducting the due diligence and the **cultural milieu** affect the types of data collected and the collection techniques.
- ❏ Countries with a history of central economic planning
- ❏ Differences in American and other legal systems
- ❏ East/West values clashes

5. Negotiations: What will be done, when it will be done, and who will do it must all be established at the beginning of the due diligence process.
- ❏ Establishing trust
- ❏ Face-to-face meetings
- ❏ Cultural nuances of yes and no

6. Key components of organizational due diligence: Successful companies increasingly use nonfinancial organizational metrics to help assess an organization's performance and prospects for the future.
- ❏ Customers
  - ◆ Retention
  - ◆ Value proposition

- ◆ Satisfaction
- ◆ Market share for each product/service
- ◆ Understanding of customer segments
- ◆ Image
- ◆ Global capability
- ◆ New-product development
- ❑ Employees
  - ◆ Innovation
  - ◆ Ability to attract and retain employees
  - ◆ Strategic training and development programs
  - ◆ Succession planning
  - ◆ Knowledge transfer processes
  - ◆ Availability of strategic skills
  - ◆ Performance-based compensation programs
  - ◆ Teamwork
  - ◆ Access to strategic information needed to do job
- ❑ Internal business processes
  - ◆ Time
  - ◆ Cost
  - ◆ Quality
  - ◆ Customer satisfaction
  - ◆ Availability of process documentation

7. **Cultural factors** may be the single most important reason a deal fails.
- ❑ National culture: the unique norms, values, and beliefs of a group of people
  - ◆ View of time
  - ◆ Task orientation versus relationship building
  - ◆ Fate versus free will
  - ◆ Leading versus following
  - ◆ Reward systems
  - ◆ Indirect versus direct feedback
- ❑ Corporate culture: the common set of values, traditions, and beliefs that influence organizational behavior
  - ◆ Self-image
  - ◆ Attitude toward risk and reward
  - ◆ Traditions
  - ◆ Requirements for "getting ahead"
  - ◆ Reward systems
  - ◆ Indirect versus direct feedback

❏ Corporate culture: the common set of values, traditions, and beliefs that influence organizational behavior
- ◆ Self-image
- ◆ Attitude toward risk and reward
- ◆ Traditions
- ◆ Requirements for "getting ahead"
- ◆ Decision-making processes
- ◆ Communication processes
- ◆ Commitment to employee development and safety
- ◆ Emphasis on people versus tasks
- ◆ Labor relations policies and philosophy
- ◆ Community involvement and concern about social responsibility
- ◆ Degree of cultural diversity
- ◆ Lifestyle indicators
- ◆ Corporate values

8. Mission, vision, and values must be reflected in a clear statement of purpose and guidelines for behavior.
- ❏ Impact of deal type
- ❏ Impact of national culture
- ❏ Potential clashes of values
- ❏ Integration into corporate culture and daily operations

9. Communication processes and patterns serve as indicators of corporate effectiveness and efficiency.
- ❏ Overall considerations
  - ◆ Impact on public image
  - ◆ Influence of national culture
  - ◆ Formal versus informal processes
  - ◆ Open versus guarded
  - ◆ Leadership styles and national cultural differences
  - ◆ Patterns of conflict resolution and national cultural differences
- ❏ Internal communication processes
  - ◆ Newsletters
  - ◆ Bulletin boards: traditional and electronic
  - ◆ Letters to employees
  - ◆ Management by walking around
  - ◆ Strategic and operational plans
  - ◆ Meetings
  - ◆ Performance appraisal systems
  - ◆ New-employee orientation programs

- ♦ Quality circles
- ♦ Corporate identity program
- ♦ Hotlines
- ♦ Employee attitude surveys
- ❏ External communication processes
  - ♦ Press releases
  - ♦ Annual report
  - ♦ Brochures and other marketing materials
  - ♦ Communications with suppliers and distributors

10. People issues: Employees are some of a company's most important assets. Postdeal loss of employees leads to reductions in the added value anticipated for the deal.

- ❏ Key tasks: early identification of senior management team, personnel to be terminated, and those to be retained
- ❏ Profiles of key management personnel
  - ♦ Basic information: name, position, education, time with the company, ethical issues
  - ♦ Unique skills and talents
  - ♦ Inclusion in fast-track programs and succession planning
  - ♦ Attitude toward advancement
  - ♦ Historical data on experience
  - ♦ Areas of responsibility
  - ♦ Compensation history
  - ♦ Perceived intent to remain with the company
  - ♦ Compatibility with investor's key managers
  - ♦ Internal and external reputation
- ❏ Staffing analysis
  - ♦ Level of staffing by function and location
  - ♦ Types of expertise available
  - ♦ Types of expertise needed but not available
  - ♦ Key personnel to be retained
  - ♦ Key personnel to be terminated
  - ♦ Compliance with employee welfare regulations
- ❏ Legal issues affecting staffing
  - ♦ Host country definition of nationals, residents, and nonresidents
  - ♦ Documentation requirements
  - ♦ Restrictions on board membership
  - ♦ Restricted use of expatriates in specific industries
  - ♦ Quotas for use of expatriates

11. Overall organizational structure: What are the implications for the future effectiveness and efficiency of the deal?
- ❏ Impact of buyer's intent to fully integrate organizations or keep them separate
- ❏ Organization structure
  - ◆ Recent and planned changes
  - ◆ Reporting relationships
  - ◆ Organizational focus
- ❏ Responsibilities of major functional areas and key leadership positions
  - ◆ Formal and informal procedures
  - ◆ Coordination of work across functional lines
  - ◆ Key measures of business success
  - ◆ Interface with regulatory agencies, labor groups
- ❏ Coordination of work between and among functional areas
- ❏ Morale and work environment
- ❏ Facilities for each functional area
  - ◆ Buildings
  - ◆ Work spaces
  - ◆ IT systems
  - ◆ Telecommunications
  - ◆ Equipment, including age and appraisal
  - ◆ Environmental issues, especially noncompliance
- ❏ Community relations for each location

12. Individual functional areas
- ❏ Information systems
  - ◆ Impact of deal's strategic objectives on systems: full integration, partial integration, little integration
  - ◆ Hardware and software inventory
  - ◆ Communications capabilities and networks
  - ◆ Technical support capabilities
  - ◆ Relationship of business requirements and systems support
  - ◆ Compatibility of existing systems with those of the buyer
- ❏ Finance
  - ◆ Impact of deal's strategic objectives on systems: full integration, partial integration, little integration
  - ◆ Budgets: types, frequency, distribution, use, time frame
  - ◆ Plans: types, frequency, distribution, use, time frame
  - ◆ Operating procedures: effectiveness and adequacy
  - ◆ Reports: internal and external

- ◆ Cost processes
- ◆ Credit and collection processes
- ◆ Information disclosure
- ◆ Staffing levels
- ❏ Sales: This is an especially important functional area for companies with little expertise in the global marketplace; due diligence should avoid national cultural myopia and describe the target's products, services, staffing, and costs. The review should consider the following:
  - ◆ Users of target's products
  - ◆ Legal liabilities resulting from those products
  - ◆ New products in the pipeline
  - ◆ Government regulations by product and national market
  - ◆ Forecasting techniques used and their effectiveness
  - ◆ Current and projected staffing needs
  - ◆ Strengths and weaknesses of current staff
  - ◆ Hiring processes
  - ◆ Turnover
  - ◆ Management expertise
  - ◆ Organizational structure
  - ◆ Product knowledge
  - ◆ Training and development initiatives (types and cost)
  - ◆ Sales systems and techniques
  - ◆ Sales approaches and strategies for each product line
  - ◆ E-commerce ventures
  - ◆ Compensation
  - ◆ Warehousing and shipping operations
  - ◆ Automated and information systems
  - ◆ Government regulations
  - ◆ Customer service
  - ◆ Key accounts

13. Marketing: There is a trend to decentralize many marketing functions to enhance reaction to local market conditions.
- ❏ Overall market characteristics
  - ◆ Maturity and market share
  - ◆ Seasonality of products
  - ◆ Marketing campaigns for each product line
  - ◆ Areas of conflict with markets served by the buyer
  - ◆ Potential legal issues affecting marketing initiatives

- ◆ Cultural differences affecting marketing strategies and their implementation
- ◆ Potential impact of industry consolidation
- ❏ Marketing support services: internal or outsourced
    - ◆ Advertising
    - ◆ Research
    - ◆ Public relations
    - ◆ Printing
    - ◆ Publications
    - ◆ Adequacy of technology to support overall marketing function
- ❏ Staffing
    - ◆ Adequacy
    - ◆ Unique expertise
    - ◆ Reputation in company and in the industry
    - ◆ Turnover

14. Manufacturing: Discover how to reduce costs and enhance synergy between the two organizations.
- ❏ Facilities inventory
    - ◆ Capacity
    - ◆ Age and condition
    - ◆ Maintenance budgets
    - ◆ Environmental regulations and compliance with them
- ❏ Manufacturing planning processes
    - ◆ Production planning
    - ◆ Materials planning
    - ◆ Order entry
    - ◆ Quality control
- ❏ Manufacturing operations
    - ◆ Technology
    - ◆ Processes
    - ◆ Inventories
    - ◆ Setup or changeover times
- ❏ Purchasing and suppliers
    - ◆ Just-in-time inventories
    - ◆ Strategic partnerships
    - ◆ Review processes for supplier base
- ❏ Staffing
    - ◆ Plant managers
    - ◆ Middle and supervisory management

♦ Equipment operations
♦ Training
♦ Location of engineers and other key personnel within the plant

15. Human resources: The role and organization of human resources is changing to enhance flexibility within the global market.
❏ Key questions for assessing the overall effectiveness of the HR function
♦ Accomplishment of performance objectives
♦ Linkage of performance objectives to key corporate initiatives
♦ Involvement in company-wide planning process
♦ Involvement in development, implementation, and evaluation of corporate strategies
♦ Internal and external reputation of HR
❏ Specific areas for review
♦ Corporate policies and procedures
♦ Benefits programs
♦ Compensation
♦ Hiring practices
♦ Succession planning process
♦ Training and organization development
♦ Performance evaluation processes
♦ Human resource information systems
♦ Communication initiatives
♦ Staffing

8 | Due Diligence Investigative Technology and Know-How

JAMES B. MINTZ

EVEN AFTER THE LEGAL, tax, accounting, and operating professionals exhaust conventional due diligence techniques, unresolved issues often remain. These professionals may need new techniques to dig deeper.

Advances in investigative technology in recent years—including the Internet and dial-up databases in many countries—have made available powerful resources that can assist those responsible for legal, financial, tax, operational, and human resource due diligence. These new ways of gathering information worldwide can be helpful regardless of the border being crossed, the type of transaction, or which party is doing the investigating.

How Investors Use Private Investigators

It will come as no surprise that as part of due diligence, investors routinely hire private investigators to check the backgrounds of a target company's executives before a transaction. But it may be less well known that investigators also help due diligence professionals resolve issues related to a company's business practices. Consider the following: Several years ago, the James Mintz Group surveyed the top ten investment banks on their use of outside investigative firms in the due diligence process. Eight responded and indicated that investigators working with their due diligence teams had uncovered executives' ties to organized crime, criminal charges, and other useful information.

But the surveyed investment banks also used outside investigators to uncover operational problems, such as whether a company was making inflated product claims. In another instance, a banker said his investigator found a company "had entered into a contract that was designed to inflate numbers to create the impression of materiality."

How Investigative Technology Can Help

The following examples show how investigative technology can provide information to help due diligence professionals resolve tough questions, and how a more traditional investigative step—quiet interviewing—is often the necessary follow-up to electronically accessed information.

The International Public Record

New technology has begun to put at the fingertips of due diligence investigators, in domestic and especially cross-border deals, the very thing that they most need: access to the international public record on the companies and executives with whom they are negotiating. That record includes regulatory filings, criminal convictions, civil litigation, bankruptcy filings, news articles, and reports by nongovernmental agencies.

Any computer plugged into a phone line can access the gigantic storerooms of public-record information that have become available in recent years around the world.

Nexis searches have become standard operating procedure for many due diligence professionals. But although Nexis (the news side of Reed Elsevier's LexisNexis Group) shows them how easy and fast it is to enter this new universe of computerized public information, less well-known databases permit them to go much further, pursuing due diligence concerns in a variety of valuable directions.

Out there is everything from Swiss corporate records to the name of the golf club to which a Japanese executive belongs; from enforcement proceedings of the Budapest Stock Exchange to the thousand people sanctioned for corruption by a commission in India; from a Swedish business association's warning list of companies engaged in fraudulent practices to a database on international shipping fraud.

The new technology shuffles together significant parts of the public record more comprehensively and conveniently in the United States than in most other countries. For example, several databases now can be used to check whether a person or company has been bankrupt anywhere in the United States. (Until these databases came along, one had to figure out each federal jurisdiction in which a subject had lived and then search each of those bankruptcy indexes in person.) A number of other countries, however, now have their own useful data services, such as Italy's Alidata, which can be consulted, for example, to check for past Italian litigation involving an individual or company.

In some countries, regulatory and other data either are unavailable or appear unreliable. In those cases, you should look for other information to bridge the gaps. So, for example, in Russia you might turn to the most reliable archive of news articles in the country, which goes back to 1991. Similarly, there is a Caribbean news service, and a service that has compiled information on lawsuits in Mexico City. In other countries, recent leaps in transparency have brought the availability, on obscure but public websites, of local enforcement actions. For example, you can download the several dozen actions documented by the Czech Securities Commission, which began operation in 1998.

The new technology provides access to other information helpful to due diligence professionals that is truly international in scope. For example, there is now a website (discussed below) that allows you to search the indexes of hundreds of investigative books. Technology thus begins to fill another hole in what amounts to the international public record.

The Hometown Newspaper

A critical rule in cross-border due diligence is: Never do consequential business with someone until you have checked the archives of his or her hometown newspaper, wherever in the world home is.

The investigator's road map for finding that Montreal's *Gazette* is on the Dialog database, and that the *South China Morning Post* is available on the Factiva service back to 1984, is called *Fulltext Sources Online*. This book also may help you decide which services to subscribe to. Due diligence investigators should consider subscribing to specialized Nexis-like news databases pertinent to the industry or location in question because the data in most publications' websites is too limited to be useful in checking a company's or individual's background.

If you subscribe to any computerized databases, the people in your office who do the searching should have an investigative mentality and be thoroughly trained. For example, even the best-known databases, such as Dun & Bradstreet's reports about companies, contain valuable tricks that due diligence searchers need to know. Here's one: Re-query the D&B database using the telephone number, instead of the name, of the company in question. This extra step can reveal undisclosed companies sharing that phone line.

Even today, not everything is online, and some investigative field work is often necessary. Small newspapers usually do not allow outsiders to have access to their morgues, but local libraries often keep clippings of people and businesses in the area. Go back ten to twenty years, if possible, and get access to the most freewheeling press outlets, such as *Private Eye* in London. Outside the world's business centers, where fewer newspapers are online, turn to local clipping services. In one cross-border transaction, for example, investigators sought information about whether the target was involved in an Argentine scandal. Nexis and other news databases turned up nothing, so the investigators called a clipping service in Argentina, which found several relevant stories.

One must dig deep for articles not only by relevant city but by relevant industry. Trade-journal searches are a good way to develop a record of someone's career and at the same time verify a résumé. Many of these (examples include publications such as *Progressive Grocer, Singapore's Computer Times,* and *Australian CPA*) are accessible online. In one instance, an American investor knew even before the translator arrived that a Brazilian business journal might have bad news about his target— the word "Watergate" repeatedly jumped out from the otherwise-Portuguese text.

Keep in mind, too, that the print media are only part of what's out there. With their increasing popularity, investigative television news shows can be an important addition to the standard news-clip search. Check the broadcast records using Burrelle's Information Services, which transcribes and indexes television and radio shows, to search for who said what on any topic. Burrelle's includes shows such as *60 Minutes.*

The Backgrounds of Key Executives

Prime Questions Investigators Must Explore

Has the executive ever been in trouble? Investigators are routinely asked to check whether a business executive has a criminal record. There is no U.S.-wide method to search for criminal charges, much less an internationally comprehensive way, so the first investigative task is figuring out in what jurisdictions a person has lived or worked in the past.

Due diligence investigators like to begin with databases that show a person's past and present addresses, date of birth, and possible aliases, confirming a person's identity along the way. Our firm has investigated many people who had never lived where our clients thought they did—some lived under other names; one woman even turned out to be a man!

Before these databases came along several years ago, uncovering a person's identity was far more time-consuming. You could hire a private eye to knock on neighbors' doors, or write to the local post office, or visit the capital of the state or country where you thought the person lived and ask the Department of Motor Vehicles or its foreign equivalent for data. Then you could have pored through phone books, city by city or country by country.

Now, however, databases such as AutoTrackXP shuffle together phone directories and real estate records with driver's license records. The latter include physical descriptions, which are particularly useful in identifying people with common names—from among all the Joseph Browns, you can pick out the one who is six feet tall and wears glasses. Other databases may duplicate what AutoTrackXP has, but AutoTrackXP particularly endears itself to investigators, for example, by preserving historical information such as out-of-date Secretary of State records on companies' registered agents.

Only after you have fully identified a person can you effectively uncover possible criminal charges that may be pending against him or her. For example, in July 2001, the press reported that a man was arrested soon after he had made a deal to buy a Manhattan restaurant. The seller of the restaurant had believed the would-be buyer's claim that he was based in California, but routine searches would have shown that he had a criminal record in New York.

In this example, a New Yorker allegedly got conned by another New Yorker, but distance and cultural differences make it even harder to see behind the masks that con artists wear. In one instance, some European investors were so thoroughly deceived by the false identity put across by a New York money manager that they continued to trust the money manager even after new criminal fraud charges had been lodged against him.

Have executives been truthful about their backgrounds? An Internet company's search for a new CEO was cited in a recent *Business Week* article for "bypassing the painstaking due diligence that averts hiring disasters." An electronic search might have stopped the CEO's candidacy in its tracks, because it would have uncovered that he made false statements about his age (according to the article), making six years of his life disappear. Then there was the executive who claimed to have credentials and expertise on population migration. A database search confirmed he was an expert on migration—but of birds, not people!

International businessmen may present themselves as local to a country where they have a clean record, covering up their messy footprints across borders. An investigative firm faced liability some years ago for conducting an entire background check in one jurisdiction but missing the subject's bad record literally across the river.

Sometimes, the *absence* of online information is a red flag of something that requires further checking. For example, a private U.S. company wanted to check out a purportedly wealthy U.K. deal maker who had expressed interest in making an acquisition. Having only a few details about the subject, investigators were still surprised that they could find no references to him in online databases. Here, the salient information they derived online was that there was *no* online information. They found out why when they followed up this electronic "dry hole" with a visit to a town where the supposedly rich investor had once lived. There they found a business creditor who told them that their subject had changed his name two years earlier. Sure enough, the original name quickly turned up on their databases: The subject turned out to be an individual who owed several parties substantial amounts of money and who had severe financial problems.

Recently, a high-profile senior executive was in the news when it was belatedly discovered that he had neglected to tell his most recent employer about some early, controversial episodes at jobs that he left off his résumé. One of those missing jobs could have been discovered electronically in a 1981 press release, for example.

Due diligence professionals should investigate any lack of candor by a target company's executives about their personal background, particularly if found in a résumé, license application, regulatory filing, or other written representation.

It's generally assumed that the most common falsehoods found in executive résumés are academic degrees that were never earned or military service that never occurred. It's far more common, however, for executives to omit brief stints at jobs that didn't work out or didn't fit well with current career goals. Consider the airline executive who for several months worked for a gambling-related company. Such individuals often hide the omission by stretching the dates of jobs held just before and just after. It's often the "little things" people edit out of their pasts that a prospective business partner most needs to know. Pay close attention to the dates in résumés and verify the story executives tell by cross-checking the facts with such external sources as news articles, press releases, regulatory filings, even college alumni bulletins.

Making false claims about college degrees is, of course, also quite common. Although these claims seem easy to check—university registrars routinely answer requests about degrees by telephone—some people have evaded disclosure by telling a well-worn story about why their schools don't have records of them. Here, you must press the candidate and college relentlessly.

Was the executive successful and trustworthy at prior jobs? People leave jobs for many reasons, but when asked, many companies confirm only a former employee's dates of employment. Thus, in investigating it's important to identify, and quietly interview, knowledgeable former coworkers for their unofficial, confidential—and candid—assessment of the ex-colleague's tenure. In these informal conversations, read their former colleague's résumé to the person to check its credibility. Most important, try to determine how the subject's past employment ended. It's the only way to separate real resignations from "resign or we'll fire you" situations.

A surprising number of executives create companies they don't tell anyone about—not their employers, their bankers, or their prospective business partners. The existence of such companies is often the clue to the presence of self-dealing issues, such as using the company to sell supplies or lease office space to the businessman's employer. In one case, a European information service helped trace a Belgian executive to his secret company in Switzerland, which he was using to siphon business away from his employer. These secret companies often surface when investigators plug an executive's home address or telephone number into a database. Other times, investigators discover a company because its name is derived in part from personal information, like the address of an executive's country house or a combination of his and his wife's first names.

Does the executive have relationships with questionable people? Investors sometimes ask if there's a list to check to see if someone is involved with organized crime. Although lists exist of the "made members" of major crime families, such lists are available only to law enforcement officials, and, in any case, the individuals listed rarely turn up in normal business situations. Determining whether an individual or company is mob-influenced is complicated, because organized crime has allegedly infiltrated a range of white-collar businesses, from stock brokerage firms to prepaid-phone-card companies.

There are several ways to determine whether an individual or a business has unsavory connections. First, you can check court records and news coverage, then make discreet calls to regulatory agencies that monitor such historically mob-connected businesses as trash hauling, casino gambling, and construction. In one instance, when an initial search proved fruitless in checking a bank's suspicions that a prospective customer had organized-crime ties, the bank's investigators called a former government investigator. He steered the investigators to the archives of a weekly newspaper that had an old article linking the businessman to a well-known mob figure.

There is now, at www.pir.org, a database called NameBase, where you can search hundreds of out-of-print books and old magazine articles about organized crime, among other things. For example, an apparently legitimate European businessman turned up with a NameBase reference identifying him as a money launderer for the mob decades ago.

Resolution through Follow-up Investigation

It's clear that database searches sometimes reveal issues that kill deals. More often, the searches raise concerns that can then be resolved through follow-up investigation. Here are several examples:

♦ A U.S. company was negotiating a joint venture with a Russian entrepreneur who held the local franchise for a service business. The U.S. company was concerned because the Russian was using armed ex-KGB agents as bodyguards. The U.S. company hired investigators whose sources in Russia determined that the Russian's lifestyle was explained by legitimate business successes and that his security concerns were justified.

♦ A U.S. businessman disclosed to a venture capital fund that he had been indicted in a fraud case years before. The indictment was dismissed before trial. The venture capital fund asked investigators to find out whether the prosecution resulted from an isolated case of bad judgment or was part of a pattern on the businessman's part. The investigators pulled the filings from the relevant courthouse and determined that the subject was only peripherally involved in the fraud, and that this was the only time he had ever been named in a criminal or civil matter.

♦ Investigators discovered that a number of real estate developers who acknowledged that they had a "rough patch" during the downturn of the late 1980s didn't admit exactly how rough. Investigators checked particularly for lawsuits by the developers' lenders, and for any role that the developers may have had in troubled savings and loans. A property developer told one prospective investor that one of his companies had filed for bankruptcy years before. The investor's investigator contacted some of the creditors listed in the bankruptcy filing and heard nothing but praise for the developer's efforts to make the creditors whole.

The Business Practices of the Target Company

Electronically available information and more traditional investigative methods are as valuable in following up on due diligence concerns about a target company's business as they are about its executives. Due diligence professionals may need company-related information on regulatory issues, business disputes, intellectual property, and many operational issues.

Regulatory Issues

Are regulators preparing to take action? It's often not possible to know if regulators are preparing to take action against a particular company, but sometimes, if you look in the right places, the handwriting is on the wall. Thus, a well-known global financial institution acquired a smaller company not long ago, even though the target had attracted hundreds of lawsuits, scrutiny from the Federal Trade Commission, and the hostility of some prominent consumer groups. Should the acquirer have been surprised that within months of completing the deal, the target was sued by the FTC, and it was forced to acknowledge integrity concerns at its newly minted subsidiary?

Documents from regulators' files that can help predict future enforcement problems include past subpoenas, consent decrees, and hearing transcripts. The challenge in digging them out is that each federal, state, and international agency makes this information public in varying degrees, and through a maze of websites, databases, and Freedom of Information procedures. To find the documents you are after, you need to know what agency regulates the target's business. Information about a trash-hauling company, for example, might be filed with a local consumer bureau, a state environmental agency, an organized-crime commission, or, if the company is public, with the SEC. Obtaining the paperwork may be just the beginning. The best nugget in regulators' files is often the name of the government investigator on the case, especially if that person is now retired. A discreet conversation with that investigator can help you understand what's on the paper record.

Does the target have tax trouble? State and federal tax liens against a U.S. company are readily obtainable from databases and may raise questions about its financial health. Red flags include long-term outstanding liens or a flurry of liens filed over a short time period. For example, a business with cash-flow problems may miss a few quarterly payments of federal employee-withholding taxes and be hit with an IRS lien. Likewise, missed payments of unemployment insurance premiums may result in a state labor department lien.

In the United States, also call the U.S. Tax Court in Washington, D.C. One call to this court checks the whole country for litigation brought by taxpayers against the IRS. Some countries, like Russia, have myriad tax laws that may be loosely enforced and difficult to comply with. Often, a good way to determine if a target company is at risk from the tax police is to check local press reports and the public record for accounts of other companies that have actually been prosecuted.

Has the target been investigated by securities or banking regulators? The SEC posts its sanctions electronically, and once one of its investigations is closed, it will respond to a Freedom of Information letter with revelations about whom it has investigated and even with copies of depositions, usually within a couple of weeks.

In one case, investigators searched a U.S. database of securities and banking regulatory actions and found that two real estate developers were the subjects of orders of prohibition filed by the Office of Thrift Supervision (OTS). This search gave the investigators enough information to retrieve the relevant documents from OTS files, which might otherwise have been impossible to find.

Many regulators abroad discipline people and companies, but the sanctions are available only at their headquarters' archives. Here you must be particularly diligent and knowledgeable to chase the paper successfully.

The numbers of disciplinary actions and sanctions on the books are compelling. In connection with its investigative activities, the James Mintz Group has compiled copies of regulatory compliance actions from around the world. The file is focused particularly on matters of money laundering, fraud, foreign corrupt practices, embargoes, and violations of securities and banking regulations. In the securities and banking area, for example, the material the firm has assembled includes the following:

♦ Two thousand sanctions against individuals and companies by Italy's Securities Commission since 1991

♦ The Reserve Bank of India's list of 5,000 individuals and entities sued for defaulting on loans and who had outstanding debts as of March 1999

♦ More than 1,000 enforcement actions brought by the Hong Kong Securities and Futures Commission since its establishment in 1989

Was the company or its executives implicated in a specific scandal? One way investigators can help due diligence professionals identify regulatory red flags is by unearthing the details of past scandals in the target company's industry. Due diligence investigators must pay close attention to the issues that arise in particular industries and regions and know how to determine whether a given company is vulnerable. In one case, a library of organized-crime exposés might be what's needed; in another, it may help to have the volume listing the German companies found to have used slave labor during the Nazi era. Due diligence investigators keep close at hand the U.S. Office of Foreign Assets Control's list of "blocked persons" (people who have violated economic and trade sanctions).

As an example of how such an investigation might proceed, assume the following:

◆ The target makes a product similar to ones that were the subject of a recent price-fixing prosecution and guilty pleas by American, European, and Asian companies.

◆ The legal due diligence team has reviewed general media coverage of the prosecution and received assurances from the target that it was not contacted or targeted in the recent criminal case and, generally, that it has not fixed prices with competitors.

◆ The due diligence team is still concerned that the target may have engaged in improper meetings with competitors similar to the ones that led to the prosecution. An investigator is asked to dig deeper.

The investigator might seek further details by: (1) accessing electronically available information, like local newspaper coverage in the prosecuted companies' hometowns; (2) pulling copies of filings in the criminal case; and (3) interviewing sources knowledgeable about the prosecution. Assume further that the investigator finds these additional details:

◆ The price-fixers used conferences of an industry association as a cover for getting together in secret meetings on prices. The few executives involved in the price-fixing stayed over for an extra day after each association conference.

◆ These meetings were never in the United States, though some of the participants were American.

◆ Each company's lawyers attended the industry conferences but did not stay over and attend the price-fixing meetings.

Armed with knowledge of these red flags, the due diligence team may want to ask the target additional questions such as: Who attended industry conferences? Any company lawyers? Were the conferences always abroad? Why? Did everyone fly back together? If the answers heighten rather than allay the team's concern, the investigator could be asked to locate and interview any of the conference and postconference attendees who no longer work for the company.

Is the company being targeted by consumer or international human-rights groups? When Ralph Nader in publishing *Unsafe at Any Speed* (1965) helped kill the Corvair, he spawned a cottage industry of consumer activists dedicated to exposing corporate abuses. You may need to know whether any such activists have exposed—or are about to expose—the target company. The challenge is to pick up signals that whistle-blowing is about to take place. After identifying the relevant activist groups in an industry, investigators often buy past issues of their newsletters, or check their websites, which sometimes contain accusations against companies. Recently, sophisticated Internet searches have made this kind of risk assessment easier.

Public-interest and human-rights concerns have gone global along with business. Increasingly, information technology and other investigative techniques should be used to answer due diligence questions such as: Is the target doing anything outside the United States and Europe in an effort to skirt environmental, labor, or human-subject testing regulations in those places?

Concerns about Intellectual Property

In an age of increasing numbers of "soft asset" transactions, it is particularly important to investigate a target's claims about its key intangible assets. Intellectual property (IP) is the key to many companies' success, and thus it is increasingly crucial in due diligence to determine their bona fides. Effective investigation requires going outside the target and finding independent sources of information and insight. Investigators of IP must have special skills and resources to do this successfully, including the following:

♦ A network of industry sources or the ability to develop them quickly

♦ Research skills for identifying obscure, specialized newsletters and websites

♦ Interviewing skills, for extracting insights and details from people who don't want to be quoted by name, possibly including competitors, regulators, and former employees

◆ A healthy skepticism about all predictions of a technology's commercial prospects and an understanding of the limits of specific IP applications

Unlike other assets, IP assets know no borders. Thus, cross-border IP investigation may require particularly creative and rigorous approaches. Away from home, where your sources are probably thinner, you must ensure that the few available sources are trustworthy. Bear in mind, too, that counterfeiting and unauthorized copying of certain kinds of IP are rampant in China and other parts of the world.

For example, assume a worst-case scenario for an IP due diligence investigator: The target's business prospects depend on as-yet-unmarketed technology that is subject to conflicting regulatory review and stiff competition in several countries, and the company's rights to the technology are being contested in litigation brought by a former employee. Databases and the Internet may help you find independent information and insight on some of the key items. Some issues and approaches are as follows:

◆ Does the technology work, and does it have the value the target claims? Check general business press coverage as well as industry-specific publications, websites, and experts.

◆ How is the regulatory process likely to go? Check newsletters that cover specific regulatory agencies, and search databases for former officials of specific agencies.

◆ What problems with this technology would competitors point out? Identify whom to contact at one of the target's competitors (unless revealing details of the technology to competitors would compromise the target's competitive edge or violate trade secrets).

◆ Did the company acquire its technology under circumstances likely to cause controversy or dispute? A good way to find out: Ask former employees.

Business Disputes

Has the company ever been a defendant in a lawsuit? It's a simple question. But there's no simple way to find out. With no national—much less international—registry of civil litigation, records on millions of cases are scattered geographically within each jurisdiction, filed in separate federal, state, and local judicial systems. (Although databases of case law—the reported legal decisions carried by Lexis, among others—are useful, they are far from complete records of a person's or company's litigation history.) For New York and several other states, a database called Superior Information Services identifies defendants and plaintiffs, as well as some of the lawyers on each side. But old cases or current ones in some areas are frequently not accessible through computerized databases.

Public Access to Court Electronic Records (PACER) is the U.S. government's service to search federal district courts and bankruptcy court dockets. Although these online searches may be unwieldy—covering the whole country requires dozens of searches—other services like CourtLink provide easier-to-use interfaces to these records.

Has the company ever been involved in "nonmaterial" litigation? Litigation brought against a target is often worth reviewing even when it is not material, active, or financially significant. Even lawsuits brought *by* a company can provide insights into its operations and vulnerabilities. A careful investor steered clear of one of the best-known corporate frauds of the 1980s, ZZZZ Best, after due diligence turned up a case in *small-claims court* that revealed part of the scam. Others who plunged in based on shallower due diligence got swindled.

Inactive and immaterial cases can also show a company's pattern of bad relationships with lenders, customers, vendors, or employees.

Depositions taken of a company's executives can be particularly revealing. There's nothing like reading a transcript of a person's sworn answers to pointed questions to see how that person responds to pressure.

Are relations with key vendors and customers at arm's length? Investigators working for due diligence professionals are sometimes assigned to determine whether the target's significant customers and suppliers have arm's-length relationships with it. Look for undisclosed ties like those reported not long ago in the business press about a Belgian software maker. Published articles alleged that the Belgian company helped set up and finance Singaporean "customers" who, in turn, bought software licenses from the Belgian company, boosting its reported revenues significantly. Government investigations ensued, and the Belgian company ultimately filed for bankruptcy.

In one case, due diligence investigators searched for the reasons behind a target company's relatively large volume of returned goods. To determine whether the goods were shipped to inflate the prior quarter's revenue, investigators considered whether the target loosened its terms on accepting returns (it had), and whether the customers doing the returning had undisclosed ties to the company (they appeared to).

One database by which to identify cross-border customers is PIERS (Port Import Export Reporting Service), a Dialog database that tracks the manifests of freighters shipping cargo into and out of U.S. seaports. A company contemplating business with an Indonesian company wanted to identify its U.S. customers before opening negotiations. At the conclusion of a PIERS search, the company's investigators had compiled a list of more than 200 imports to scores of U.S. companies and were able to build a comprehensive picture of the Indonesian company's business relationships with U.S. companies.

Is the target associated with questionable people? Check the backgrounds of various kinds of individuals who are tied to a target, including the following:

♦ Local agents in corruption-prone countries, whose reputations might be worrisome in light of the U.S. Foreign Corrupt Practices Act

♦ Brokers and other financial consultants from obscure securities firms who have stock-purchase warrants, board seats, or other ties, and who may have checkered regulatory histories

♦ Labor relations consultants, finders of financing, and other agents of the company who may have questionable reputations

Increased Pressure on Due Diligence Professionals

Due diligence professionals ignore at their peril information available through new technology and through the old tried-and-true investigative methods. The vast expansion of available data (and the misperception among companies and the public that the Internet has put all information within easy reach) spells trouble for professionals who do not use or keep abreast of the evolving technology. At the same time, it is clear that the new technology, while extraordinarily useful, is not a substitute for old-fashioned legwork, interviews, and other data-gathering methods.

As an example of the former, consider the case of a large accounting firm that conducted due diligence on a U.S. company on behalf of a European investor. The accounting firm ran its standard background check on the president of the American company, which was, let's say, in Miami. The transaction went forward. As soon as it became public, the client received a fax from someone in Miami: Some months before, the local newspaper had accused the president of securities fraud and revealed an active SEC investigation of him. It turned out that the accountants' due diligence check had used a standard database of news articles, and the Miami newspaper was searchable only on a more obscure database.

Another example: Until recently, due diligence professionals, seeking to learn whether a public interest group in another country had negative information on the target, would have spent many hours making inquiries. Today, that information is likely to be cited on the group's website, a few hours of quiet research away.

The new technology has expanded the concept of the international public record, which opens new opportunities for due diligence professionals. Thus, electronically available information can provide certain avenues on which to proceed, outside the confines of the target and its representations, toward independent information and expertise.

The new technology, however, is not a panacea. Although it provides valuable leads to the truth about some issues, the team also may need a more old-fashioned detective's skill: that of eliciting the truth from strangers. In that regard, the electronically available data can lead due diligence professionals to knowledgeable, reliable people. Such people—regulators, activists, competitors, former employees, academics, reporters, litigation opponents, and so on—are clearly free to hang up the phone. But surprisingly often they don't, and the information elicited from them can move the due diligence process dramatically forward.

Due Diligence Investigative Technology and Know-How

BACKGROUNDS OF KEY EXECUTIVES

1. Where has the executive lived and worked?
❏ Check for current and past addresses.

2. Confirm his/her identifiers, such as date of birth.
❏ Check for possible aliases in databases such as AutoTrackXP.

3. Start your press searches with the hometown newspaper.
❏ Use "Fulltext Sources Online" to identify relevant papers.
❏ If the hometown paper isn't online, call or visit the local library, or try a clipping service, which is especially helpful in international searches.

4. Search large media databases like Nexis, but don't limit yourself to them.
❏ Include searches of television and radio transcripts through Burrelle's Information Services, for example.

5. Check to see if he/she has a criminal record or has filed for bankruptcy.
❏ Be sure to check all jurisdictions where he/she has lived and worked.
❏ Double-check any representations he/she makes about where he/she is from.

6. Investigate any lack of candor, especially in a résumé or other written statement.
❏ Pay close attention to the dates in résumés for any evidence that they have been "stretched" to cover undisclosed past jobs.
❏ Be persistent in drilling down on possibly false claims: Keep calling that college registrar's office until it opens its records to you.

7. Was the executive successful and trustworthy at past jobs?
❏ Identify and quietly interview former coworkers for their candid assessment of his/her tenure and how his/her job ended.

8. Check for self-dealing issues, as manifested in secret "side companies."

❏ Run his/her home address and telephone number through a database such as Dun & Bradstreet to see if any company names appear.

❏ Be wary of any companies run from other addresses, such as a P.O. box or a country house.

9. Does the executive have relationships with questionable people?

❏ Search news coverage and court filings for business associates.

❏ Run his/her name through websites like www.pir.org, which has indexed out-of-print books and magazine articles.

CONCERNS ABOUT THE BUSINESS PRACTICES OF THE TARGET COMPANY

10. Are regulators preparing to take action, or have they already done so?

❏ Identify which agencies regulate the target company's industry and search those agencies for material such as past subpoenas, consent decrees, and hearing transcripts.

❏ Familiarize yourself with any relevant freedom of information laws, which can facilitate the gathering of regulatory information.

11. Has the company had tax trouble?

❏ Pay special attention to any long-term outstanding tax liens, or to a flurry of liens filed over a short time period.

❏ Make inquiries with the U.S. Tax Court in Washington, D.C.

12. Was the company implicated in a specific industry scandal?

❏ Pull copies of filings in any relevant criminal cases, and quietly interview sources knowledgeable about the prosecution.

❏ Keep in mind resources like the U.S. Office of Foreign Assets Control's list of "blocked persons," who have violated economic and trade sanctions.

13. Has the company been targeted by consumer or international human-rights groups?

❏ Obtain past issues of relevant consumer-group newsletters and check their websites.

❏ Be certain that the company isn't doing anything outside the U.S. and Europe in an effort to skirt environmental, labor, or human-subject testing regulations in those places.

14. Concerns about intellectual property
- ❏ Research the viability of IP technology in industry-specific trade journals.
- ❏ Check databases for former regulatory-agency officials with expert knowledge of how the regulatory process is likely to go.
- ❏ Pay close attention to whether the company acquired its technology under circumstances that may cause controversy or dispute, and whether any such dispute is being litigated in U.S. or foreign courts.

15. Has the company been involved in litigation?
- ❏ Consult databases such as Superior Information Services, Lexis, and CourtLink to help identify whether the company has litigated on the federal, state, or local levels.
- ❏ Pay attention to seemingly "insignificant" or small-claims litigation that can provide insights into the company's operations and vulnerabilities, or show a pattern of behavior with respect to lenders, customers, vendors, or employees.
- ❏ Remember that not all courts can be accessed online.

16. Are transactions with key vendors and customers at arm's length?
- ❏ Look for indications that the company has financed any of its key customers.
- ❏ Databases such as PIERS (Port Import Export Reporting Service) may help to identify cross-border customers of the company.

17. Is the company associated with questionable people?
- ❏ Vet any of the company's local agents in corruption-prone countries whose reputations might be worrisome in light of the Foreign Corrupt Practices Act.
- ❏ Examine any of the company's brokers or other financial consultants from obscure securities firms who have stock-purchase warrants, board seats, or other ties.

APPENDIX: Cross-Border Due Diligence in an Age of International Terrorism

The seismic events of September 11, 2001, have had profound effects on the political, social, and economic fabric of the United States and elsewhere. What these events and others following in their wake portend in a period when no nation is immune from the specter of terrorism only time will tell. Surely, however, those engaged in cross-border transactions need to consider the potential impact of terrorism not only in those areas of the world where such activities have long been a part of the landscape but also in places that, until very recently, were thought to be havens of domestic tranquility. In the checklist that follows, the chapter contributors offer their visions of how the threat of terrorism may affect cross-border due diligence. Like any checklist, not all of its suggestions will apply in every working environment. It is one thing to investigate security measures taken by a company headquartered in the Empire State Building or with a manufacturing facility in Peshawar, Pakistan, and quite another when the target is located in a small office complex in rural France. Therefore, use this checklist as appropriate in the context of each cross-border due diligence investigation.

STRATEGIC DUE DILIGENCE

Apart from their baleful effect on specific industries like airlines and tourism, the events of 9/11 have accelerated a global slowdown whose duration is anybody's guess. Thus, those events should cause corporate planners engaged in cross-border due diligence to consider at least two major new questions: (1) How will the increased international turbulence of the post-9/11 era affect the value creation premises of the proposed transaction, and (2) What added cross-border due diligence complexities should be considered in light of the new era?

1. Regarding the value-creation premises of the deal

❏ What has been the impact on the market in which the target participates? Should the market's growth prospects be revisited and projections (up or down) revised? What is the expected short-term versus long-term impact of terrorism? Thus, for example, growth in the U.K. tourism industry will be negatively affected by a likely decrease in the number of U.S. tourists; however, this is likely to be somewhat offset by an increase in British tourists deciding to vacation at home instead of abroad. In the markets under consideration in the transaction, it is critical to consider the potential impact on the drivers of growth described in the main text of this book.

❏ Have we properly defined the market? What is the likely impact of terrorism on the customer and geographic segments in which the target participates? Consider the fact that the prospects for casualty insurers may be different from those of life insurers. Incorrect market definition could lead to an improper assessment of the potential effects.

❏ How (if at all) have the events of 9/11 and since affected the competitive position of the target company? Since 9/11 is the target's position better, worse, or the same in an absolute sense and versus its competitors? How do terrorism and possible cost increases in its wake affect the target with a superior cost position? Could such a company aggressively cut prices to stimulate demand and use bad times to take market share away from competitors?

❏ Does increased turbulence affect the deal's strategic rationale? If the buyer's intent is to pursue adjacency expansion, are the markets still attractive? If it proposes to gain scale in purchasing, how have the events of 9/11 and thereafter affected supplier costs?

2. Regarding the additional complexities of the deal process

❏ Will market dynamics change? Will consumers react the same way in all markets? For example, purchasing patterns of Americans may change dramatically. Throughout the year following 9/11/01, Americans were spending less on air travel and more on cars. Will this trend continue, and if so, for how long? Meanwhile, changes in consumer spending in the United Kingdom probably will not be as pronounced or prolonged, given Britain's distance from the disaster and British citizens' unfortunate familiarity with terrorism.

❏ Will the regulatory/legal environment change? Could trade restrictions be imposed on certain countries? Might increased security measures adversely affect the buyer or the target? For example, growth prospects for a German target with significant exports to the Middle East and Asia may be significantly reduced if trade restrictions are imposed in the latter regions by the European Union or the United States.

OPERATIONAL DUE DILIGENCE

The events of 9/11 require revisiting the assumptions made by one or both parties before that date about the size and character of the market, as discussed above. Given a material change in the assumptions, the pricing of the transaction itself may require revision. In addition, the events highlight systemic risk issues related to the target company's positioning in a world where there is likely to be a greater long-term focus on security needs.

❏ It is generally assumed that transportation of goods will become more cumbersome, costly, and time-consuming as security measures are ramped up. What are the resulting implications for the target's suppliers and customer relationships?

❏ Does just-in-time inventory management need to be revisited?

❏ Are there other scheduling effects that require revision, such as a need to adjust critical path analyses?

❏ Describe whether (if at all) the target's products/services and its value production cycle will need to be altered to respond to employees' and the public's greater awareness of security risks (e.g., enhanced screening of employees, improved information gathering and dissemination regarding possible risks, tightened physical security, improvements in materials handling, need for evacuation plans).

❏ Are there critical raw materials that are at greater than historical risk in the changed or uncertain political environments that have been affected by the events of 9/11? If so, can they be stockpiled or otherwise safeguarded?

❏ Are information systems adequately backed up on a "hot backup" basis and otherwise sufficiently redundant and robust? Are there physically dispersed personnel who can handle systems recovery and switchover to the backup?

❏ Are advertising and marketing messages properly positioned in light of the public's current heightened and varied sensibilities?

❏ What are the likely effects of recent events on the company's insurance needs and the cost and availability of coverage?

❏ Are the company's facilities and personnel optimally sited, weighing the benefits of physical proximity against mitigation of risk? If not, should there be a rapid redeployment or just a gradual evolution toward a different building/staffing model?

❏ Revisit utilities and other infrastructure support—water, electricity, and communications. What are the implication for the target of any air travel or other transport disruptions?

❏ Are there some areas of business where the risk profile has changed so dramatically that a pullback should be considered? Or are there opportunities for the target in the changed environment?

❏ Does bioterrorism offer a real threat of product contamination? If so, what steps have been taken to mitigate the risk?

❏ Is there a policy to scan, for electronic retrieval and backup, documents received (other than online) from third parties?

FINANCIAL AND ACCOUNTING DUE DILIGENCE

The effect of terrorism on financial due diligence will vary somewhat depending on whether the target was directly or only indirectly affected by acts of terror.

1. For those targets directly affected by terrorism

❏ How was the loss and the recovery recorded? Was the accounting applied in a correct and appropriate manner for the circumstance?

❏ What additional costs have been or were likely to be incurred over the subsequent two years in the wake of 9/11? Have financial projections been revised to reflect these costs?

❏ Have any assets become impaired as a result of the business disruption? Did the target have business interruption insurance?

2. For those targets indirectly affected by terrorism

❏ Has the target's industry been adversely affected? What steps, if any, has the target taken to replace lost revenues or to decrease its costs? Have any discount pricing measures been implemented? If so, with what prospective outcome?

❏ If revenues have decreased, and such decreases are expected to continue, have any assets been impaired? Are there assets whose recoverability is not assured, and if so, have appropriate accounting adjustments been made?

❏ If the target had made recent investments or acquisitions and goodwill was generated, has the goodwill (or other intangibles) generated from such acquisition been impaired, and is an impairment adjustment required? Consider whether the financial projections prepared in conjunction with any investment have been made obsolete by the events of 9/11 and thereafter.

❏ Is the target company considering any workforce reductions or any other operational measures, such as plant or office closings, which may be accounted for using a restructuring charge?

❏ Is the target company considering any security enhancement measures that will require additional capital investments? If so, what is the likely impact of such investments on the target's operations and liquidity?

❏ Has the target recorded any unusual, one-time increased revenues resulting from the events of 9/11? Consider nonrecurring revenues. For example, companies in industries used to remove the debris from the World Trade Center would have received substantial payments, which should be considered one-time opportunities.

❏ Does the target own any products, patents, or other assets that terrorism or its consequences may have caused materially to increase or decrease in value?

LEGAL DUE DILIGENCE

The events of 9/11 and those that have followed (such as anthrax by mail) and may follow add to the risks to be explored, uncovered, and evaluated in due diligence on inbound and outbound transactions. Among the risks calling for close scrutiny are the following:

1. Insurance

❏ Was there adequate insurance in place for a target directly affected by the events of 9/11 to recover its losses?

❏ Have claims been timely and properly notified to the insurers? What has been the response thus far from the insurers?

❏ Do existing insurance policies (casualty and business interruption, in particular) make acts of terror an exception? If so, what is the availability and cost of policies specifically designed to cover such an exposure?

❏ Is acts-of-terror coverage sufficient to cover reasonably foreseeable terror scenarios (e.g., evacuation and temporary idling of facilities due to bioterror, such as happened at post office facilities)?

2. Other material agreements

❏ In the event of a terrorist incident affecting the target or its contractual counterparties under material agreements to which the target is a party, to what extent does the wording of the agreements excuse performance by either party? Examine "force majeure" and "commercial impracticability" provisions, considering also any mandatory provisions of relevant decrees under applicable foreign law.

❏ To what extent would "material adverse change"/"material adverse effect" clauses in pending agreements be triggered by a terrorist event?

❏ Has the target or any of its contractual counterparties invoked or threatened to invoke any such provisions excusing performance?

❏ Do notice provisions in any material contracts provide for notices to be sent to the World Trade Center or other destroyed or interrupted locations? Check that notices sent on or about 9/11 were subsequently effectively given.

3. Real estate, raw materials, and finished goods

❏ What do provisions in real estate and equipment leases (and pending purchase or sale contracts) say about complete or partial destruction of the structure or equipment or its temporary unavailability? Will the target be compelled to return to the property or continue to use the equipment upon repair or replacement, or can it enter into long-term replacement arrangements?

❏ Does the target have adequate security arrangements in place at each of its facilities? Is there a centralized security policy on a worldwide or national basis, taking into account the heightened security called for at higher-profile facilities (e.g., where hazardous materials are used, power plants, etc.)?

❏ Are security arrangements in compliance with applicable laws (e.g., freedom of speech; avoidance of potentially unlawful screening based on race, national origin, or religion)?

❏ Have the target's products, or the raw materials used by the target, been made subject to any special security-related rules, surveillance, or transport or use requirements (e.g., crop-duster aircraft; materials usable in explosives)?

4. Management, employees, agents, customers, and suppliers

❏ Do the target's employment and contracting procedures and record keeping (e.g., end-user certificates) ensure that it properly knows its employees, agents, customers, and suppliers? If not, should reviews be conducted?

❏ Have there been any government or law enforcement inquiries about the target or any employees, agents, customers, or suppliers, and has the target prepared for such inquiries (taking into account applicable rights of privacy and contractual confidentiality obligations, as well as disclosure obligations)?

❏ Does the target suspect that any employees, agents, customers, or suppliers may be connected with terrorist organizations or activities, and if so, have any remedial steps been taken? What steps?

❏ Have operations been affected by departure of military reservists, and have applicable regulations been followed as to their tenure, benefits, and other rights?

❏ Have applicable regulations been followed in connection with charitable solicitations by well-intentioned employees, as well as by the target itself? Check that the target is not making donations to proscribed charities or permitting fund-raising by them on the premises.

❏ Is the target subject to the USA Patriot Act, and if so, is the target in full compliance with this new anti-money-laundering legislation? (It requires, among other things, that U.S. financial institutions having certain accounts for non-U.S. persons establish "appropriate, specific, and where necessary, enhanced due diligence policies, procedures, and controls that are reasonably designed to detect and report instances of money laundering through those accounts.")

5. Pending legal and regulatory matters

❏ Have lawyers or other professionals involved in the target's current legal or regulatory matters been directly affected by the events of 9/11 and thereafter? If yes, have any necessary original documents been lost, or has the progress or prospects of the matter been materially affected?

❏ Has the terror risk itself affected the prospects for any sought regulatory approvals?

TAX DUE DILIGENCE

The tragedy of 9/11 has clear and immediate implications for the tax due diligence process. Among them are the following:

❏ As a result of the President's or the IRS's federal disaster declarations for five New York counties and Arlington County, Virginia, the need to obtain details by the regular due date for each taxpayer claim for relief from performing any of the filing or payment obligations set forth in the six items listed below
  ♦ Filing any income, excise, harbor maintenance, alcohol and tobacco, or employment tax return
  ♦ Payment of any of such taxes, including installments due thereon
  ♦ Contributions to a qualified retirement plan
  ♦ Filing a petition with the Tax Court or for review of a decision rendered by the Tax Court
  ♦ Filing a claim or instituting a suit for tax credit or refund
  ♦ Any other act specified in a revenue ruling, procedure, notice, announcement, news release, or other guidance published in the Internal Revenue Bulletin
❏ The need to obtain details concerning original books and records, financial information, tax return reporting information, or other relevant tax due diligence data lost or missing as a result of the 9/11 federal disasters, without regard to the taxpayer's location, including the following:
  ♦ Nature of items missing
  ♦ Existence of backup data
  ♦ Degree of difficulty to replace
❏ The need to obtain details of any 9/11 claimed casualty loss deduction.
❏ The need to obtain details of any unresolved insurance matters existing as of the tax return filing claiming a casualty loss deduction.

❏ The need to obtain details of any secondary data sites for tax-related information existing prior to or installed after 9/11, including the following:
  ◆ Site location
  ◆ Breadth of data
  ◆ Degree of detail
  ◆ Security of data
  ◆ Results within the past twelve months of testing secondary site for reliability

PEOPLE AND ORGANIZATIONAL DUE DILIGENCE

Before 9/11 fewer than 30 percent of U.S. corporations had terrorism response plans and more than 40 percent had no policies to deal with potential employee Internet sabotage, although nearly that many had experienced such acts in one form or another. In the people/organizational due diligence effort, the team should ask the following key questions:

❏ Is there a corporate security officer, and if so, to whom does that person report?
❏ Has the target evaluated the impact of September 11 on employee morale and the ability to successfully recruit attractive new hires?
❏ What steps has the target taken to evaluate the risk of terrorist attack and, in the event of such attack, to reduce its risk, including the following:
  ◆ Cessation of operations in or near areas likely to be subjects of attack
  ◆ Use of contractors in high-risk areas
  ◆ Workplace security awareness programs
  ◆ Regular surveillance reports on potential terrorist threats
  ◆ Evacuation procedures
  ◆ Increased security measures such as guards and executive protection
  ◆ Evaluation of expatriate risks such as kidnapping of executives and their families
❏ Is there a disaster succession plan in place for key management? If yes, does it include backup corporate authorizations for important banking, regulatory, and securities matters?
❏ Is there a disaster contingency plan for the target and its units (perhaps modeled on pre-existing Y2K contingency plans)?

INVESTIGATIVE TECHNOLOGY IN DUE DILIGENCE

Companies do business with all sorts of people, including some they really know nothing about other than the name such persons claim to have. These persons may be visitors, the cleaning lady, or even some employees. Since 9/11, corporations are increasingly focused on the flight-manifest analogy: He gave me his name, but do I know the real identity of the person who just walked into my conference room? Confirming that people have the identities they claim is as important as patting them down for weapons. There are still Class A buildings where one can get through the "security check" in the lobby by signing in as "Superman." Often people suspected of engaging in harassment are questioned, causing companies to ask "How did we ever hire that person?" In the personnel file search that follows, often it is discovered that a background check was performed but revealed nothing wrong, because the putative harasser gave false identifiers. Thus, persons on either side of the due diligence negotiating table may properly ask the following questions:

- ❏ Has there been adequate assessment of the risk that either company could be hiring or doing business with people associated with terrorism?
- ❏ Have steps been taken to confirm the identities of people with whom the company comes into contact?
- ❏ If something went wrong with a particular individual with whom the company comes in contact, could the company readily document the person's identity in order to follow up?
- ❏ Has the target taken adequate precautions to ensure that unvetted people do not have access to its facilities?
- ❏ In unstable parts of the world, has the target satisfied itself that the employment agencies it uses are free from terrorist influence and that such agencies check for unsavory ties in the backgrounds of the people they recommend to be hired?

Index

333